A CUT ABOVE THE REST

A CUT ABOVE THE REST

THE BIOGRAPHY OF
THE WORSHIPFUL COMPANY
OF BUTCHERS

NICHOLAS COURTNEY

SINCLAIR-STEVENSON

LONDON

First published in Great Britain by
Sinclair-Stevenson
3 South Terrace, London SW7 2TB

British Library Cataloguing in Publication Data
A CIP catalogue record for this title is available from the British Library

ISBN 0-9543520-7-6

Typeset by Rowland Phototypesetting Ltd, Bury St Edmunds, Suffolk
Printed by St Edmundsbury Press, Bury St Edmunds, Suffolk

Contents

This is a significant year for the Worshipful Company of Butchers and as an Honorary Freeman I much enjoyed the dinner at the Mansion House in February 2005 to mark the 400th anniversary of the granting of their Charter.

The direct links between the Crown and the Worshipful Company of Butchers go back before the twelfth century, when rents were extracted for markets and grazing. Then there was the famous fine of one mark for operating as an 'adulterine' guild, that is one without a Royal Charter. After more than 800 years, the fine is still unpaid, but it does show a certain spirit of independence.

Apart from a slight lapse of loyalty during the Civil War, the Butchers' Company has been unswerving in its allegiance to the Crown, particularly when their Royal Charter was in the offing in 1605! No Monarch would enter the City of London without being lauded by the Worshipful Company of Butchers, just as no Royal Banquet was complete without the meat supplied by one of their number. This close connection with the Company continued with my grandmother, Queen Elizabeth The Queen Mother, also an Honorary Freeman of the Company, who often referred to them as 'my Butchers'. It is the Livery brooch that the Company presented to her that I wear with such pride.

'A Cut Above The Rest' is a biography of the Worshipful Company of Butchers, not the often dry Livery Company history. I am sure you will enjoy reading it.

Anne

Acknowledgements

I knew it would happen. This biography of the Worshipful Company of Butchers is finished, done and dusted, leaving me with withdrawal symptoms from this thoroughly enjoyable work, made so agreeable by the fascinating subject and all whom I met in the Livery and the staff. Advice was freely given (and generally taken), often with the rare roast beef and claret at a Carvery Lunch. It was a privilege to attend so many of the great functions and to see, first hand, the inner workings of Company.

My research was made even more pleasurable by meeting, or talking to, the octogenarian and nonagenarian brigade, naturally led by Terence Bonser, father of the Company, who with a sharp memory fielded a constant stream of questions, both major and trivial, and who put me on the right path at the very outset, steering me the whole way through. Austin Kingwell spoke to me from his hospital bed: Mrs Newall Wallbank, widow of the Rector of St Bartholomew-the-Great, gave another insight to the Company from her pretty cottage in Eton.

The younger team was invaluable too. John Brewster added much colour to the text, Fred Mallion, as ever a tower of strength, was a mine of precise information. Graham Sharp put me right on so many items, as did Douglas Noakes, Doug Brydges and John Edkins. John Jackman, David Franks and John Tuckwell were always there for much-needed material and guidance. Help came too from Miss Rosemary Smith, granddaughter of William Long, the Beadle through the War years and beyond, and Mrs Charles Woods widow of his successor.

Colin Cullimore, the Master throughout the 400th anniversary year, gave unstinting encouragement and support. But it is to the 400th Anniversary Committee, under the Chairmanship of the Deputy Master Michael Richardson, who commissioned me to write this biography that I owe much, not least for their sage guidance and helpful suggestions. Martin Lingeman, with his critical eye, did much to polish the text. Finally, there is the Clerk, Anthony Morrow, who initially introduced me to the Company and during the whole project, has made it appear that he has had no job other than to steer the book through to its conclusion.

To them all, and those unnamed, I give heartfelt thanks.

List of Illustrations

MONOCHROME

COLOUR

Introduction

'Parade will advance . . . by the right . . . quick . . . march!'

The stentorian command echoes around St Bartholomew Close as the column moves off as one from the Butchers' Hall. A pair of motorcycles from the City of London Police lead the way. Next, the Royal Logistic Corps' Corps of Drums march four abreast, the stirring beat of the bass drum marshalling the Master of the Worshipful Company of Butchers, Colin Cullimore, the Clerk and the Beadle with the rest of the Court behind, as they struggle to keep up with the punishing pace. Behind them is the fanciful plastic representation of a boar's head carried by four soldiers, each an Army specialist learning the butchers trade. A mounted escort of the City of London Police bring up the rear, the nostrils of the two grey horses blowing clouds of steam as their breath condenses in the chill December air.

In a trice, the procession moves out of the Close into Little Britain on their way to the Mansion House to deliver this symbolic boar's head to the Lord Mayor of London, as they have done in past centuries, but this is the fiftieth anniversary of the revival of the custom. As the parade moves on at a steady pace, passers-by on the pavement photograph this unique spectacle with their mobile telephones, testament, were it needed, that this is an ancient custom played out in a modern world. The chosen route too is bound in history, with links to the past at every step of the way. The procession swings into King Edward Street, formerly Stinking Lane or Fowle Lane, named after the filth created by medieval butchers as they slaughtered their beasts in the street. The name changed again in the sixteenth century to Butchers' Hall Lane, one of the first streets in London to be paved, in honour of their Guild's second hall. Then, as the parade swings into St Martin-le-Grand, work stops on scaffolding and in office alike as spectators admire the spectacle below. Here, the statue of Sir Rowland Hill, founder of the Penny Post, stands high on a plinth before the General Post Office, his stare fixed on the buildings opposite, the very site of that second Butchers' Hall and the Guild's church of St Nicholas Shambles. A dark blue plaque was once fixed to the walls of those office buildings, showing the position of that hall which burned in the Great Fire of London off Angel Street. The great dome of St Paul's Cathedral is glimpsed as the parade moves into the top of Cheapside, once the haunt of the sellers of offal when it was known as Bladder Street. Behind is Newgate, home to the former street market of St Nicholas Shambles. The Great Fire of London put paid to the broad street lined with butchers' stalls, with more stalls, back to back, down the centre. This is true, historic Guild of Butchers' territory, the very heartland of their trade.

By now, the procession has moved along Cheapside, named after the Old English word *ceap* meaning market. For centuries, it was known as West Cheap, as opposed to East Cheap, the other stronghold of the first freemen butchers of London. On and on they go to the end of the street, past evocatively named places: Butter Lane, Bread Street, Milk Street, Ironmongers Lane, to Poultry, another landmark of the flesh trade. The end is in sight. With a final flourish from the Corps of Drums they wheel into the courtyard before the Mansion House. Again the butchers should feel at home, for this was the site of yet another flesh market, the Stocks that also lasted until the Great Fire of London. The Lord Mayor, Alderman Michael Savory, is waiting to receive the Master, the Deputy Master, the Wardens and Assistants and their gift to him at the Walbrook entrance. There was a time when the ceremonial boar's head was real, suitably scalded and dressed as a fitting present for the Lord Mayor, but that was before Health and Safety regulations put an end to such a natural display. So the Master presents the Lord Mayor with the facsimile head, a fanciful affair in shocking pink, its mouth parted in a contrived grin with the aid of a plastic orange. He reminds the Lord Mayor of the tradition of the gift. He tells of the perpetual trouble of the 14th century butcher, of their difficulty in disposing of the blood and the guts and the ordure. He continues in his authoritative way to tell of how John Hamond, the Mayor of London in 1343, came to the Butchers' aid by allowing the Guild to purchase a parcel of land by the Fleet River where they could slaughter and clean their beasts. In return, the Mystery Guild of Butchers had to 'repair and maintain a certain wharf, they and their successors for ever, rendering yearly to the Mayor of London at Christmas a boar's head,'[1] as the Master quotes from the statute.

The Lord Mayor thanks the Master and the Company of Butchers for their kind present in this very special year – the four hundredth anniversary of the granting of the Royal Charter to the Worshipful Company of Butchers. He leads them into the Mansion House and up the Red Staircase to the Ball Room on the second floor, where at the far end of the room is the real boar's head. It is a triumph of the butcher's art and belies the nine days it took the Army School of Butchery to prepare – the boning and soaking, the bandaging and stuffing, the boiling and decorating with aspic. Real wild boar's tusks and glass eyes complete the splendid creation. The Clerk presents the Court to the Lord Mayor who, after a short acceptance speech, takes the knife to carve the first slice off the back of the boar's head. He carves it wafer thin, as indeed he should as a Liveryman, indeed Past

Master, of the Worshipful Company of Poulters. Past Master Fred Mallion of the Butchers takes over with equal skill.

The occasion passes all too quickly. The Court disappears in all directions, leaving the Beadle under a mound of discarded gowns and Tudor bonnets. The faux boar's head is returned to the Butchers' Hall to be stored until the next year. Although the boar's head ceremony is pure tradition, symbolic of a past that stretches back well over 1,000 years, it also reinforces the close links between the Worshipful Company of Butchers and the City of London, two great institutions, one within the other, whose roles are firmly set in the future.

1 The Saxon Hall
1545–1666

T OWARDS DUSK, on the evening of 18 October 975, a member of the Craft Guild of Butchers made his way from his stall in Eastcheap to the Butchers' Hall for the feast of St Luke the Evangelist, the Patron Saint of all butchers. It was a fair step to the Ward of Faringdon Without, just outside the old Roman city wall and moat around London. On he went, skirting the pens of scrawny cattle and sheep awaiting slaughter at Smithfield Market, then past the great horse pond and the stand of elm trees until he reached the Butchers' Hall, a single-storey, wooden building, open to the eaves under a tile roof. It was not large, but typical of all important town dwellings of the period being comparatively newly built after the great fire that had swept away the cathedral church of St Paul's and the surrounding houses just fourteen years before.

Once inside, the butcher was familiar with the scene, not that he saw much from the faint glow of the few tallow candles set on spikes in an iron circlet hanging from the roof, nor through the smoke that filled the room from the fire at the centre of the Hall. At one end, on a dais, the Master of the Craft Guild of Butchers was seated on a rudimentary chair placed beneath an embroidered canopy of state. The Guild was not rich, and, most likely, there were no other hangings in the hall. The Master, however, would have been attired in keeping with his station – a long, violet cloak over a short tunic held together with an embroidered girdle, and a Phrygian bonnet, a small felt cap with a pointed crown, the same design that was adopted centuries later for the Cap of Liberty. Before the Master would have been a long trestle table with benches on either side for the Court, the officers of the Guild. Below the dais, on a floor strewn with rushes that contained all manner of filth, were more trestle tables and benches for the rest of the Guild.

Once the Master, Court and Members of the Guild were all assembled, the feast was served – great cuts of beef spit-roasted over charcoal in a kitchen hut separate from the Hall, along with flagons of ale, specially brewed for the occasion. Each butcher carved the flesh with his own knife, laying the strips of sinewy beef on a

I

piece of bread that doubled as a plate and a sop for the fat and the juices. This being a special feast, there was also boiled mutton, known as 'sodden', to which 'pot herbs' (a mixture of vegetables and herbs) had been added. Such feasts were generally accompanied by music; and, dinner over, more ballad singing and other entertainment, possibly a troupe of jugglers or even an acrobat. Feasts in Butchers' Hall were to be enjoyed, for the Anglo-Saxon Craft Guild of Butchers was above all a close-knit fraternity.

Feasting was certainly an important function of the Saxon Craft Guild, so much so that the word 'guild' (correctly 'gild') was thought to have come from the Danish *gilde* meaning 'banquet' where the 'Company . . . meet on stated occasions for the purpose of feasting and merry making'.[1] Although the primary origin of the Old English word was a *feast*, the meaning later developed into the *assembled company* eating together. However plausible this explanation, the brief of the early Craft Guilds was far wider than mere revelry, and the now accepted derivation of the word 'guild' is from the Anglo-Saxon *gyldan* (variously *gildan* or *geldan*) meaning 'to pay'.

At the turn of the first Millennium, when many believed that the world would end, the Anglo-Saxon dynasty founded by Alfred the Great, that first ruled England as one nation, collapsed in ruin with the arrival of a new wave of Vikings. What the invading Norsemen found, however, was a framework of society whereby the country was divided up into shires and counties, that were, in turn, broken down into a series of 'hundreds' in the country, and towns, (or 'tuns' as they were then termed). Each unit had its own *moot*, a court under the king's appointee, to mete out justice to the community. It was an admirable system whereby all of the king's subjects were accountable by law to their own small community, which in turn was answerable to the next higher authority, and so on right up the scale to the king himself. A part of that accountability was the law that decreed that:

> every freeman at fourteen years of age should find sureties to keep the peace, or be committed, upon which the neighbours entered into an association and become bound for each other, either to produce him who committed any offence, or to make satisfaction to the injured party, in order to do which, they raised a sum among themselves, which they put into a common stock, out of which they, upon occasion, made a pecuniary compensation, according to the quality of the offence committed.[2]

As the law required freemen (as opposed to serfs and villeins who were bound to the feudal lord on the land) to form an association with a corporate responsibility for the good conduct of their members and their mutual liability, it clearly made sense that the members were like-minded or engaged in the same trade operating in the same part of the city or town – as with say the butchers of Eastcheap. So associations were formed by freemen in all major towns and cities, and as a payment, *gyldan*, was due from the *gegilda*, the subscribing members, these associations became known as gilds or guilds.

> These Trade Guilds were of two orders – Merchant Guilds and Craft Guilds; the former being composed of men of substance, in many cases landowners as well as traders, early obtained State recognition by a clause in the Charter of Incorporation of the Borough or town in which the guild was held. In London and Florence, we do not hear of the Merchant Guilds; there the Craft Guilds early asserted their associating powers and independence, and gradually took a place in the organisation of the town government.[3]

By the nature of their trade, the butchers were always a craft guild or 'mystery' (from *misterium*, the Medieval Latin for craft or professional skill). When the Mystery Guild of Butchers was first formed in London, they were one of a few select craft guilds in the City. While the merchant guilds in the provincial cities took over the municipalities, they were never established as such in London. This meant that the law and code of practices of the craft guilds were predominant in the City, and so magnified their importance.

Although there are many parallels between the first Anglo-Saxon craft guilds and those voluntary associations for commercial, social and religious purposes of ancient Rome, the *collegia*, there is no foundation for the widely-held view that the one led to the other. Nor is there definite proof to support the other theory, that the English craft guilds were modelled on those of Western Europe (the Carolingian *geldoniæ* or *confratriæ* outlawed by the Emperor Charlemagne during the ninth century), despite the close trading links between the two regions. However, the most credible theory is that the Anglo-Saxon craft guild simply adopted the Christian principles of the family group 'for the support of the body and the salvation of the soul' being

> an institution of local self help which, before the Poor Laws were invented, took the place in old times of the modern friendly benefit society, but with higher aim, while it joined all classes together in the care for the needy and for objects of common welfare, it did not neglect the forms and the practice of Religion, Justice or Morality.[4]

Self-help within the Craft Guild of Butchers (as indeed with all the other craft guilds) was a vital part of their code. The sick were cared for, and the dying knew that they would receive a proper funeral. Furthermore, they knew that the Guild would pay for the clergy to say masses for their souls and care for their widows and children. This corporate family also extended to those butcher freemen who came to London from the provinces, where the Guild took the place of the close family bond within a rural community.

Although the spiritual and temporal side of the guild, together with the feasting, were central to the company, the prime function of the Craft Guild was to regulate their own trade. The officers 'of the Craft Guilds provided for the maintenance of the customs of their craft, framed further ordinances for its regulation (including care against fraudulent workmanship), saw those ordinances properly enforced, and punished the Guild brothers who infringed them'.[5] The system was based on a hierarchy. The master craftsman, as in this case the master butcher, had the premises and owned the tools of his trade. With the freedom of his guild, he carried on his trade with the help of craftsmen or journeymen, his employees. These were freemen who had completed their apprenticeship and hoped, in time, to become master butchers themselves. While the merchant needed to raise large sums of money to set up on his own, the journeyman butcher needed comparatively little. Thus the inevitable conflict between labour and capital was avoided, so making it easier for the journeyman butcher to progress to master in his own right.

In the eight century the Venerable Bede wrote that 'London is the mart for many nations resorting to it by sea and land'.[6] Largely through its position on the River Thames it continued to grow, and soon became the most important trading centre (or *wic*, as in Lundenwic) of England. With this steady growth of trade, both at home and with the Continent, the population of London expanded rapidly. The craft guilds – not least to those of the Mystery Guild of Butchers – were there to service this ever-increasing population, to their lasting benefit.

The main London market was at Cheapside, from *céap*, Old English for both market and cattle or stock. Here butchers, bakers and fishmongers traded every day except Sunday, a fine of thirty shillings and forfeiture of goods being payable by those who transgressed. Although the toll, based on the area of each stall, was due to the King, it is thought that the market originated from the place where the Chapter of St Paul's disposed of their surplus food collected as rent. Nor did the butcher have far to go for his supply, as livestock had been sold at Smithfield (from the flat, triangular pasture of about six acres known as *smeth field* a corruption of the Saxon *smoothfield*) for centuries. It was later described by William FitzStephen, clerk to Thomas à Becket, in 1174 as 'a smooth field where every Friday there is a celebrated rendezvous of fine horses to be sold, and in another quarter are placed vendibles of the peasant, swine with their deep flanks, and cows and oxen of immense bulk'. It had in fact been well established as a cattle market by the end of the tenth century, being fed from a series of ancient drove roads that eventually led to the village of Islington to the north. In the main, the cattle that were sent to Smithfield were either cull animals that had ended their working life as draught oxen, or cows that had finished milking, although at that time most of the milk came from ewes. Likewise, mutton came from sheep that were either barren or dry, in both cases the wool, milk and leather being only marginally less important than the meat.

With the shortage of winter fodder there tended to be a glut of animals killed in the late autumn, although salting carcases was common, particularly with bacon. From the bones excavated in the old Lundenwic, it can be seen that the slaughtered domestic animals were roughly half the size and twice the age of those of today, although later the compromise between beasts that worked in the field and those needed for the table much reduced the age of killing.

Part of the commercial success of London was due to the rigid controls of the Craft Guilds – in the case of the Butchers' Guild, they ensured the quality of the meat and the butchering skills. But the role of the Craft Guilds within the framework of London went far further. By that time London had long considered itself virtually a 'federal state', being a city 'composed of Wards governed by Aldermen'.[7] Each Craft Guild was therefore answerable to their local 'Wardmote' – the moots of the Hundreds – or court that in turn was made up of their number. For the butchers, their legislation was, in the main, well thought out to protect both the buyer and seller: 'Two witnesses', for example, 'are required when stock is killed, the slaughterer is to keep the head and hide of the beast or sheep for three days for production upon an inquiry'.[8] Prices were also controlled, as the legislation laid down that 'the horn of an ox is worth ten pence, the horn of a cow is worth two pence, the tail of an ox is worth a shilling, and that of a cow five pence'.[9]

London acted as a sovereign state or independent power, raising an army for the defence of the City. For this, the Craft Guilds were called on to provide part of the finance and some of the manpower for the *fryd* or the militia. The well-fed butchers, with their expertise in slaughtering and the tools of their trade, knives, axes and poleaxes, would have been particularly in demand in resisting the Viking hordes. Notwithstanding the repeated attacks of the Norsemen, London continued to trade with the Continent – a visiting Icelandic poet in 1001 recorded the scene whereby 'merchants from Rouen, Flanders, Normandy, Liège and other places . . . brought in wool, and cloth, and planks, and fish, and melted fat; . . . and in turn the mariners bought pigs and sheep for their journey homewards'.[10]

Although the citizen army 'would not yield, but resisted with full battle',[11] London finally surrendered to the Danes in 1013 after a long siege. When Cnut was eventually crowned king in 1016, a tribute was levied on the whole nation, one-eighth of the whole being raised in London. Once again, the country was subjected to a new dynasty, and the citizens of London serviced the new Danish population. Likewise, after the Norman Conquest, life within the City and the Craft Guilds went on very much as before, largely due to the foresight of William the Conqueror – in his charter to the City of London he pledged that 'I, William, king, greet . . . all the burghers within London, French and English, friendly; . . . And I will not endure that any man offer any wrong to you. God help you'.[12] Assured of such royal patronage, the economy continued to expand, particularly through the twelfth and up to the fourteenth century. With this period of great affluence, the Craft Guilds, including without doubt the Mystery Guild of Butchers, all prospered considerably.

Part of this increased prosperity was due to the strong government of Henry I, the fourth and ablest son of William the Conqueror. Nicknamed Beauclerc, later 'The Lion of Justice', he reorganised the *Curia Regis* (King's Court), or the English judicial system, a royal court-of-all-work that also supervised the taxation of the whole country. In 1130, towards the end of his reign, the first Exchequer Pipe Roll was drawn up. This was a written record of the King's financial account for the year 1129–30, Michaelmas (29 September) to Michaelmas. The series runs, virtually uninterrupted, from 1155 until 1832. Two copies were made of each account, the second version being known as the Chancellor's Roll. The King's accounts were written in abbreviated Latin (apart from a short time in the 1650s when they were written in English) until 1733, when they appeared again in English. Each pipe roll consisted of a number of sheepskin parchments stitched together, head to head (Exchequer style) or head to tail (Chancellor style), and known as rotuli, from the Latin for a roll. They were then rolled up all together in waxed parchment for protection and looked like a section of a drain pipe. On the last parchment of the Pipe Roll for the fiscal year 1179–80, there is the entry *Gilda bocheorium unde Willelumus Lafiete est aldermannus debet I m* – The Guild of Butchers of which William Lafeite is Alderman owes one mark.

The one mark payable by the *Gilda bocheorium* to the King's Exchequer was a fine for operating as an adulterine guild, that is, one practising without the authority of the Crown. Nor were the Butchers' Guild the only defaulters; amongst the other seventeen guilds mentioned in the same passage, four were Craft Guilds. Like the Butchers, the Clothworkers were fined one mark, the Pepperers 16 marks, while the Goldsmiths were liable for 45 marks. At that time, it is known that only two of the Craft Guilds held a Royal Charter – the Bakers, who paid £6 per annum in lieu of a toll on baking, and the Weavers who had held their charter (granted by Henry II) since 1155. In return for these fines their existing privileges were ratified, for example those not of the Guild of Weavers were forbidden to work in London or Southwark. It is certain that there were many more than these six craft guilds operating in London at that time, yet only those four guilds were singled out for fines. This indicates that this was a *political*, rather than a *judicial*, move. Further, as the fines imposed were trifling amounts, and remained unpaid, there had to be an ulterior motive for exacting them. The chosen four Guilds were not only rich, especially the Goldsmiths and the Pepperers (the forerunner of the Grocers, number two of the Great Twelve today), but each was also associated with a prominent Aldermen, such as William Lafeite of the Butchers – a well-established family in the City of London prominent from the early twelfth century onwards. Thus it would appear that these four craft guilds (along with the fourteen other religious and sundry guilds) were being fined by the Exchequer merely as an example in order to reinforce the Crown's authority over them all, and to bring them into line like the Bakers and the Weavers. To pay the fine to the Crown would have acknowledged that total authority, which is why they went unpaid.

This obvious ploy by the Crown to bring the Craft Guilds into line was not only for a ready source of income, but also to curb the increasing independence of the City of London that it had enjoyed since the original Charter of Liberties of Henry I. But the fine in 1180 was only a little more than a decade away from the City's support for Prince John in his bid to usurp his brother, Richard I – the same Prince John who notoriously stated that he would have sold London if he could have found a rich enough buyer. In return for its support, the City received the Prince's assurances to ratify its 'inalienable right ... to form its own commune as a self-governing and self elected city-state, to which all the nobles of the kingdom, and even the very bishops of that province, are compelled to swear'.[13] This led to 'the barons of the City of London' being given the right to choose 'for themselves each year a mayor from amongst themselves'[14] to be assisted by aldermen, the *probi homines*, 'the honest men'. Henry Fitzailwin is credited as being the first Mayor of the City of London in 1192.

It would appear that, despite the enhanced powers of the City of London, the Craft Guilds, which naturally included the Guild of Butchers, still operated outside the authority of the Mayor and Aldermen. Yet the Mayor of London was answerable to the Crown – one, Richard Renger, was heavily censured by Richard, Earl of Cornwall (brother of Henry III) for not punishing the Bakers for selling defective bread. On the downside, if the Craft Guilds did not submit to the Mayor's authority they could not expect his support if their authority was flaunted. By the general Ordinances of 1262, the Butchers, in common with the other Craft Guilds, were all-powerful within their own organisation. As the regulations from each Guild were so similar, it can be presumed that the Guilds colluded in imposing restrictive practices and in legislating to protect their members against all outside competition, that is from 'foreigners'. However, without the authority of the Mayor and Aldermen, there was no real way of enforcing their orders.

But things were to change, particularly for the Mystery Guild of Butchers. After Parliament met for the first time at the rebuilt Westminster Abbey, an Act (51 Henry III) was passed in 1266 to prohibit the sale of infectious meat. The self-regulating Butchers' Guild had had an identical ordinance in place for at least two centuries, so this further piece of legislation was superfluous for them, but not for the foreigners who remained outside the Guild's jurisdiction. But, as with the fine imposed on the Butchers in 1180, the Act was more to do with the control of the Guild rather than a necessary piece of legislation. The passing of the Act marked the end of the independence of the Mystery Guild of Butchers, and through the City's links with the Crown, they came under the ultimate authority of the King. Regulations from the City to control the price of meat followed soon after. The power of the City was further endorsed by another Charter of 1268 granted by Henry III. One of the first Acts was to ban 'forestalling', when stock is bought before it reaches the market to be sold on at a profit. The Act stated that:

> no merchant or other do meet any merchant coming by land or by water with their merchandise or victuals, towards the City, to buy or sell again, till they come to the said City and there have put the same to sale, upon the forfeiture of the things brought and pain of imprisonment from whence he shall not escape without great punishment.[15]

Notwithstanding these Acts, the Craft Guild of Butchers had long been answerable directly to the Crown, not in statute, but through payment of rent. The revenues paid to the Crown from the City of London in 1268 included the sum of £42 0s 5d for various 'stallages' in the City markets and for 'Haw and Annual Socage of the Butchers of London'.[16] This entry shows that the Guild leased a parcel of enclosed land close by the City for which they paid *socage,* an annual rent, which was either for holding stock before slaughter or for a 'killing field', common outside certain Medieval French cities like Orleans. The *stallage*, the site of the butchers' stalls and shops, was the rent paid to the Crown for the various flesh markets, principally Eastcheap.

There seems to be no good reason why the early butcher should congregate around Eastcheap, other than for the convenience of his customers. The vintners and the fishmongers gravitated to the wharves beside the Thames for ease of transport, just as the dyers, who needed vast quantities of water, worked over the river itself. Other crafts producing noxious fumes and smoke were relegated to the City walls, quite often right outside them. But the butcher, who traditionally slaughtered the beast as well as preparing it for the table, was allowed to operate in the street at the very heart of the City, regardless of the offal, blood, ordure and noise connected with slaughter. Besides Eastcheap, an important thoroughfare remodelled on the instructions of Henry I at the beginning of the twelfth century so that it 'should be wide enough for 16 armed knights to ride abreast',[17] butchers also congregated around the Church of St Nicholas de Westmacekaria, dedicated to St Luke the Evangelist, Patron Saint of all butchers, and central to the their spiritual life. It was here that the Guild's plate and valuables were stored, as well as the hearse pall, an embroidered cloth that was draped over a freeman butcher's coffin. They traded out of the 'Street of the Butchers', as it was described in a lease with the Fishmongers, later known as St Nicholas Shambles Lane and then simply as St Nicholas Shambles – the 'shamble' being the table where meat, sometimes fish, was sold. The main street from the City Wall to Poultry by Cornhill was one continuous street-market selling all manner of goods, where each craft grouped together in a particular area, like at the Shambles (the present Newgate) where 'all the stalls of the butchers are to be numbered, and it is to be asked who holds them and by what service and by whom'.[18] Those who held the stalls were usually simply called by their Christian name and trade, such as Ralph the Butcher, or Richard the Butcher who is recorded as paying six shillings per annum for his space to the Holy Trinity Priory, as did Robinel the Butcher, who paid 4s per annum for half a stall.[19] Collectively they were referred to as either the 'Butchers of the Shambles' or the 'Butchers of Eastcheap', which presupposes that there were separate organisations responsible for each separate flesh market. And that was before the Butchers of Le Stockkes, or the Stocks Market.

Such was the demand for meat in thirteenth-century London that a third flesh market was established on some waste ground (the site of the present Mansion House), a gift to the City from Edward I in 1283. Unlike the open street markets of the Shambles and Eastcheap, the Stocks was a covered market with stalls let to both butchers and fishmongers. It was then known as Le Stockkes, thought to be named after the stocks, or pillory, that were presumed to be there, but, like the shambles, its name in fact comes from a 'stock', a table or block on which butchers and fishmongers cut up their wares – as in stockfishmonger. The rent from the Stocks went towards the repair of London Bridge, then in a sorry state. It was paid weekly, and, such was the reputation of the butcher stallholders that the bailiffs were given an extra allowance for drink when they went to collect the rent.

This allowance could well have been needed, as the rivalry between all of the Craft Guilds was legendary, through either guild loyalty or trade disputes. Some were comparatively minor, such as the dispute between the Butchers and Fishmongers of the Stock Market over whether Christmas Eve and the Saturday before Easter Day were fish or flesh days, as it determined who had the stalls inside the market, and who was relegated outside. Christmas Eve was later judged to be a flesh day, as set out in the original agreement of 1324. At the other end of the scale, the inter-craft guild rivalry could erupt into a full-blown riot, when the lessons of fraternity were temporarily forgotten. In 1394 a fight developed from a quarrel between the Goldsmiths and the Merchant Tailors, and all the other crafts joined in. Although the Butchers were not specifically mentioned, it seems most likely that they were involved as the fight raged around them for several days. Many were severely injured, some killed, including an innocent bystander who was hit by an arrow fired indiscriminately into the crowd. Eventually peace was restored and the ringleaders arrested and hanged.

Like his Craft Guild, the early medieval master butcher had come a long way in comparison with his Anglo-Saxon counterpart, particularly in his standing within the City of London. During the Christmas week of 1299, the King's Writ to the City was ratified, whereby 'pollards and crockards' (clipped and crooked coins) were devalued from a 'sterling' (an English silver penny) to a halfpenny. It was further ordained that the price of meat should be fixed –

The carcase of the best ox	1 mark
The carcase of the best cow	ten shillings
The carcase of the best pig	four shillings
The carcase of the best mutton	two shillings[20]

To enforce these price controls, and to oversee the currency devaluation, the Mayor and Aldermen appointed Wardens of 'the butchers at St Nicholas Masecrue [butcher] . . . Estchep . . . and Le Stocke',[21] together with three stockfishmongers and three poulterers: one of the seven chosen Butcher Wardens was Luke de War.

Luke de War and his wife Agnes were prominent members of society. Beside his position as one of four wardens of the 'Butchers of the Shambles', he owned three shops there, and a well furnished house in the neighbourhood, built of stone and with a reasonable garden. The shops were of timber, as they had developed from 'stall boards . . . set up by butchers to show and sell their flesh meat upon, over which they first built sheds to keep off the weather; but since that, encroaching by little and little, they have made their stall boards and sheds fair houses, meet for the principal shambles'.[22]

Each of his shops would have had a journeyman and a servant, and almost certainly an apprentice, maybe two. Each apprentice would have been bound to the master to learn the skills of his craft and, equally important, to accept the standards of the craft. Twelve butchers' apprentices' names appear on the rolls for 1309 to 1312, with eleven apprentices becoming freemen. The origins of apprenticeship lay with the Romans, or even, according to some, with the Ancient Egyptians, and by the thirteenth century it was the standard means of becoming a freeman of the Guild (freedom could also be purchased). Many butcher apprentices came from the provinces – a London apprenticeship and subsequent freedom was an attractive proposition – but records show that most returned home to practise their craft. In theory, the period of apprenticeship was 'open-ended' and only finished when the masters of the mystery could testify that the apprentice was 'able and well instructed in his craft'.[23] More usually, 'no apprentice was received for a term of less than seven years according to the ancient and established usage'.[24] An ingress (entrance

a. A medieval butcher working at his 'shamble'. The term 'shambles', as in St Nicholas Shambles, a meat market, comes from the name of this stall.

1b. *Margarita Philosophica*, engraved by Gregor Reisch in 1508, depicts Boethius (with the new Hindu-Arabic numerals) competing against Pythagoras working a counting board, similar to those used by butchers for accounting in Roman numerals.

c. The first written record of the Guild of Butchers in the Pipe Roll of 1170-80. They were fined by the Crown 1 mark as an 'adulterine' guild, that is, one operating without a Charter. The fine was never paid.

2a. The official Arms granted to the Guild of Butchers in 1540. Although they adopted the supporters, the winged bull of St Luke, patron saint of all butchers, they were only officially licensed to use them in 1922.

2b. Butchers' broom *(ruscus aculeatus)*, with its stiff, sharp leaves, was used for scrubbing down butchers' blocks, hence its depiction in the Company's Arms.

2c. The original Arms adopted by the Butchers' Guild and worn as a distinguishing badge by the livery.

a & 3b. Drawings of St Nicholas Shambles and Eastcheap from Hugh Alley's *Caveat: the markets of London in 1598*, a remarkable collection of drawings showing sixteenth century London. The originals are now at the Folger Shakespearian Library, Washington DC.

4a. Daniel Defoe, the famous writer, became a Freeman of the Butchers' Company through the patronage of his father, James Foe, a former Warden and butcher from Cripplegate.

4b. Butcher's halfpenny trade token issued in the 1650s by Thomas Taylor, a Warden of the Butchers' Company. Although not legal currency, trade tokens were widely used to overcome the paucity of official small denominations.

4c. Drawing of Hungerford Market in 1830 by Thomas Hosmer Shepherd. There was a large meat section in the market that supplied the fashionable new West End. The Market was finally demolished to make way for Charing Cross Station.

fee) of 2s 6d payable to the City was mandatory. In return, a freeman would stand 'in *loco parentis* to the apprentice who lived in his house, sat at his board, and associated with him in the workshop and the home on terms of the most personal intimacy'.[25] More likely, journeyman and apprentice alike slept on the floor in the shop.

The butcher's shops owned by Luke de War were just three of dozens lining both sides of St Nicholas Shambles, as well as a row of narrow stalls (both for meat and fish) back to back down the centre of the street, and all controlled by the Guild of Butchers. Like the stalls, the selling place in the shops would have been in the open (albeit with a canopy) as the Guild ordained that meat should be sold in the open air. Selling meat from inside the shop 'by candlelight' was outlawed, as much as a fire precaution in wooden buildings as to prevent the customer being deceived. To avoid further congestion in St Nicholas Shambles, the Guild specified that the 'stall-boards' should be no more than thirty inches wide and, presumably for the look of the street, that they should all be the same height. The City authorities confined the sale of meat to the limits of the three flesh markets, St Nicholas Shambles, Eastcheap and the Stocks, which were rigorously policed on behalf of the Mayor and Aldermen by inspectors appointed and paid for by the Guild of Butchers. At the beginning of the fourteenth century, for example, they fined a group of butchers and confiscated their wares for setting up in Poultry to escape the high rents of the Stocks.

Another important function of the Guild of Butchers was to protect its own good name so that of its freemen could be trusted. When buying stock, the freeman butcher could either buy at Smithfield Market, or go direct to the producer (but not half way between the two, as in 'forestalling' which was illegal). When the butcher went to the country, the Guild expressly proscribed the taking any form of credit, for:

> whereas some butchers do buy beasts of country folk, and as soon as they have the beasts in their houses kill them, and then at their own pleasure delay the peasants of their pay, or else tell them that they may take their beasts, it is provided that on conviction before the Mayor, the butchers shall pay unto the seller double the value, and also pay damages, or in default be put in the pillory, and remain there one hour in the day at least, a Sergeant of the City standing by the side of the pillory with good hue and cry as to the reason why he is so punished.[26]

The Guilds and the City authorities operated by way of Ordinances passed for the benefit of all, and those that defied them did so at their peril. Despite this, there are frequent references to transgressors. One, William Sperlyng, a butcher from the Stocks, fell foul of the Guild in 1319. :

The sworn Wardens of the flesh meat brought to the Shambles called 'Le Stockkes' seised two carcases putrid and poisonous taken from William Sperlyng of West Hamme, he intended to sell the same at the said Shambles. The said Sperlyng being taken before the Mayor and Alderman acknowledged he intended to sell the beef, but insisted that it was good clean, and fit for human food, and demanded inquisition thereon – and the jury of twelve say, on oath, that the said carcase are putrid and poisonous and have died of disease.

The Mayor and Alderman order the said Sperlyng to be put in the pillory, and the said carcases burnt beneath him. Of the jury of twelve five consisted of the sworn Surveyors of the market.[27]

In the same account, William Le Clerk of Higham Ferrers was punished in the same manner for selling 'certain putrid and poisonous meat unfit for human food, and the same having been found to have died of disease'. The punishment was particularly severe. At that time, the miscreant would have been used to noxious smells, but the meat being wet would have produced a great deal of smoke which, coupled with the heat from the fire, could well have killed him. But, as the punishment was only to humiliate, a constable of the City would have freed him before death.

Bad meat was endemic throughout the country, particularly after the terrible 'murrain' that swept the country during the last quarter of the thirteenth century. It was caused by foreign import from 'a rich man of France [who] brought into Northumberland a Spanish ewe, as big as a calfe of two years, which ewe being rotten, infected so the country, that it spread through all the realme.'[28] It caused great hardship, and its effect was long lasting, particularly in the later legislation against the importation of meat or livestock from the Continent.

The Guild of Butchers also looked after their own. For the convenience of the freemen of St Nicholas Shambles, they arranged for the 'curriers of ox-leather [to hold] two plots of land nearby for a market for their leather'.[29] Warden Luke de War was one of the signatories along with the Mayor, John le Breton. At that time, the hide was worth about a third of the value of the beast, while the hooves and horns, with their multiple uses such as buttons, combs and drinking vessels, were also valuable. The considerable worth of the cattle and their by-products led to huge numbers of cattle being bred and brought to London to cater for an affluent population. The same applied to sheep, with the demand for mutton and all the ancillary products.

While the armies of Europe had been marching back and forth across the Continent for centuries, the island kingdom of Britain had enjoyed comparative peace. These foraging armies on the march first killed the stock of the conquered, particularly the sheep which were easily killed and butchered. Consequently, having lost their breeding stock, it was hard for the invaded to build up their herds and flocks again. With a paucity of sheep, there was always a shortage of wool and cloth, particularly in the Low Countries with their great tradition of weaving. The resulting demand for wool, both for the home and overseas markets, led to a vast increase in the numbers of sheep in Britain. Great flocks were run by the monasteries and by the lords of the manor and, along with those owned by the peasants, it can be deduced from the amount of wool produced that there were some 12 million sheep in England and Wales in the early fourteenth century. This also implies that a prodigious amount of mutton was being sold for consumption by all classes through-out the country by this time.

Traditionally, pork was the fare of peasants who kept the odd house pig for their own consumption. Likewise in London, pigs were kept in sties and allowed to scavenge in the streets until prohibited by order in 1277. Thereafter, no pigs were permitted

> in the street or lanes of the City or suburbs, nor in the ditches of the City, and if found to be killed by whoever finds them, and the killer to have them without challenge, or redemption, for four pence from the owner. If anyone wishes to feed his pigs, let him feed them in the open away from the King's highway or in his house.[30]

The only pigs in London allowed to scavenge were those belonging to the Hospital of St Anthony, an order situated on the north side of Threadneedle Street. St Anthony was

> universally known for the patron of hogs, having a pig for his page in all pictures, though for what reason is unknown, except, because being a hermit, and having a cell or hole digged in the earth, and having his general repast on roots, he and hogs did in some sort enter-common both in their diet and lodging.[31]

Those pigs belonging to the Hospital of St Anthony had been bequeathed by Guild of Butchers' inspectors appointed to oversee the three markets, who collected up those 'pigs starved or otherwise unwholesome for man's sustenance'.[32] One of 'the proctors of St. Anthony's Hospital' would then tie a bell around its neck and 'let it feed upon the dunghills; [where] no one would hurt or take it up; but if any one gave it bread or other feeding, such it would know, watch for, and daily follow, whining till it had somewhat given it'[33] – hence the proverb 'To whine like a Tantomy [St Anthony] pig'.

With the new-found wealth and increased population of the City of London, the butcher's trade was much in demand. Feasting was an essential part of medieval life, and the master butchers would have catered solely for the more affluent, the rich burghers and their fellow tradesmen. The poorer citizens bought what little they could afford from street hawkers, who were usually men, as opposed to hucksters, who were generally women. Sometimes the hawker worked for a freeman butcher – like bakers who gave their sellers thirteen loaves, 'a baker's dozen', with the last one being their profit – others worked on their own account. The advantage to the poor of the hawker over the butcher was that he would sell small quantities of meat at a time when the penny, the lowest denomination, would buy about 2½ pounds of beef.

The real competition for the freeman butcher came from the 'foreigners', those from outside the City and not members of the Guild. They were allowed to trade in the flesh markets, but only under severe restriction from both the Guild of Butchers and the City authority. Unlike the freeman butcher who slaughtered his animals in the street, or behind his shop, the foreign butcher was made to

> bring the hides, and pelts, of every beast, together with the flesh, under pain of losing the price of such hide. That is to say, for the price of an ox hide, two shillings and six pence. The price of a cow hide, two shillings; for a pelt of a woollen mutton, six pence.[34]

The foreigner came between the hawker and the butcher and sold his meat in one of the three markets, 'in pieces both small and large'.[35] After midday was 'rung at St Paul's', he was forbidden to cut up any more meat, and had to 'expose the same for sale, up to the hour of vespers [about 4 p.m.].'[36] The foreigner was in a difficult position. He was not allowed to keep any meat that he had brought 'either secretly or openly, or putting it in salt, or otherwise so that by such time he shall have fully made his sale',[37] nor could he store it. If he was caught and 'any such shall be found in town carried into the house that is forbidden, the same shall be forfeited unto the Sherrif.'[38] There was a further restriction whereby he could not 'buy meat from the Jews to sell again to Christians, or meat slaughtered for Jews and by them rejected'.[39]

The City authorities and the Guilds were always at pains to distinguish between their freemen and foreigners. When John le Perer, John Estmar, and Reginald ate Watre, described as foreign butchers, were arrested their meat was confiscated 'as they had exposed the said meat for sale by candle light at Les Stockkes, after curfew rung at St. Martin's-le-Grand'.[40] The meat was forfeited to the Sheriff, but when it was discovered that John le Perer was 'free of the City', his was returned.

The City authorities and the Guild of Butchers worked closely together on all matters affecting their trade. In 1321, the price of meat was fixed:

The best carcase of an ox was not to be sold for more than 1 mark, the middle quality for more than 10 soulz [shillings], and the other according to the discretion of the Mystery.

The carcase of cow, bullock and heifer to be sold for 8 soulz, and the others according to the discretion of the Mystery. The carcase of pork, the best to be sold for 40 deniers [pence], the middle quantity for 30 deniers, and the other for 2 soulz.

The best carcase of mutton to be sold for 12 deniers, and the middle for 8 deniers and the rest to be fixed by the Mystery.

Four inspectors to be chosen for each of the three Butchers' Markets by the Mayor and Alderman, and who do not belong to the Mystery.[41]

That reference to the 'Mystery' confirms the existence of a single governing body with overall control of the three 'Butchers' Markets' – it was, after all, easier to deal with one organisation than three separate ones. Soon after, Edward III granted his famous Charter to the City effectively banning any new market within seven miles. The next year, 1328, twenty-five of the most senior Mysteries in the City were authorised to nominate their own members to their council, and it is a measure of the importance of the Butchers that they appointed a total of twenty-four, the same as the Fishmongers, to the Tailors' twenty and the Vintners' thirteen. Of the twenty-four senior butchers, three are of particular interest being the first butchers to be appointed Aldermen of the City. One is William le Clerk, formerly described as a foreigner from Higham Ferrers, Northamptonshire, who had been pilloried for selling bad meat, only to reappear eight years later as a respectable freeman (most likely through purchase) and an elected member of the Council. The other two are Nicholas Crane, a former Warden of St Nicholas Shambles, and Nicholas Dereman, a warden of the Stocks. In fact, Nicholas Crane owned several properties in St Nicholas Shambles, including a house with a garden, and was exceedingly rich. Along with two corn merchants and a fishmonger, he is distinguished by paying the highest tax in London in 1332. Dereman and Crane both made their fortunes as 'carcase butchers', or wholesalers, whose clients included the Royal Household.

This period of great economic expansion gave rise to the wholesaler, like those members of the Guild of Pepperers who became the Guild of Grocers, those who sold goods by 'the gross'. Dereman was a substantial butcher in his own right. He supplied, and paid for, all the meat for the banquet given by the City to celebrate the marriage of Edward III to Philippa of Hainault. The feast cost the City £95 13s 6d, that included Dereman's gift of '10 carcases of beeves, price £7 10s: 20 pigs, price £4: and for the Queen, 5 carcases of beeves, price 75/; 12 pigs, price 48/-.'[42]

Another lucrative market for the carcase butcher was supplying the cook shops, where they lived and operated side by side. Cook shops played a vital role in medieval London. Meat was obviously difficult to keep fresh and only the larger houses had a stove and fuel to cook. So, the customer could either buy a hot dish ready for eating to take away, or send his own cut of meat to be cooked – to cook a goose, for instance, cost two pence 'for the paste, fire and trouble'. By the same Ordinances of the Guild of Piebakers, prices were fixed: 'the best roast pig, for 8d. Three roast thrushes, 2d. Ten eggs, one penny ... The best capon baked in a pasty, 8d.'[43]

Under the strict canon law of the Catholic Church, meat could not be sold on a Friday, during Lent, or on fish days. This was rigorously enforced by the City authorities and the Guild, with large fines for those who broke the law. Nor could meat be consumed on any of those days either, although there were always those who found a way round the law, like the order of monks in Ireland who were 'convinced' that barnacle geese grew on trees and that it was therefore perfectly permissible to eat their flesh on fish days.

By the end of the fourteenth century, the Mystery Guild of Butchers was playing a significant role in the workings of the City of London, with a number of their Wardens acting as Assistants to the Aldermen. Their appointees were also founder members of the emerging Common Council, at that time made up of forty-seven Mysteries. While the larger Craft Guilds sent five or six representatives, the Butchers sent just three, Richard Stoneham, Henry Asshelyn and John Tikhulle, their numbers rising to four the next year in 1377. However, five years later the Butchers sent the full six representatives to the Common Council. Having now achieved parity with the likes of the Goldsmiths, Drapers, Mercers, Grocers, Vintners, Fishmongers and Tailors, it would appear that the Butchers were about to join their exalted ranks. But it was not to be, for the very nature of their trade was to count against them, in particular, the slaughter of their animals in the street. This great contagion in the City was outlined in a command from Edward III to the Mayor and Sheriffs:

> Because by reason of killing great Beasts, &c. from whose putrefied blood running down the Streets, and the Bowels cast into the Thames, the Air of the City is very much corrupted and infected, whence abominable and most filthy Stinks proceed. Sicknesses and many other Evils happen to such as have abode in the great City, or have resorted to it; WEE willing to prevent such danger, and to provide as much in Us lies, for the Honesty of the said City, and the Safety of our People, by the Consent of our Council in our present Parliament, have ordained, That all bulls, Oxen, Hogs and other gross Creatures, to be slain for the sustenation of the said City, be led as far as the town of Stretford [Stratford le Bow] on one part of London, and the town of Knightbrugg [Knightsbridge] on the other; and there and not on this side be slain. And that their bowels be there cleansed: and being so cleansed, to be brought, together with the Flesh, to

the said City to be sold. And if any Butcher shall presume anything rashly against this Ordinance, let him incur Forfeiture of the Flesh of the Creatures, which he has caused to be slain on this side of the said Towns, and the punishment of Imprisonment for one Year. This Ordinance to be publicly proclaimed and held; and all Butchers doing otherwise to be chastised and punished according to the Form of the Ordinance aforesaid. Witness the King at Westminster, the 25th February, 1363.[44]

In the main, the Butchers were an unruly lot. Ordinances were introduced, and the Butchers complied – for a time. Then, they slipped back into their old ways and a new Ordinance was necessary to keep them in line. So it was not long before slaughter was resumed in the streets – if ever it stopped, as the Guild fought vigorously against the order, appealing time and again. The King was petitioned: the Mayor and Aldermen were lobbied by the citizens of the City, Acts were passed – in 1371, and again in 1379 when Richard II decreed that 'no butcher should kill any flesh within London, but at Knightsbridge, or such like distant place from the walls of the City'.[45] But still the Butchers flouted the law, which can hardly have endeared them to the voters in the Ward elections. But, notwithstanding the fact that the Butchers failed to consolidate their position as one of the senior companies, their status as a Craft Guild within the City of London was never higher than at the end of the fourteenth century.

2 The First Hall

1423–1545

T HE GOOD BROTHERS of the Order of the Friars Minor could stand it no longer. The gardens that surrounded the monastery, where they grew all manner of medicinal herbs, were becoming untenable through the filth in the ditch that ran through their grounds and into the moat beyond. Even in the height of winter, the stench was appalling. On closer examination, the friars saw that the water ran red with blood, and that there was the hair of cattle and the short bristles of hogs. Entrails and dung, too, floated down in the 'lotura'[1] or washing water. Brother Robert de Madyington, the guardian (the abbot) of the Friars Minor followed the kennel (ditch) back to find the cause of the Order's misery. He walked up to St Nicholas Shambles, along the street with its stalls and shops, towards Poultry. Although there were remains of carcases in the street, they were not the cause of the Friars' discontent. On he went, turning north into Pentecostlane where he stopped outside a tenement.

It did not take much for Brother Robert to identify the source of the nuisance, for 'Bocher' Richard Bayser and his wife Emma had built a 'skaldyinghous' onto the side of their dwelling. This would have been a simple lean-to with a tile roof, housing a large wooden tub and a cauldron slung over a fire for boiling water. If the friar had caught Butcher Bayser working, he would have seen the hogs, with their razor backs and long legs, awaiting slaughter. There would have been the carcases of the slaughtered animals lying in pools of their own blood, alongside great piles of viscera heaped on the dirt all around the yard, with Emma Bayser adding to the filth by squeezing out the entrails to make sausage skins. Behind her, Bayser would have been working on another carcase in the tub, ladling boiling water over the flesh and then scraping away the hair. When the whole process was finished, Bocher Bayser would then have tipped up the tub and brushed the remains of the slaughter into the open ditch for it to end up in the Friars Minor's herb garden.

Although the butcher was doubtless sympathetic to the Friar's problem, he declined to change. It was then that Brother Robert decided to act. He engaged the services of an attorney, Robert de Watlynington, who was well known at the London Assize of Nuisance. The attorney then served a notice on the butcher and his wife to desist. They in turn ignored it. Playing for time, they requested that the matter be delayed. Eventually, de Watlynington arranged for the Mayor, John Chychestyre, and five Aldermen to view the Baysers' scaldinghouse for themselves. After the inspection, both parties were given just a day to prepare their cases. The assize court met on Friday 15 February 1370 before the Recorder, William de Halden, who found for the plaintiff.

The Order had been there before. The Brothers of the Friars Minor, or Greyfriars, were the largest of the mendicant orders of the Franciscans. Their funds came predominantly from the leading merchant families and the urban upper middle classes, and so through them they wielded a certain amount of power and influence. When they complained that the Butchers of St Nicholas Shambles had discarded their offal and ordure in the street so that the friars could hardly pass, the Civic Authorities acted.

By an order dated 12 March 1343, the Butchers of St Nicholas Shambles were granted a parcel of land in Secollane Lane by the City where they could clean their carcases and dispose of the offal in the Fleet Ditch, the 'vilest of all abominations which London then contained'. It was, in fact a small stream that was further fed from some mineral springs outside the City walls. When the water from the springs was diverted, the ditch became stagnant and 'creepeth slow enough, not so much for age, as injection of city excrements wherein it is obstructed'.[2] The rent for adding to such an 'abomination' was 'to repair and maintain a certain wharf, they and their successors for ever, rendering yearly to the Mayor of London at Christmas a boar's head'.[3] The cost of this gift was met out of the Guild's funds – and one of the earliest entries to survive in their account books reads 'Pd. For a boar to my Lord the Mayor . . . £1 4 0d.'[4]

The chosen site had the advantage that the river was tidal at that point and, in theory, the entrails would have been washed into the River Thames, and then out to sea. Ten years later, there was an exceptionally hot summer which can only have brought matters to a head. The Prior of the Hospital of St John of Jerusalem claimed that his predecessor had been dispossessed of the wharf and land, and still smarting at the loss, petitioned the Crown for its return. In addition, the Prior sought to have the butchers of St Nicholas Shambles evicted, complaining that the stench was 'injurious to the inhabitants of the Free Prison of the Fleet [Ludgate Prison] and neighbourhood'.[5] The prison, also known as 'le Frenche Prison', was on the east bank of the river, while Secollane, later Seacoal Lane, named after the wharf where sea-coal was unloaded, ran south from Snow Hill Street.

The Mayor and Sheriffs could find no evidence that the land and wharf had belonged to the Hospital of St John of Jerusalem, they being some way north in

St John Street, West Smithfield. However, the petition to have the Butchers removed from the banks of the Fleet River appears to have succeeded, as the next year they, the Butchers, were petitioning the Crown Authorities for another site to dispose of their offal. At last, the King ordered the Mayor to find them somewhere else, and the City Authorities came up with a parcel of land on the banks of the Thames for the Butchers of St Nicholas Shambles to 'deposit the entrails of slaughtered animals'.[6] The 'suitable place' was between the House of the Teaching Friars – an order of Dominicans or Black Friars – and the tenement of a William Hercy, close to Baynard Castle. The purchase was backed by the Mayor, with 'orders for the arrest and imprisonment of anyone found disturbing the said butchers and their servants in the execution of their duties to the butchers of the Shambles of St Nicholas for the said purpose'.[7]

The Butchers built a bridge – more likely it was a landing stage or platform over the river – that became known as the Bochersbrigge – butcher's bridge. There, the offal was cut up into small pieces and left on the staging until the tide was on the ebb, when it was shovelled into the Thames and taken out to sea. The butchers of Eastcheap had a similar arrangement a little way downriver at Pudding Bridge. This too was a rudimentary stage (later known as Fresh Wharf) at the bottom of Pudding Lane, so called 'because the Butchers of Eastcheape haue their scalding House for Hogges there, and their puddings [bowels, entrails, and guts] with other filth of Beastes, are voided downe that way to theyr dungboats on the Thames'.[8] Later the butchers of Eastcheap actually bought this narrow strip of land, a 'barroway' called Katherine Lane

> situated in the Parishes of St Magnus and St Botolph, London, between a tenement formerly belonging to Gilbert Maughfeilde, on the part of the east, and a tenement of Henry Bosworthe on the part of the west, and the King's Highway called Thames Street towards the north, and the River Thames towards the south.[9]

As with the Bochersbrigge, the butchers of Eastcheap had a similar setup. This was particularly successful as their 'Podyng-house', according to the Patent Roll, was still being used in 1549. In 1402, the Eastcheap butchers were further allowed to 'make a bridge upon the Thames, and to build houses upon the same, and the intestines of beasts and filth and offal of the said beasts, to carry little by little at the reflux of the tide . . .'[10]

The butchers of St Nicholas Shambles did not fare as well. The constant trail of spilt entrails from the wheelbarrows, and the resulting smell to and from their wharf, was too much for the grandees living around St Paul's. Some even blamed the butchers for another plague similar to, but not quite as devastating as, the Black Death of 1348. So a writ was issued for the removal of Bochersbrigge in 1369.

The King having received grievous complaints from diverse Prelates, Nobles, and other persons of the City, having buildings in the streets, lanes, and other places between the Shambles of the Butchers of St Nicholas, near the mansion of the Friars Minor of London and banks of the water of Thames, near to Baynard Castle, in the said Shambles and the carrying of entrails and offal, etc., through the streets to the river, at a place called Bochersbridgge, so that no one, by reason of the corruption of the same and filth, can hardly venture to abide in his house. We . . . order the said Bridgge, before the Feast of the Blessed Virgin [15 August], to be entirely pulled down, and such slaughtering of beasts shall be done on penalty of £100.[11]

Typically, nothing was done, and two years later the Mayor and Sheriffs were reprimanded by the King for their failure to enforce his orders. The bridge was finally removed in the early New Year. Following the loss of their bridge, the butchers had huge vaults constructed at vast expense beyond the Holborn Bridge, with streams and underground drains diverted through them to carry the offal away. With this new facility, the Butchers had the 1488 Act (against slaughtering cattle in the street) repealed in 1532. Another vault was constructed in Thames Street and linked by a ditch to Fresh Wharf for the use of the slaughterhouses of Eastcheap. This was originally a ditch covered over with a few planks of wood, but later it was completely enclosed by a brick arch. It apparently remained in use for the next century, as the account books are littered with entries for repair to the brickwork, pumps and gullies.

But still the butchers of St Nicholas Shambles were in trouble, and legislation was passed against their using the Holborn vaults through the nuisance they caused to 'the burghers of Middlesex'. The following year, the butchers were dumping their offal directly in the Thames again, 'whereat the King is wroth'.[12] The Mayor was ordered to arrest the offenders and confiscate their meat. With the slaughter of beasts outside London, coupled with the difficulties of disposing of the offal, came the inevitable rise in the price of meat, anathema to the citizens of London. This spurred Parliament to action. The Mystery Guild of Butchers was allowed to buy, through compulsory purchase, an existing dunghouse by Queenhithe, later known as Brooks Wharf, where they built a house to take the offal from St Nicholas Shambles. It arrived in enclosed carts and was cut into small pieces prior to being dumped by boat in the centre of the Thames on the ebb tide, so long as it was not 'between the Palace of Westminster and the Tower'.[13]

Occasionally, individual butchers were fined for leaving entrails in the street. However, contemporary court records show that it was the women, either butchers in their own right or those married to a butcher, who were fined in their husbands' stead. The fine was the same for both men and women, but with the wife being fined, the butcher's record was clear if he wanted to go on to higher office.

Besides their 'Podyng-house', the Eastcheap butchers owned their own scalding-house off Pudding Lane. This eventually became the property of the Butchers' Company, and was later the site of their third Hall. It was here that, in 1504, the butchers of Eastcheap were ordered by the Court of Aldermen to scald their hogs, but only in 'Vanners Hall in Podyng Lane',[14] doubtless named after a former incumbent, a senior Eastcheap butcher named John Vannere, living in a house named Vannershawe.[15]

Notwithstanding this catalogue of harassment, it was a time of plenty for the Butchers. The Black Death of 1348 had destroyed over 40 percent of London's population (around 50,000 people), and it had been said there were not enough of the living to bury the dead. But, for those who survived 'the great pestilence', it was a time of great opportunity. A third of the City within the Walls was still unoccupied a decade later, but towards the end of the fourteenth century these houses were taken over by merchants, craftsmen and labourers. They had come from the provinces, lured, as in the apocryphal story of Dick Whittington, by the notion of London as *cockaigne*, the realm of gold. For the Guild of Butchers it was precisely that, particularly when Edward III (after a heavy 'contribution' from the City) ordered in 1371 that 'no strangers, *i.e.* none except freemen, should be allowed to sell by retail, within the City and the suburbs. This privilege had always been resented by the citizens who were in favour of free trade'.[16] Nor was the Guilds' contribution to the City at that time particularly onerous. Apart from the earlier monetary contributions to the Crown for the expensive wars with France, they were required to provide 40 men at arms and 60 archers. These were to keep watch between the Tower of London and Billingsgate after French galleys were sighted off the Foreland of Thanet in Kent. The Guild of Butchers produced just two soldiers, who kept watch with the Fishmongers every Thursday.

But the threat of France was never far away. The memories of the great victories of Edward III were slowly being eroded with his advancing age. The Black Prince was sick, and shortly to predecease his father who died in 1377. The new king, Richard II, granted Letters Patent to the City, whereby they could levy murage, a toll for the upkeep of the City Wall. For the Butchers, a tax of 1d was levied on both an ox and a cow, $\frac{1}{2}$ d on a lamb and a porker (or 2d for 5 pigs) and $\frac{1}{4}$ d for a calf and a lamb.[17]

Life for the Guild of Butchers and its freemen throughout the extravagant reign of Richard II went on very much as usual. An Irishman, Richard Whyte, was caught stealing a leg of mutton from Walter Beawe, a butcher of St Nicholas Shambles. His punishment was half an hour in the pillory with the stolen leg of mutton hung around his neck. That same year, 1391, the Guild was ordered not to allow a best lamb without wool to be sold for more than 6d, and that it should not be 'dubbed'[18] with extra fat from another lamb.

Besides overseeing these trading restrictions, ordinances and their role in the administration of Ward and City, the Guild of Butchers were still true to their Saxon origins. They cared for their sick and arranged decent burial for the dead, supplying both the hearse-pall and the candles for the actual service. There would have been four separate meeting places, one for each of the markets, and one for the general Mystery Guild of Butchers. The individual market guilds met in their local churches as guests of the relevant church guilds with whom they were loosely associated, such as the Fraternity of St Luke centred on the church of St Nicholas Shamble and the butchers of St Nicholas Shambles. However, it is certain that the Butchers were burned out of their original Saxon hall, there having been several major fires over the centuries, both within and outside the City walls. In addition, there are written accounts of land and buildings (such as the Pudding House in Katherine Lane) being held by the Guild in the fourteenth and fifteenth centuries. Had there been a hall owned by them, it would certainly have been recorded as well. When the Mystery and the three market guilds met up together, the hall of another guild was hired, the first mention of this being an entry in the Court Minutes of the Brewers' Company in 1422–3. The Brewers Hall, built in 1418, stood in Addle Street, the name corrupted from the Old English word *adela* meaning 'stinking urine'. However, its nomenclature seems inappropriate as it was reported that 'the street had fair buildings on both sides'. Fifty years later the Butchers were using the Carpenters' Hall by London Wall, as evidenced by the entry 'Resseyuid of the Bochers for the Halle Ijs'.[19]

It was in those two halls (doubtless along with many others over the years) that the Guild of Butchers met for court meetings, for dinners and for feasts. Although the fraternity was as strong as ever, the menu had developed somewhat from its Saxon origins. To the original roast and boiled meats was added what became traditional butchers' fare – marrow bone pie,[20] a fine concoction of bone marrow, eggs, cream, and saffron in a pastry case.

While ale would still have been the staple drink, wine was becoming more popular, particularly at the more important dinners such as the election of the Wardens or their Saint's day. On these occasions, all members of the Mystery would have worn their distinctive livery. As a senior Craft Guild, the Butchers would have been amongst the earliest in livery by around the mid-fourteenth century, exactly as Chaucer wrote of freemen who 'were clothed in the same livery, All of one solemn, great fraternity, freshly and new in their gear, and well adorned it was'.[21]

Strictly speaking, livery was not only the uniform but food and wine as well – a 'livery cupboard' was where food was stored, often to be dispensed to servants or the poor. The earliest liveries were inspired by the habits of the various monastic orders, with their distinctive and distinguishing coloured cloaks and cowls. Although the blue and white hoods that marked the Butchers' Company have not been worn since the middle of the nineteenth century, there is no reason to suppose that blue and white were not the chosen colours of the medieval guild, particularly as these chosen colours were also those adopted by allied crafts, notably the Tallow Chandlers, Basketmakers, and the Fishmongers. The gowns 'were of party colours, as the right side of one colour [white] and the left side of another [blue]',[22] the hood embroidered with the badge of the Guild (see page 37).

It can only have been a glorious sight as the Mayor, Sheriff, Aldermen, and members of the various guilds, wearing their polychrome liveries, were processing, their banners flying in the wind, or lining the route to witness any of the dozens of events in the City calendar. There were royal occasions too, as when Henry V received his queen, Catharine of Valois, at Blackheath and presented her to the City. The route was lined by the Guilds, 'standyng yn order'[23] and the King 'was received worthily and royally by the mayor and aldermen with him there'.[24] When they reached the cross at Cheap, there 'was made a castelle and there was moche solemnyte of angelys and virgenys syngyng'.

Two years later, in 1422, the King's mortal remains were taken with great ceremony through the City to lie in state at St Paul's Cathedral. The corpse was met by the Mayor and Aldermen, and escorted by three hundred freemen 'clothed in black vestments, together with 300 torches borne by 300 persons clothed in white gowns and hoods'.[25] The route was also lined by the Misteries, the Butchers providing eight of the 211 freemen with torches, 'the remains of which were returned to them'.[26]

Likewise, when the young king Henry VI received his queen, Margaret of Anjou, the City turned out to greet them. Five hundred freemen were conspicuous with their 'conysaunce of everych Fellyshypp brawderid upon theyr slevys that oon Craft mycht be known from an othir'[27] – their Guild badges embroidered on the sleeves of their gowns. The standing of the Butchers' Guild must have been high in 1445 as, like the Salters, Vintners and Haberdashers, they contributed a full £20 towards the cost of the event.

Nor were the Butchers above advancing their station. On the Lord Mayor's Day of 1427, there was an altercation with the Goldsmiths

as to which should stand before Goldsmith's Row, the Goldsmiths claiming to stand there by ancient right, the Bochers refusing to give up their place. The Bochers complained to the Mayor, and both companies agreed to abide by his award. The Mayor [John Gedney] sat in his Parish Church of St Christopher, next the Stockkye, and had before him the Wardens of the Goldsmiths and the Bochers, and he awarded that the Goldsmiths should have their standing in the same place as of old time, and charged the Wardens of both crafts to take each other by the hand in sign of love and peace, and love and cherish each other as they ought to do.[28]

Despite the odd inter-Guild rivalry (that frequently erupted into a full-blow riot), they were united in the love of pageantry. From the very beginning, the Mayor of London marked his appointment with a show, a grand affair with 'drumes and flutes and trumpets bloyhing'.[29] At that time, the show was usually a water pageant, where each Guild had their own barge, although some were hired for the occasion. Each was richly decorated and hung with flowers, streaming ribbons and the Guild's banners. Led by the Mayor's barge, they 'processed' in order of precedence between the Tower of London and the Palace of Westminster. Then, the Mayor would entertain them all to a feast at the Guildhall, whose 'new edifice' had already been transformed from 'an oylde and leytle cottage' into 'a fayre and goodly house'.[30] One major benefactor among many rich City merchants was Richard Whittington, four times Lord Mayor.

Just as the standards of dress, entertainment and status of the Mystery of Butchers advanced through the fifteenth century, so their authority over the members of their Guild became absolute. In 1423, they submitted an Ordinance for the governance of the Mystery consolidating their former set of rules. Amongst many other provisions, the total ban on Sunday trading was relaxed, where 'no butcher shall keep his shop open or expose meat for sale after 10 o'clock in the morning on any Sunday under penalty of 40d'. Another requirement was that 'no bull be killed for sale before it has been hunted and baited'. Since the days of Ancient Greece, it has been accepted that

> before killing of any beast or bird; namely, how to make it tenderer if it be too old, and how to make it of the best rellish: Petrocles affirmed, that a Lion being shewed to a strong bull three or four hours before he be killed; causeth his flesh to be as tender as the flesh of a Steer: fear dissolving his hardest parts and making his very heart to become pulpy. Perhaps upon the like reason we used to bait our Bulls before we kill them: for their blood is otherwise so hard, that none can digest it in the flesh, but afterwards it is so far from being poisonable, that it becometh tender and nourishing food. Perhaps also for this cause Old Cocks are coursed with little wands from one another, or else forced to fight with their betters before they are killed.[31]

Plutarch wrote that sheep killed by wolves, birds by hawks, geese by foxes, hares or deer by greyhounds, 'eate much sweeter, kindlier, and tenderer, then if they be killed by sleight or violence'.[32]

Another original clause in the 1423 Ordinances decreed that 'no butcher find fault with a stranger for demanding pence for victuals sold to him',[33] in other words, demanding the exact money for the purchase. At that time, one penny would buy between two and a half and three pounds of beef, and slightly more of pork or mutton. After 1216 the Exchequer, tired of their pennies being bisected or quartered, introduced a silver farthing. A halfpenny, also made of silver, came sixty years later. Naturally, these lower denominations made a great difference to the butcher, as smaller quantities could now be sold to his customers.

For the ordinary marketplace butcher, Roman numerals were perfectly adequate for quantifying objects. He had no trouble serving his customers, nor giving change with the new found denominations. In larger transactions, however, where advanced accounting such as multiplication and division was required, the more substantial butcher found it extremely difficult before the more straightforward Arabic numeric system, with its decimal point and zero, was adopted in the sixteenth century. The simple solution to the problem of calculating with Roman numerals was to use a counting board with a number of jettons or counters. It was an ancient system whereby a polished wooden board was marked off in a series of parallel lines, each space designating a different value. A calculation was made by moving the jettons, usually copper discs with a hole in the centre, between the grooves, rather like an abacus. It was extremely quick and accurate. The pub game shove ha'penny developed from this simple counting board.

Further Ordinances followed those of 1423, and as the Mystery of Butchers became more self-regulatory, so the Wardens capitalised on their increased power. Journeymen lost the right to elect their wardens, the vote being the prerogative of the livery alone. In 1466, the journeymen Butchers complained to the Mayor and Aldermen 'of the various suits and dissentions which had taken place concerning the election of the Wardens of the Butchers'.[34] The Mayor and Court of Aldermen found for the liverymen, but in their judgement they specified that the elections of Wardens should be held annually. This judgement was incorporated into the Ordinances of the Royal Charter of 1605. To show their total authority over the Mystery of Butchers, the Court of Aldermen gave themselves the right to remove unsatisfactory Wardens, and to replace them with those of their own choice.

Within the City, the power of the Mayor and Aldermen was absolute. They pronounced on every aspect of the Guilds, including the inter-Guild transactions. For instance, in 1461 there was a shortage of tallow, and the Butchers' Guild, who had always fixed their own price, raised it to 13s 4d taking the scarcity into consideration. The Mayor and Aldermen stepped in and not only legislated against the price increase, but also forbade them to take tallow out of London and so their jurisdiction. The Mystery retaliated by fixing their own price of 12s a wey (a weight that varied locally). But the Mayor and Aldermen were determined to make sure that candles were available in London at an affordable price, and decreed that the

Butchers [were] not to sell their tallow after Shrove Tuesday next but at such a price that the candlemakers could sell one pound at 1d., and 13 lbs at 12d., and that if any scarcity should happen they should go to the Mayor to fix the price, and that the Butchers should not sell to strangers until the City be supplied; and the candlemakers were ordered not to sell 12 lbs. of candles beyond the price of 14 d and to sell 13 lbs. at 12d.[35]

Clearly with such a small profit margin allowed by the Mayor and Aldermen, the purchase price of the tallow was crucial to the candle maker. But still the Butchers flouted the rules, and they were summoned before the Court of Aldermen:

> Whereas candles are daily sold in London at a more excessive price than in days past to the great hurt of the people, particularly the poor folk of the City of London, which price is caused by the covetousness of the butchers and the agreements made among them whereby the tallow is brought into a few hands and sold out of the City, and also they melt the same tallow so they may keep it from corruption so that they may keep it and sell it at a price which pleases them . . .[36]

Nor was that the end of the Butchers' misdemeanours. They were accused of making candles themselves and selling them outside the City, thereby inflating the price of candles ever further. The Mayor and Aldermen were incensed by the Butchers' behaviour and their disrespect, and decreed that they could not sell any tallow at all, either inside or outside the City, until the Mayor and Aldermen gave their permission, and even then only at a price fixed by them. Making candles, other than for their own use, was also prohibited on 'pain of forfeiture'. Through their transgressions three Wardens were removed from office and replaced by the Mayor's nominees. They were also collectively fined £40, which they did not pay, so the fine was 'reduced to £20'[37] the next year which, although still heavy, they did pay.

The Wardens were all butchers appointed by the Guild to police the three flesh markets. In the thirteenth century there were twelve, but by 1426 their numbers were reduced to just two per market. Although these surveyors were in fact Court appointees, they had sworn an oath of allegiance to the Mayor and Aldermen, and acted under their jurisdiction. Nor was the warden's task easy enforcing the orders of the Common Council and Aldermen. In 1484, they complained in an involved bill that, despite their City authority, the butchers were being 'disrespectful' in the extreme, either swearing at them or blatantly ignoring their orders. When they finally managed to prosecute an offender, such as William Coc, 'bocher of Eschep', who was fined 26s 8d for 'mysbehavyng',[38] either swearing or selling bad meat, or both, half the fine went to the Wardens and the other half to the City. Later, speaking 'seditious words' against the Wardens earned a custodial sentence, as in the case of John Hyggyns who was sent to prison in 1525, or Robert Normanton who was sent to Newgate Prison when he 'spoke many unfitting words of the Wardens'.[39] On his release, he was brought before the Court, where he was compelled to sink to his knees to confess that he had slandered his Guild and to beg their forgiveness. Often the friction between Warden and butcher was caused through inter-market rivalry, or when a member of one market guild was appointed as Warden of another.

Another feature of the Wardens' bill from the Council of Aldermen was his power to examine any pig brought into the City for sale, and to seize any that were measled (*Cysticercus cellulose*). Such a disease would have been obvious, while other conditions, whose 'signs of putrefaction, a fevered carcase, signs of dropsical or oedematous animals',[40] although harder to identify, would still have been well within the diagnostic capabilities of the experienced butcher and Warden alike. The penalties for selling meat that was 'unwholesome for man's body'[41] were increased to:

> First offence: grievously amerced
> Second offence: pillory
> Third offence: imprisonment for a year
> Fourth offence: outlawry[42]

Such penalties might have seemed harsh, but they were a considerable improvement on the regulations enforced by the Kingdom of Naples and Sicily where those caught selling animals that had died a natural death incurred the following punishments:

> First offence: fine of a lire of gold or corporal punishment
> Second offence: cutting off a hand
> Third offence: hanging[43]

Back in England, by the middle of the fourteenth century, the pillory was commuted to a fine, as in 1452 when William Scalon was charged £20 for attempting to sell two putrid oxen, the fine being divided ⅔ and ⅓ between the City and the Butchers' Guild. Other punishments were more shaming than financial, as with John Pinkyard who sold four flitches of rancid bacon. He was made to ride on his own mare with two of them slung around his neck, and a sign over his head 'For puttyng to sale of mesell and stynkyng bacon'.[44] A 'basyn' was beaten in front of the horse in case anyone missed his shame. Another punishment was meted out to John Clerk who was taken from Newgate prison and made to sit on a scaffold in Leadenhall Market for two hours, wearing hog's ears and a sow's udders over his shoulders. It is likely that Clerk was a foreign butcher, but he would still have come under the jurisdiction of the Warden of Butchers' Guild.

Leadenhall Market, named after its lead roof, had opened as a general market in

1445 at the direction of the then Lord Mayor, Sir Simon Eyre. It had originally belonged to the Neville family, who sold it to the City for a granary. Although poultry and fish were the mainstay of the market, foreign butchers were admitted to sell flesh in 1533:

> The foreign butchers for a long time stood in the high street of Lime Street Ward on the north side, twice every week, namely Wednesday and Saturday, and were some gain to the tenants before whose houses they set their blocks and stalls; but that advantage being espied, they were taken into Leadenhall, there to pay for their standing to the chamber of London.[45]

At that time, 'the number of butchers then in the city and suburbs was accounted six score, of which everyone killed six oxen apiece weekly, . . . or seven hundred and twenty oxen weekly'.[46] In the first Butchers' Guild returns of 1544, it is recorded that there were 102 members of the livery who paid quarterage (along with 25 freemen not of the livery), which leaves just 18 foreign butchers in Leadenhall Market. This seems somewhat unlikely, particularly as the importance of Eastcheap and St Nicholas Shambles appeared to have declined. With the ever-increasing demand for meat from an expanding and increasingly affluent population, the non-free butchers crept back and were officially allowed to sell their meat within the City limits. They mostly operated in Leadenhall Street where they set up their stalls on the pavement, paying a small fee to the owner of the house. They were allowed to sell their meat on Wednesdays and Saturdays, but only during the mornings. These foreigners were encouraged by the City authorities, as they had long held that the 'inflated' freemen butchers' prices were the major cause of inflation, and that competition from the non-freemen butchers would keep the price of meat down. By 1533, however, the foreigners were forced back inside Leadenhall Market and so paid their dues to the City. The restriction was lifted by 1540, and once again the foreigners were on the street with the payment 'of ½d for cleansing the street to such person as the Alderman of the ward should appoint'.[47] A few years later, they were back solely in the Market at a rent of 8d a week, but their hours were extended to the afternoons as well. Predictably, the Wardens of the Butchers petitioned the Court of Aldermen to allow one of their number to police the foreigners, but nothing came of it until 1573 when the Wednesday market was suspended, and the foreign butchers were enjoined to bring to the market 'jaws, midriffs, feet and heads, on which the poor would very gladly bestow their small portion of money'.[48] The authorised presence of the foreigners was, of course, a serious blow to the monopoly of the free butchers, but as they had recently been at serious odds with the Crown, the Mayor and the Council of Aldermen, they were powerless to resist.

A series of poor harvests and bad weather conditions, coupled with the rising demand from an increasing population, were the real causes of the high price of meat. In 1529, the 'King's Most Honourable Council' or the Privy Council, fixed the price of beef at $\frac{1}{2}$d a pound, veal at $\frac{5}{8}$d and mutton at $\frac{3}{4}$d a pound weight, until an order from the King released them from the controlled price. Furthermore, each butcher was bound to the King for £100 to keep to these prices, and to sell 'indifferently to any person that would buy at the said price without any fraudulent excuse and to give true weight and poise without affection or any other corruption.'[49] The idea was to control the exact price of meat by weight, as opposed to an arbitrary price for the piece, or a 'pennyworth' as had been the practice in the past. For this, each butcher was required to have an accurate steelyard that was inspected regularly by the City authorities.

Steelyards had been used by butchers (and other tradesmen) since the 4th millennium BC. The Greeks, then the Romans, improved upon the earlier Egyptian balance, producing a highly effective weighing apparatus. This was usually made of bronze, with a straight bar with a ring and hole pivot, mounted with unequal arms. This meant that a heavy load could be weighed at a short distance from the fulcrum by using small, standard weights. Sometimes there was a pan for lighter cuts, otherwise a hook was used to suspend a heavy carcase. Often the weights were highly ornamental, such as a bronze head. Little changed over the centuries as butchers adopted the Roman system of weighing. During the reign of the Anglo-Saxon King Edgar it was ordained that 'one measure and weight should pass through the king's dominions such as is observed at London and Winchester',[50] and again in Magna Carta there was a clause relating to standardised weights. An act of Parliament in 1340 decreed that 'from henceforth one measure and one weight shall be throughout the realm' with standard sample weights being sent to each county. At that time the Roman balance was also being used by a group of German merchants, of the Hanseatic League, which had its warehouses beside the Thames just above the present London Bridge. In one part of the complex was a place where all the imported goods were weighed, called in old German, *stãlhof* – sampleyard, which corrupted became 'steelyard'.

Change to selling by weight was naturally resisted by the Butchers, and as was so often the case in their early history, they totally ignored unpopular legislation. This meant that a further Act was passed in 1533 for the 'poor people [who] could not gain sufficient money by their labour to provide their common victual of beef and other flesh owing to its excessive price'.[51] In other words, the butcher was ordered to sell meat in whatever weight was required by the customer and at a controlled price. The weight was known as *Haberdepayes* (today's *Avoirdupois*) with both beef and pork restricted to $\frac{1}{2}$d a pound, with mutton slightly more expensive at $\frac{5}{8}$d a pound. There was a fine of 3s 4d for any butcher who failed to sell by weight at the fixed price, half going to the Crown, half to the informant.[52] It was further enacted that the graziers should sell their beasts on the hoof at a price that would allow the butchers a reasonable profit. Even before the Act was passed, the freemen of the Butchers' Guild wrote to the Court of Aldermen saying that they were withdrawing from all City affairs in protest at their enforced price control. The Committee of Common Council then met with the Privy Council and the Butchers' Guild, as well as a representation from the foreigner butchers, when they were both ordered to abide by the Act. The Butchers wrote to the Common Council twice more, repeating their threat to have nothing to do with the City. The Privy Council then ordered the Mayor and Aldermen to reappraise the price structure, but it was still not acceptable to the Guild. During this stalemate foreigners were given ever greater freedom to sell within the City.

But the Butchers were not to be intimidated. They immediately stopped slaughtering, and sold their store cattle back to the graziers in the vain hope that there would be such a public outcry over the lack of meat that there would be no alternative but to repeal the Act, so that they could 'do as they did before'. The Mayor and Aldermen tried to persuade the Butchers to change their minds, accusing them of 'wyldful frowerdnes [perverseness] . . . [as they had] utterly refused to serve our seid subjectes'.[53] The King too was livid. On 29 July 1533, the Court of Aldermen ordered all 53 freemen[54] butchers to appear before them at 8 am when they were summarily disenfranchised. At a stroke on Lammas Day (1 August), they each lost the privileges, franchises and liberties as freemen of the City of London. Such a large expulsion was unprecedented in the history of the City, and demonstrates not only the power of the Council but the resolve and unity of the Butchers' Guild.

A Royal proclamation followed, confirming the disenfranchisement of the butchers. It also opened up the City to non-freemen butchers, who for the first month were allowed to sell at an open market price. This was extended to another month, which was all that the freemen butchers wanted themselves, but were denied by law. Later, the ex-Wardens were summoned to the Court of Aldermen and were asked to recant, which they steadfastly declined to do. In retaliation, the Court expressly forbade the ex-freemen butchers to negotiate prices with their customers, and encouraged the public to report them if they did. This was particularly unfair as they were bound by an Act that did not apply to the foreigners.

The Butchers continued to flout the law without fear of reprimand and regardless of consequence. After a series of complaints, a second Royal proclamation followed, even more forceful than the first. The King's authority was not to be trifled with. The Mayor and Aldermen enacted the statute with a vengeance, imprisoning the offenders without bail.[55] A further reconciliation was sought by the Court of Aldermen, but still to no avail. Eight butchers were appointed to speak on the Guild's behalf, and the stalemate was partially broken when it was agreed that they would resume the steady supply of meat after Easter, but the 'other answer they cannot make'. Finally, at the intervention of Thomas Cromwell, by then Master of the Rolls, and the Lord Chancellor, the offending statute (25 Henry VIII, c. 1) was finally suspended. The authorities agreed that it was unjust that butchers should buy on the hoof and sell by weight, regardless of the purchase price of the beast. The price of beef and veal was increased marginally to ⅝d a pound for beef, while mutton remained the same at ¾d a pound. The price increase was a step in the right direction, but still the Butchers refused to stand down.

Feelings ran high on both sides of the argument and there were many prosecutions. The City folk had become used to their diet of meat and were now being deprived. When Emanuell Lucar attempted to buy a quarter of veal by weight, Butcher Normanton refused, saying that he could have the piece for 14d or not at all. Lucar's brother Francis reminded the butcher of his obligations, to which Normanton replied that there had been two Royal proclamations which he had ignored and doubtless there would be many more which he would continue to flout. A woman joined in the argument, screaming at him that he should sell by weight. Normanton rounded on her telling her that he would rather see her die, than sell his meat by weight. Incensed, Lucar complained to the Lord Mayor, Thomas Whyte, whose presence was enough to sway Normanton. The Aldermen tried yet again to persuade the Butchers to conform and so 'to avoid the King's high displeasure'[56] but, yet again, there was stalemate.

By now, July 1534, everyone was heartily sick of the dispute. The City authorities then decided that Wardens of the Butchers Guild were no longer fit to supervise the meat markets, and appointed two Upper Wardens from other Guilds and Companies. The first were the Wardens from the Drapers' Company, then the Mercers, followed by the Grocers and Goldsmiths. Their authority was backed up by two officers appointed by the Lord Mayor and Sheriffs who carried white rods 'two yards long' as symbols of their authority. Other Companies and Guilds followed, serving a week at a time in each of the four flesh markets. It was deliberately humiliating for the Butchers to be supervised by not just one Company, but by a whole series of Companies.

Matters finally came to a head when John Long, who had had a record of dissent over the years being one of the freemen who had been disenfranchised, took the case of his fellow Butchers to the Court of Aldermen. He informed them that, as there was no living to be had by selling meat by weight at the City's prices, as from 1 August he and the rest of the Mystery would close down for good and seek alternative employment. The Court could see that he was not bluffing, and became extremely worried. They set up an enquiry and travelled to the surrounding grasslands, interviewing the graziers and drovers. The deadline was extended for a month, then two, while the King and his Privy Council decided what to do. By the end of October the authorities climbed down. They admitted that the free butchers were further penalised by the expense of living in the City – the cost of servants, their premises, scot and lot (City tax and duty), the rent for holding grounds for stock outside the City walls, but most important of all, the fluctuation in price of the stock between the winter and the summer. The King relented marginally and allowed the Butchers, 'his loving subjects', an increase of $12\frac{1}{2}$ percent, but only for beef and pork to $\frac{7}{8}$ d a pound weight. The notice of the price increase was posted all over the markets and the main gates into the City.

For the Butchers, 27 October 1534 was an important day, as the Act of Parliament (25 Henry VIII, c i) was finally ratified. By this Act any butcher, his wife or servant who refused to sell by weight, using a new set of weights specially struck for butchers, was to be imprisoned. It was also the day the Council of Aldermen received a petition from the Butchers pleading for reinstatement to their freedom and liberties. This complete *volte face* was prompted by the Butchers' need to employ journeymen and to keep apprentices. They could not operate without them, so if they were not empowered to have them, there was a real danger of losing them and their businesses as well. The authorities took six weeks to review their case, and on 10 December 1534 the livery and freedom of the Mystery Guild of Butchers was restored. The whole sorry affair had lasted sixteen months, but their reinstatement had still not resolved the thorny question of selling by weight. On the positive side, they did, however, keep their position of twenty-fourth in the order of precedence of the Livery Companies and Craft Guilds in the City.

The question of foreigners could now be addressed, they who had recently had all the advantages of the freemen, but none of their restrictions and expenses. The Court of Aldermen considered the Butchers' plea, but concluded that the non-free butchers posed no real competition to the freemen and that they should be allowed to continue as before. To reinforce their authority over the Butchers, they reinstated the supervision of the markets by other Companies, beginning with the Grocers.

Royal Proclamation followed Royal Proclamation fixing the price of meat by season, and still the Butchers petitioned the Court of Aldermen to intercede on their behalf to be allowed to sell by the piece. Surprisingly, the Aldermen managed it, and a specific order allowed the butchers to sell their wares by the piece providing there was no complaint of 'their greed and covetous appetites'.[57] The price paid for this success was for eighteen of the principal members of the Butchers' Guild to be bound to the Lord Chamberlain for £100. This was to oblige the Wardens and their successors to ensure that there would always be a ready supply of meat in the City. To keep the peace, further proclamations suspended the 1533 Act so long as the Butchers 'took no courage or boldness'[58] from this favour. The City authorities can only have been heartily sick of the intransigence of the Butchers, as petition followed petition demanding that the clause stating that meat could only be sold by weight be repealed, rather than suspended. In early 1544, the Court of Aldermen accused the Butchers of being 'blynded in averyce and syngler gayne and lucre'[59] when complaints were received by the Privy Council that freemen butchers had exceeded the ¾d a pound weight for beef and 1d for mutton, despite the threat of a custodial sentence for the miscreants. The penalties for the third offence of overcharging were later increased to time in the pillory and the loss of an ear.

The Mayor and Aldermen's power in the City was absolute, even covering the amusements of apprentices. In 1479, they forbade 'all labourers, servants and apprentices of any artificer or victuallers'[60] to play tennis or football, or to use cards and dice, on pain of six days' imprisonment. They were encouraged to practise archery, however, 'or other semblable games which be not prohibit nor forboden by the Kynge'.[61] The charge of playing dice with an apprentice was serious – as late as 1577 William Parllnbye was fined 3s 4d 'for playenge at the dyce with a prentyce'.[62] An earlier proclamation had made it illegal to act in a Christmas mumming (a silent play) wearing false beards or 'disfourmyd or colorid visages'.[63] It would appear from this that the apprentice's life was unexciting and dull – but in truth there was much entertainment in the streets of London. There was 'merrymaking on the vigils of the great feasts, with dancing in the streets, and the houses decorated with flowers, and oil lamps burning throughout the night'.[64] To celebrate Midsummer Eve, the richer citizens would have an open house, with bread, biscuits and wine served on trestle tables outside their houses for all comers. The dancing continued right up to the seventeenth century when Puritan zealotry put paid to such jollity.

Plays, specially commissioned and often performed by members of the Guilds, were another popular form of entertainment. For the Guild of Butchers, the plays were frequently staged on election day, 18 October, the same as their patron saint St Luke's name day, when it was certain that they had hired a hall for both occasions. However, by 1485, they had a hall to call their own, St Gylus [Giles] Hall in Monkwell Street, close by Cripplegate,[65] not that far from their old quarters in Addle Street. The rent was £7 per annum. Monkwell, or Monkswell, Street led off from Silver Street, with its silversmiths and 'in which be divers fair houses'[66]. It was named after a well used by a hermit who lived in a cell called 'St James in the City Wall'. Next to the cell, by then a monastery, stood the Bowyers' Hall and beyond them were the Barber Surgeons – the Brewers, Curriers and Plasterers were all close by. On the opposite side of the street was the church of St Giles, with seven almshouses behind. It would appear that the Butchers' Hall was the parish house of the church, which they certainly shared with its owners, the Fraternity of St Giles. As the church 'was very fair and large', it can be assumed that the hall was of similar standing.

Inside the City wall, space was already at a premium. The hall itself would have

a. Smithfield as a livestock market finally closed in June 1855 after nearly 900 years continuous trading. Its place was taken by purpose-built market, Copenhagen Fields, in Islington.

b. Newgate was the principal dead-meat market of London until it finally closed after the new Central Meat Market, Smithfield pened in 1868.

6b. A pen and ink drawing of the entrance to Butchers' Hall from Eastcheap by Thomas Hosmer Shepherd, 1855. The Hall, set in a courtyard, was reached by a long alley. Shepherd also made a separate sketch of the Company's Arms protected by a lead cowl.

6a. Portrait of William Collins, Master 1828, who was largely responsible for the rebuilding of the fourth Butchers' Hall. His contribution was marked by a sketch of the new Hall on a paper by his right hand, the only known representation.

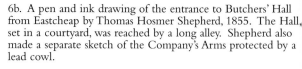

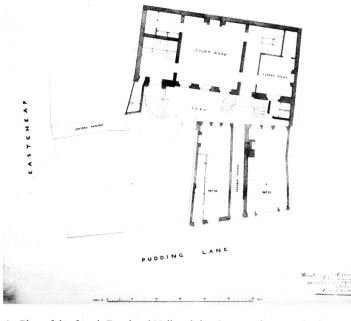

6c. Plan of the fourth Butchers' Hall and the Company's properties in Pudding Lane drawn shortly before it was destroyed by fire. It was a grand building with a double-flight staircase to the entrance hall.

a. The Nathanial Edwards Loving Cup, 1724. Edwards
referred to donate this remarkable silver cup to the Company
lieu of a fine for not accepting the position of Master.

7b. The 'Charles II Goblet' was presented to the Company by
Richard Taylor, a butcher from Cripplegate, in 1669. Three
hundred years later, Terence Bonser gave a replica to the
Butchers. All three pieces were stolen in the silver robbery of
Easter 1981.

c. The 'Fury' locomotive hauling carriages carrying cattle on the Liverpool & Manchester Railway, 1833. The spread of the
lways finally put paid to the drover.

 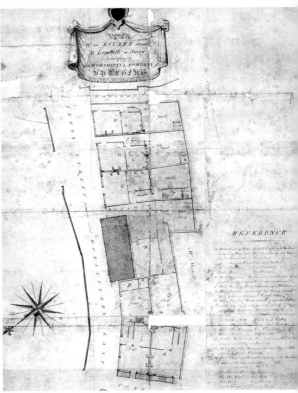

8a & 8b. Fore Street, Lambeth in the 1860s. The plan shows the extent of the property, a bequest from James Leverett in 1663. At one stage it was the centre of Lambeth stone-glaze pottery with several kilns and let houses. The whole was finally sold to Sir Henry Doulton, the largest manufacturer of sanitary fittings in the area.

8c & 8d. Plate commemorating the centenary of the first refrigerated cargo of New Zealand mutton and lamb landed in 1882 in London aboard the sailing ship *Dunedin*. A carcase of lamb was presented to Queen Victoria on her birthday at Buckingham Palace. The actual cleaver used to butcher the lamb was presented to Queen Elizabeth The Queen Mother who passed it on to the Company.

formed part of a long terrace that stretched the length of Monkwell Street. St Giles Hall would have been typical of the period, being certainly two, possibly three, stories high. On the ground floor was a staircase hall with store rooms and offices leading off it. A contemporary inventory shows that the ceremonial regalia, banners, flags, and torches were stored there, along with military equipment that included eight cressets, a form of iron basket on a pole in which grease, wood or coal was burnt for illumination, six banner staves, four 'sheffs [sheaves] of arrows, one payre of almayne revytts [light armour] with spents and salett [headgear]'.[67] This is the first record of the possessions of the Company.

On the first floor of the building there would have been a double height hall, most likely with a fireplace. As the building was shared with the Fraternity of St Giles, which was comparatively well off, the decoration would have been lavish, with carved beams, certainly a carved wood and painted statue of St Giles, and various woven wall hangings. At one end, there was a minstrels' gallery, at the other a raised dais for the Warden and the Court. The Warden could well have had his own chamber off the dais, with another room above it. The kitchens were situated off the hall at the other end of the room, and were entered around the side of a carved wooden screen. By this time, the timber frame and the brickwork would have been rendered, and painted with a lime wash. All in all, it was a grand but serviceable room that served needs of the Butchers well for sixty years.

Although the Butchers shared their hall with the Fraternity of St Giles, they remained loyal to their patron saint, St Luke. By the end of the fifteenth century the 'Fellowship of the Craft of Bochers' had founded a separate body, 'the Fraternitie of St Luke'. They had endowed a chapel in his honour at St Nicholas Shambles, where they kept the 'herse cloth with the box yt is in with lock and four torchis,. . . [and] a great chest standing in St Lukes Chapel with sertyn things in it' including the Guild's plate and other treasures.

St Luke the Evangelist, the patron saint of the Butchers, was further honoured when his symbol, the ox, was incorporated into their arms 'Granted by Thomas Hawley, Clarenceux [Herald of the College of Arms] 7th February 1540/41'.[68]

The actual armorial bearings, which are the same today, are registered as:

Azure two poleaxes in saltire or blades inwards, between two bulls' heads couped in fesse argent, on a chief argent a boar's head couped gules, tusked or, languid azure, between two bunches of holly vert, banded or.

Crest: On a wreath of colours a bull statant with wings adorsed or lined with argent, the head, forequarters, hoofs, and tuft of the tail or, the hindquarters argent, armed gules, about the head a nimbus or.

Mantling: Gules double argent[69]

This technical description translates as a pair of blue poleaxes crossed, their blades turned inwards. It is interesting that they chose the grander war poleaxe as opposed to the heavy, hammer-like version used by butchers. Being competent butchers, the bulls' heads, silver on either side of the poleaxes, are cleanly cut (as opposed to being wrenched off) at the neck. The livery colours were silver (often just white) and blue, and this is reproduced in the shield colours – the chief argent, a strip of silver being the top third of the shield. Again the boar's head is neatly cut off, couped, at the neck and coloured red with gold tusks and a blue tongue. The bunches of holly, neatly bound in gold, are not true holly (*ilex*) but common butcher's broom or knee-holly (*Ruscus aculeatus*). The branches of this knee-high shrub (hence one of its names) has small, sharp leaves on a stiff branch, ideal, when bound together, for scrubbing butchers' blocks (hence the alternative name). Another name is Jew's Myrtle as it was used in the service of the Feast of the Tabernacles. Incidentally, there seems little that butcher's broom will not cure being used variously as an aperient, diaphoretic, diuretic, as well a cure for dropsy and scrofula, while the young shoots eat like asparagus.

The crest is the winged bull of St Luke standing squarely on all four feet on a 'wreath of colours', a small pad of twisted material (in this case silver and blue) that originally disguised the join between the identifying crest and the helm or helmet. The bull's wings are swept back and upwards, addorsed, in gold, lined with silver, with a golden body, hooves and tip of the tail. The horns, under a golden cloud, are gules or red, like the tongue. Unusually, the mantling – the decoration around the shield and the helm – is red and silver, although it would have been more normal had it been the same as the livery colours of silver and blue. The allusion to St Luke is derived from the description of the heavenly liturgy in *Revelation* of the animals seated at the throne of God: 'And the first beast was like a lion, and the second beast like a calf, and the third beast had the face of a man and the fourth beast was like a flying eagle.'[70] This in turn was probably inspired by the vision of the cherubim to Ezekiel: '. . . they four had the face of a man, and the face of a lion on the right side, and the face of an ox on the left side, and they four had the face of an eagle'.[71] The ox was assigned to St Luke as his symbol as he begins his Gospel, with the priest Zacharias sacrificing one in the temple. The face of a man, or an angel, was the symbol given to Matthew, the lion to Mark and the eagle to John.

The supporters, 'on either side with wings addorsed, the head, forequarters, wings, hoofs, and tuft of the tail or, the hindquarters argent, armed gules, about the head a nimbus or', were 'Granted by Sir Henry Farnham Burke, Garter [King of Arms]'.[72] Although the supporters were used for many centuries, they were only formally granted to the Company on 28 June 1922 at a cost of £55. The motto, *Omnia subiecisti sub pedibus, oves et boves*, was taken from *Psalm* 8, verses 6 and 7 –

'Thou madest him to have domination over the works of thy hands; *Thou hast put all things under his feet. All sheep and oxen*, yea and the beasts of the field'.

The arms of the Worshipful Company of Butchers granted in 1540 are, of course, the same that are used today. It is most likely that their armorial bearings were granted much earlier as it had long been recorded that the Butchers wore a distinguishing badge on their cloaks or livery (see page 24). In the Vincent Collection, an unofficial volume in the College of Arms entitled 'Two Ears of Wheat' of around 1530, there is an entry for 'The Bochers'.[73] There the arms are recorded as: 'Azure two poleaxes in saltire, blades outwards, or, between four roses argent',[74] in other words, two crossed poleaxes in blue, their golden blades pointing outwards with four silver roses. That there is no extant record of the grant of these arms does not prove that they were not granted.

England was thrown into turmoil when Henry VIII died on 28 January 1547. His eighteen-year marriage to Catherine of Aragon had failed to produce a male heir, so he had the marriage annulled with the connivance of Cardinal Wolsey, the ambitious son of a butcher from Ipswich. This led to the break from Rome, and to the dissolution of the monasteries. This in turn spawned the suppression of the chantries – benefices established for chanting masses for the soul of the deceased. These were most often a chapel within a church, or sometimes a hall attached to the church. The Act of Henry VIII was finally ratified in 1547 whereby all the chantry revenues, including those of St Giles Hall, were vested at a single stroke in the Crown. It has been suggested that the Butchers left St Giles Hall in 1547 as a result of this new Act. While this could well have been the case, it is far more likely they left their hall as it was burned down, along with the church, in the same year. The burned out site was bought by the then Lord Mayor, Sir John Gresham, and given to endow a school founded by him at Holt in Norfolk. While St Giles was being rebuilt on the other side of the City Wall, the Butchers began a two year search for a new hall.

3 The Second Hall
1547–1668

MISTRESS JACKSON was distraught, for not only had her husband Benedict Jackson, a senior Warden of the Bochers of the City of London, just died, but she did not consider the 40 shillings he had left in his will for a feast to be adequate to honour his memory. So she petitioned the Wardens, who promised to cover any extra costs out of Fraternity funds – as it happened, they added a further 17s 6½d to the bequest. So, on 13 August 1555, the good man was buried with all the pomp and ceremony due to his station. The heavily embroidered Butchers' pall was draped over his coffin while 'a Pryste for goying abowt the herse of Bene[dic]t Jackson'[1] was paid just 4d for his services. The whole of the Guild, resplendent in their livery and accompanied by their wives, turned out for the funeral. This was held at Christ Church, Newgate Street, the Butchers' Church of St Nicholas Shambles having been demolished by 1547. Those who did not attend could have been fined, but with the promise of a magnificent dinner there were no defaulters.

In life, Benedict Jackson was not only a successful butcher (with four shops and a large house with a garden near St Paul's), but one of the prime movers within the Mystery Guild of Butchers. Although he escaped being disenfranchised in 1533 (see page 31) he was instrumental in the subsequent wrangling over the selling of meat by weight with the Crown and the Mayor and Court of Aldermen. Such was his standing that it was he who was summoned to appear before Sir Rowland Hill, a merchant of the staple from Wolverhampton and Lord Mayor of London. In his best clothes, Jackson presented himself to Sir Rowland to hear the latest Royal Proclamation whereby the price of sheep and cattle was to be fixed. Known as the King's Price, it alternated around three seasons – midsummer when the 'grass was lush', November to Christmas, and Christmas to Lent. Hill explained that, if the price of beasts was fixed there would be no reason not to sell by weight. Three months later, Jackson and his fellow Wardens were back before the Lord Mayor.

Sir Rowland Hill was incensed. He himself had been summoned to appear before the Privy Council and answer the charges that, despite all the Butchers efforts to understand the problem, they still flouted the law and overcharged. Jackson was commanded to investigate the whole matter, and to supply the names of all those who had bought at the King's price and of those graziers who had refused. He was further charged to solicit his fellow Wardens and the Livery to find out what they needed to charge in order to show a reasonable profit. Ten days later, Benedict Jackson returned with his findings, and the price of meat was fixed accordingly, with an increase of around 25 percent on the old price. And so the insoluble problem continued throughout the century with order after order – even senior members of the Guild, including Wardens John Launde and Gamalyon Pye went to gaol for selling 'hotte [overpriced] flesh'. Tempers rose, on both sides of the butcher's block, and an order was even passed commanding butchers, their wives and servants to use 'gentle and honest language to customers'[2] when a customer required a piece of meat to be weighed.

Nor were the Butchers alone in their constant clashes with authority. The Poulters were in equal trouble with the price of chickens and eggs, as were the Brewers. Even the Bakers came in for heavy criticism, as directive after directive went to the Lord Mayor and Court of Aldermen who in turn enforced the price controls. This was the Tudor way of keeping the masses happy (around 120,000 in London alone by 1565), the 'bread and circuses' syndrome of ancient Rome.

Although when Benedict Jackson died in 1555 the matter of selling meat by weight was still far from resolved, his contribution to the Mystery Guild of Butchers during his lifetime was one of which he could be justly proud. He had been Senior Warden three times (1544, 1547 and 1552) and Warden once in 1549. As Senior Warden, he is the first to be named in the earliest accounts of the Butchers to have survived:

> This is the Accompte of Bene[dic]t Jackson and other Wardens of the Bochers of the City of London, and containing their receipts, as also of all their payments from the Feast of Saint Mychell the Archangel [Michaelmas] in the 36th year [1544] of the reign of our Sovereign Lord King Henry VIII by the Grace of God, King of England, of France, and of Ireland, Defender of the Faith and of the Cherche of England, and also Ireland. To the same Feaste of Saint Mychell next and immediately following for the space of a whole yere complete.[3]

From these accounts, much contemporary history of the Mystery comes to light. The Livery numbered 102 men, who paid quarterage of 1s each, and, as £4 6s 8d was received for ingress money at the rate of 6s 8d each, it can be deduced that there were thirteen new liverymen that year. Another entry shows that 53 indentures for apprentices at 8d each were presented. There were also those who were not directly of their number, like the Basketmakers, who held their Freedom of the

City of London through the Butchers. They later left to join the newly-formed Guild of Basketmakers in 1570.

The 'Accompte of Bene[dic]t Jackson' details the feasting and the ceremonies, including the items of 'botte hire' to take the Wardens and Liverymen to the barge they had hired for the day. Every year from 1454, and right up to 1857, the Butchers celebrated the inauguration of the Lord Mayor and Sheriff, joining the procession on the Thames from the Tower to the Palace of Westminster 'where the Mayor took his Oath'. In the year in question, the barge was decorated, besides the usual banners and flags, with flowers and rushes. There was a feast afterwards for the Liverymen. These expenses were indeed small in comparison with those dues connected with Crown and City.

There are items paid to 'Master Cauldwell and to Master Baynston, Collectors for the Kyng's Subsedye'. The King's Subsidy was a tax of one fifteenth of the Company's landed (as opposed to personal) property – that included the scalding houses and the 'podying' house owned by the Company beside the Thames. There was also a 'benevolence' that was collected by a 'Master Peckham, the Kyngge's Cofferar', another due levied by the Crown to extract money from the City Companies. The greatest item of all was that to the 'Chamberlayn of London towards the provision made for whett [wheat]'. There had long been a place for storing wheat in London 'lest the bad harvest and unkind season of the year should beget great want',[4] as well as ensuring cheap food for a poor, overcrowded London. Leadenhall Market had originally been purchased by the City as a granary (see page 28), but in the late sixteenth century the granary was the converted Bridge House by London Bridge. The money was in fact a 'prest and lone', the amount of the forced loan being set by the Lord Mayor and Aldermen of all Mysteries and Companies.

Nor did the weather help. 1555 was a wet year with violent winds and rainstorms during September that ruined the late harvest. The next year there was such a drought that the very springs dried up. The price of wheat rose six-fold, and 'the scarcity of bread was so great in so much the plain poor people did [eat] of acorns and drink water'.[5] But these failures of the harvest were only a small part of the problems that beset the new reign. After a century of near-stable prices, inflation was rife. Henry VIII, always short of money, had debased the coinage. By 1550, the amount of silver in each coin was reduced to one sixth of what it had been fifty years before. Added to that, Spain's conquests in the New World meant that European money markets were being flooded with gold and silver coinage. The whole country was affected, particularly the landowners who looked for ways to maintain their incomes; to this end they moved away from the old system of peasant strip farming and began large-scale sheep husbandry. Waste and common land began to be enclosed, the start of a process that was to last for three hundred years, creating the fences, ditches and hedges that can be seen today. Many cottagers and small farmers were dispossessed of their land and grazing rights and obliged to become wage-earning labourers at best, otherwise taking to the open road as vagrants. For the landowner and the more substantial tenant farmer, sheep farming was highly profitable, for both wool and mutton. In addition, it needed very little labour – a shepherd or two and a few dogs could manage the largest flocks. The change was deeply unpopular and far-reaching:

> The more shepe, the dearer is the woll.
> The more shepe, the dearer is the mutton.
> The more shepe, the dearer is the beefe.
> The more shepe, the dearer is the corne.
> The more shepe, the dearer is the white meate [dairy products].
> The more shepe, the fewer egges for a penny.

Enclosures were as much about cattle as about sheep, particularly as by the mid-century beef and veal were the Englishman's favourite fare. According to Sir Thomas Eylot, author of the *Castel of Helth*, 'Beef of England to Englishmen which are in health bringeth strong nourishing',[6] but meat was only for the privileged who could afford to pay for it. Despite the King's Price for livestock, the average market price for crops and livestock doubled between 1550 and 1600. Much of the livestock that was sold in London had come from the farther reaches of the country, brought along drove roads from as far afield as Scotland and Wales. The drove roads were well-established, even before the fifteenth century when the troops of Henry V fighting in France were all provisioned from Wales. Cattle and sheep were driven in the summer and fattened on pasture around the Home Counties, before moving to Smithfield for the final sale to the London butchers. The cattle destined for the royal table were held at the Neat House, the country seat of the Abbot of Westminster in what is now Victoria – 'neat' being an archaic term for cattle or oxen.

By the middle of the sixteenth century, by which time the Abbot of Westminster had kept his see but lost his lands to the Crown, the long-term effect of the dissolution of the monasteries was beginning to be felt, particularly by the wool merchant and the butcher. The monasteries, which had collectively owned a quarter of the agricultural land in the country, had been at the forefront of the wool trade and the supply of livestock. They had also been responsible for such matters as the roads (which now devolved on the parish) and the care of the poor, the mentally ill, and the sick. In London, one of the main charitable organisations was St Bartholomew's Hospital which had developed from a small hospital house, founded by Rahere in 1123, into an important shelter for the sick, the poor and abandoned children. The Priory was also well endowed to carry out this vital work.

By 1539 St Bartholomew's had been suppressed. Although their assets were seized by the Crown, the Hospital continued to operate. But, their future was far from assured, and it was soon realised that London was about to lose one of its most crucial institutions. A petition was sent to the King requesting that the City take over the Hospital, with its original endowments, to help 'the miserable people leying in the streete, offendyng every clene person passyng by the way with theyre nasty fylthye and nastye savors'.[7] After an interval of six years, the King's Commissioners made a survey of all the property and contents, then took possession of the Smithfield buildings, finally granting the City by Letters Patent the Hospital formerly known as St Bartholomew's 'hereinafter to be called the House of the Poore in West Smithfield in the suburbs of the City of London, of King Henry VIII's foundation', which accounts for his statue over the main gate in West Smithfield that can still be seen today. Within the grant, the King included the sites of the demolished parish churches of St Ewen and St Nicholas Shambles, along with all the houses belonging to St Sepulchre Without Newgate and the site of the former monastery of Greyfriars, all in Newgate Street. It was through this grant of Letters Patent that the Mystery Guild of Butchers secured their new hall, one that was to last them for the next one hundred and thirteen years.

Throughout 1545, the Wardens of the Butcher's Company were casting around for a replacement hall. They began by petitioning the City authorities for a part of the former Greyfriars Monastery 'to make them a Common Hall',[8] but by that time the monastery's chapel had been co-opted into the new parish church of Christ Church, under its first incumbent, the Reverend Thomas Brigotte. The old parish of St Nicholas Shambles had already been incorporated into the new parish, so making the church itself, the vicarage and other buildings redundant. The Lord Mayor of London, Sir Martin Bowes, was charged with pulling down the church of St Nicholas Shambles (the site of the present British Telecom Centre in St Martin-le-Grand), and disposing of the building materials and the effects, including the remainder of the glass that could not be utilised by St Bartholomew's Hospital. Once the Reverend Brigotte had turned down the vicarage, known as the Mansion House, for his residence, a lease on 'the building and void ground' was granted to the Fellowship of Butchers in response to their 'humble suit'[9] dated 12 January 1548. The lease was granted to the Senior Warden, Benedict Jackson, and the four Wardens by name, then their successors, to run from 29 September (St Michael the Archangel's saint's day) for a term of eighty years at an annual rent of £6 'of good and lawful money of England'.

The Guild of Butchers was clearly delighted with their new premises, even more so when they saw off a challenge by a printer to build on another part of the void ground, the City Viewers declaring that it would infringe their light. Moreover the hall, sandwiched between Stinking Lane (perennially associated with butchers) and

Pentecost Lane, was situated in exactly the right place, close by the Shambles, not too far from the other flesh markets and near to Smithfield. The house and land was carefully measured by two Aldermen and the Chamberlain, and the lease was prepared by M. Blackwell, the Town Clerk. All parties in the transaction were rewarded, the Aldermen with gifts of wine, the 'towne clerke for the drawtte of the leese'[10] was paid 6s 8d, while Benedict Jackson sold a sheep and a lamb to the Fellowship of Butchers as a gift for 'Syr Marten Bowys'. The new Lord Mayor, Sir John Gresham, was given a fine gelding at a cost of £8 for his part in the proceedings. It would appear from the Wardens' accounts that the curtilage of the hall was enlarged when the neighbouring garden, formerly part of Greyfriars, was leased from a Dr Borman for the initial payment of £27. Both transactions were completed by 8 November 1548, by which time all the repairs and improvements had been carried out.

The Wardens were responsible not only for negotiating the lease, but also for raising the funds to convert the building – in fact, the building works cost nearly £180 with a shortfall of a little over £13. From the two leases, it can be deduced that the new Butchers' Hall stood on a site of nearly forty feet by sixty, with the actual hall being around twenty feet by thirty-eight and three storeys high. A good picture can also be built up of the Hall itself from the schedule of payments. For a start, the old Mansion House or vicarage appears to have been in a state of disrepair, judging by the money spent on the renovation. They began with a completely new tiled roof, then stripped out the whole house from top to bottom. A large, new front door now opened into a staircase hall laid with stone flags, with a lean-to kitchen built on to the back. The ceiling must have been comparatively low, as the replacement staircase, with turned 'barley twist' balusters and an elaborately carved newel post, that led to the first floor, had only fifteen steps. The walls that formerly divided the parlour, closets and back chamber were removed to form a single, and undoubtedly grand room open to the eaves. Judging by the price of the timber, the lower wall was panelled with wainscot oak, probably imported from Holland or Germany. Above, the walls were plastered on new laths, with a deep red-ochre pigment added to the final coat. Although there is no reference to any further adornment or carving, there would undoubtedly have been some further decoration, such as a tapestry or the carpet (most likely a Turkey rug) that appears in a later inventory as having been repaired. Three new chimneys were built, two of stone and one, in the kitchen, of brick. Then there was a new fireplace in the main hall with a grand, carved stone mantel and a tile surround, the other on the ground floor having a wooden mantel. The room would have been light and airy, with windows (leaded with twenty panes of glass, two bearing the arms of the King and the City) overlooking the garden. The most expensive items were the locks and door furniture, amounting to nearly a tenth of the total cost. A new jakes, or outdoor lavatory, with a wooden stool reinforced with two iron bars, was installed in one of the outhouses in the garden. There was also a cellar that was let to Robert Baylye for 40s per annum.

Also included in the accounts is the expenditure for tables, benches, (all with turned legs), three settles and a chair for the Senior Warden, giving weight to the theory that, as the Butchers needed all new furniture, they must have been burned out of St Giles Hall, rather than losing it through the dissolution of the chantry. The final entry was for a 'topping out' breakfast for the workers at the end of the contract. The grandeur of the hall, 'now callyd Boccars Halle', shows that the Butchers were a substantial organisation, with a membership quite able to meet the heavy demands, raised by subscription, for the repairs. Further evidence of their standing, or of that of one of their number, is that they owned a clock with a case of 'joyner's work'. This would most likely have been a table clock, possibly mounted on a wall bracket, or a clock with weights. Either way, at that date, it would have been a very prestigious item – so much so that those owning a clock were generally painted with it in the background. The City, too, obviously regarded the Guild highly as they changed the name of Stinking Lane (sometimes Fowle Lane) to 'Butcher's Hall Lane' (the present King Edward's Street). Whether it was by coincidence or by design, the street was amongst the first in London to be completely paved, along with Chancery Lane, Long Lane in Smithfield, Holborn, Cannon Street and Petty France. The roads were paved with round cobbles, with a gutter or channel running down the middle.

The comfort of the new hall too was much improved. The settles and Senior Warden's chair were draped in green cloth; linen diaper (woven with a diamond pattern) tablecloths and napkins were either bought or donated. Eighty-nine pounds of pewter was purchased to be turned into '6 chargers, 18 platters, and 12 sawcers'[11] and used for the feasts. Then, like now, the hall was hired out for private functions, plays and wedding receptions.

But however grand the Butchers' Hall undoubtedly was, or whatever the level of power and influence they wielded, it all paled by comparison with those of continental Europe, the cradle of the Merchant Guilds. Each town and city of any note in Holland, Flanders, Germany, Italy, Switzerland and France had their own craft guilds that exercised considerable control within the municipality. In Antwerp, the Guild of Butchers was particularly rich and powerful. Not for them the *Groot* Market, the general market-place for other traders, but their own magnificent hall, the *Vleeshuis*, built between 1501 and 1504. The tallest building in Antwerp, it was sited beside the Scheldt River to carry away the 'blood and guts'. The ground floor had space for sixty-two stalls and was approached by a flight of steps known as the *Bloedberg* – Blood Hill. Above was a very grand banqueting hall, meeting rooms and a chapel.

The butcher guildsmen held a total monopoly of their trade, as meat could only be sold at the *Vleeshuis*: it was the same in Ghent, at the equally magnificent *Groot Vleeshuis* that was built between 1407 and 1419. These monopolies not only produced the wealth to fund such magnificent buildings, but also gave those guilds great power in the cities and the country. With the threat of invasion from the Spanish Duke of Parma in 1585, for example, the government decided to flood the polders to the north of Antwerp as a first line of defence. The Butchers of Antwerp vetoed the idea, as it would have destroyed their grazing lands.

The London Guild of Butchers, and those in the provinces, had no such power, but they (along with the Bakers, Cordwainers, and Tailors) were at least better off in terms of influence than most of the other craft guilds. Like their European counterparts, all the British medieval guilds benefited over the centuries through restrictive practices, by controlling competition and prices, and by regulating employment. This had formerly worked equally well for all three types of guild – the grander wholesale merchants or traders, the manufacturers, and the craftsmen, who sold their wares directly to the customer. By the nature of their trade, the merchants (often importers and exporters as well) tended to be the richest, and as such held the most sway within the municipalities of the cities and towns where they operated. The Lord Mayor, Mayors and Aldermen were more often than not of their number. The cottage industry system, where home-workers carried such crafts as weaving, tanning and dyeing away from the cities and towns to their own houses in the country, weakened the influence of the municipal craft guilds. These guilds were further undermined when they became dependant on the merchants for the supply of their raw materials, such as wool for the weavers, and then for the sale of their finished cloth, so losing direct contact with their customers. Conversely, those craft guilds that operated from a premises, either out of a shop or a stall in the town, and who provided a vital service to city dwellers and townspeople alike, fared far better and held their own in a changing society. Some butchers became extremely rich, particularly the new breed of 'grazier-butcher', like those who owned the rich grasslands such as the Welland Valley, around Leicester, as these became the principal fattening lands in the country. Vast fortunes were made for both the owners of the land and the butchers who took the grass keep. The grazier-butchers in turn dominated their city affairs in Leicester as in other cities such as York and Newcastle-upon-Tyne.

In London too, where it was said that there were as many butcher's shops as taverns, there was a good living to be had for the butcher, as although the majority of the population were very poor, there were enough who could afford the luxury of a regular supply of meat throughout the year. According to Stow, there were 120 butchers in the City and suburbs, each killing around six oxen apiece each week. In addition, there were vast numbers of sheep, lambs, calves and pigs killed that made for a significant amount of meat consumed throughout London. Foreign visitors were struck by this consumption of meat by the English – Paul Henzner commenting in 1598 thought that 'they are more polite in eating than the French, devouring less bread, but more meat, which they roast to perfection'.[12] This appetite for meat also extended to the poor. Apart from what they managed to scrape together themselves from a meagre income, there were donations from the rich – if the meat was not 'broken', that is cut, it was given to the servants, if it was, it went to the poor.

The observance of Lent had long been prescribed by law, but this was difficult to police and even harder to enforce. One of the acts of defiance of the Puritans was to eat meat on forbidden days. Queen Elizabeth ordered that no meat was to be sold or eaten on 'fish days' – the forty days of Lent, Ember (fasting) Days, Rogation Days (the three days before Ascension Sunday) and Fridays – but even at that time, fresh fish was at a premium, and many had to resort to stock- or salt-fish. Her decree, however, was more to do with maintaining a healthy fishing industry than being based on either religious grounds or sound husbandry. A fishing fleet with seasoned fishermen was the best source of recruits for the Navy and the burgeoning mercantile fleet, while the total abstinence from meat during the forty days of Lent partially allowed the stocks of animals to recover after the winter. With the enclosures and changing agricultural practices there was usually a ready supply of beef and mutton throughout most of the year. For those who wished to consume meat legitimately during fish days, there was also a legal loophole where a licence was issued on the grounds of 'bodily infirmity', that was for those who were forbidden to fast. The cost was on a social sliding scale of charges, set by the Privy Council, that ranged from 26s 8d per annum for a nobleman, 13s 4d for a knight, right down to 6s 8d per annum for a mere commoner.

Up to the middle of the sixteenth century, little notice was taken of those who were caught selling or consuming meat during fish days. When Benedict Jackson and his other Wardens reported Greene of Eastcheap and Playfote from St Nicholas Shambles to the Court of Aldermen for slaughtering sheep and lambs in their houses during Lent of 1545, it would appear that no action was taken as Playfote, at that time Purveyor of Flesh to the Royal Household, was elected Senior Warden of the Butchers the next year. The practice continued for three years, more or less unabated, until the House of Lords raised the question with the Lord Mayor as to why forty butchers were allowed to kill during Lent and why 'eating flesh is common in the City'.[13] Shakespeare refers to the practise in *Henry IV Part II*, when Falstaff addresses his hostess in the Boar's Head Tavern:

'Marry, there is another indictment upon thee for suffering flesh to be eaten in thy house contrary to the law, for which I think thou will howl.'

To which the mistress of the tavern replies:

'All victuallers do so; what's a joint of mutton or two in the whole of Lent.'[14]

For another keeper of a London tavern, serving 'a joint of mutton or two in Lent' resulted in an hour or two in the pillory.

After consulting the Senior Warden of the Guild of Butchers, the Mayor reported to the House of Lords that there were in fact only five, not forty Lenten butchers. Even so, the Wardens were charged with policing their own and reporting those who sold without a licence. But their Lordships were still not satisfied, and by way of retribution, outlawed the sale of meat on Saturdays as well as Fridays, during Lent and the other fish days. By this time, 1587, the Mayor and the Wardens of the Guild of Butchers were thoroughly irritated by the House of Lords' continual carping, and suggested that the Lords themselves should do the Lenten licensing. They declined. Like so much of the history of the Guild of Butchers, matters dragged on without there being a proper resolution. The Fishmongers, protecting their trade, also had their say, frequently reporting the butcher miscreants to the Court of Aldermen. The scarcity of meat on sale during Lent, combined with a population loth to give up their favourite food, inflated the price of meat to such an extent that the risks of killing and dressing beasts, or smuggling them in to the City from outside, far outweighed the fines if caught.

But the City of London was changing. Parliament had usurped many of its old powers, and eroded some of its independence – Henry VIII had even taken over the nomination of Lord Mayors. On the other hand, London became the acknowledged capital of the nation, where the municipal ethos was displaced by a national ideal. As before, London was in a state of adjustment. Throughout the second half of the sixteenth century few could boast more than a generation or two as Londoners, although a sixth of the population lived there having been drawn in from the farther reaches of the country. A Swiss medical student noted that 'London is not meant to be in England, but rather England to be in London'.[15] As before, foreigners came in great numbers to settle in London, making it a truly international city. There were 'brewers and book-binders from the Low Countries, tailors and embroiderers from France, gun-makers and dyers from Italy, weavers from the Netherlands – even an African or "Moor" in Cheapside who made steel needles without ever imparting the secret of his craft'.[16]

At that time, London was a city in a hurry, for the mortality rate was the highest in the land, the two 'great harvesters being the plague and sweating sickness'.[17] The plague was particularly rife amongst the squalid tenements of the poor, where life expectancy was little more than twenty-five years. The middle classes fared little better, living to an average of between thirty and thirty-five. And so their places were filled by hopefuls, who came from the country in search of those golden streets, when the average age of the whole City was under thirty. Many were apprentices, and in the Guild of Butchers the list for 1551–53 shows that all but five of those taking up articles were from the provinces, and only two of the Londoners being the sons of butchers. The Statute of Apprentices Act of 1563 for the first time standardised the terms of their service throughout the country, where they were bound for a minimum of seven years to a master (or in a few cases, a mistress) who had himself served out a full apprenticeship. Nor could anyone who had not served the full term be employed by a butcher, and the ratio between journeymen and apprentices was fixed. As an apprentice could not become a freeman before the age of twenty-four, and as life expectancy was comparatively short, the future for the journeyman butcher was bleak. Furthermore, Elizabethan standards of excellence were high, and had to be maintained at every level throughout the realm, as a contemporary wrote:

> The prentice that is bound for less than seven years does not commonly prove to be an expert artificer, so that thereby ignorance and imperfection in divers arts and occupations do enter; yet many are bound for five, four, three, yea two years or less, and take upon them to bring up others under them, whom they make as evil and unskilful workmen as themselves, which doth only impair good and perfect workmanship or knowledge in occupations, but also it means whereby the number of artificers do so multiply that one of them do as it were eat out and consume another.[18]

As in previous centuries, however, life for the apprentice London butcher was far from grim in a city that was essentially for the young. They 'would ether bee at the taverne, filling their heads with wine, or at the Dagger in Cheapside cramming their bellies with minced pyes: but above all other times it was their common costome, as London prentices use, to follow their maisters upon Sundays to the Church dore and then leave them, and hie unto the taverne'.[19] Often this drunken good humour spilled out on to the street. The butcher apprentice was as xenophobic as the rest, and foreigners were treated as fair game. The servants of the aristocracy and the gentry were also regularly attacked, a law even being passed warning the apprentices not to 'misuse, molest, or evil treat any servant, page, or lackey of any nobleman, gentleman, or other going in the streets.[20]

Football hooliganism too was rife amongst the apprentices; after one match at Cheapside, three were jailed for 'outrageously and riotously behaving themselves'.

The annual Bartholomew's Fair, held at Smithfield and attended by all classes, was another venue noted for violence and disorder. Henry I had granted the Prior and Convent of St Bartholomew the right to hold a fair, partially on their own land

and partially on a neighbouring parcel belonging to the City. For centuries, this area had not only been an area for trading cloth and cattle, but also one of entertainment – not least as the site of the gallows and the stocks, and the haunt of prostitutes in the aptly named Cock Lane. In the fourteenth century, the fields were used for jousting tournaments, and it became the traditional place to fight duels. The fair was held for just three days over the Feast of St Bartholomew (24 August). By the middle of the sixteenth century (when the merchants rather than the weavers sold their cloth), the textile element of the fair had gone. However, 'the privileges of the fair'[21] were inherited by the City who turned it into a fortnight of every conceivable form of entertainment and distraction. There were plays and sideshows, gaming booths and freak shows. There were drinking tents and dancing marquees, with the inevitable 'affrays' that followed in their wake. Whether as an antidote to the violence, or as a spectacle in its own right, Bartholomew's Fair was renowned for its wrestling matches. Chaucer's 'stoutly built, broad and heavy'[22] miller was a noted wrestler, who 'wolde have alwey the ram', as did the Knight, Sir Thopas, who, 'Of wrastlyng was ther noon [none] his peer'.[23] The wrestling prize at Bartholomew Fair was also in the form of livestock and traditionally donated by the Guild of Butchers. The earliest record for this prize is in 1500, but there are two references to the ram in Chaucer's *Canterbury Tales*, leading one to suppose that it was common before.

The wrestling matches became the highlight of the Fair, and turned into a great City occasion. The Lord Mayor and Aldermen presided over the games amidst great ceremony from a brightly decorated stand. The Sheriff's sergeant read the proclamation, where contestants and spectators alike were charged to keep 'the Kynges peace' and that only true wrestlers should enter the ring. The wrestler who 'the most falles gyveth' in the first round would receive a horse or '1¾d in money thereof' from the Guild of Innholders, 'for the seconde game of the Bochers a bull or 10s[hillings] in money therefore, for the thyrde game of the Bochers a bore or 8s in money therefore, and for the fourthe game of the bochers a ram or 4s in money'.[24] Although Bartholomew's Fair continued in various forms right up to the middle of the nineteenth century, the wrestling transferred to the fields of nearby Clerkenwell in 1460, where the prizes of varying amounts for the different matches continued to appear in the Butchers' accounts right up to the Commonwealth, when all such sport was outlawed. These payments for prizes were an undoubted drain on the Butchers' coffers, often when they could least afford it, but at least they kept the Guild, later the Company, in close touch with the City authorities.

Despite all the legislation, both within the Guild of Butchers and from Parliament, and all the innovative methods employed in disposing of dung and offal, the Butchers continued to be harassed by the City authorities and public alike. For example, at the end of the fifteenth century a number of butchers were being beaten by members of the Inns of Court for dumping offal in Holborn. Towards the end of the sixteenth century two unexpected new areas of disposal opened up – the Common Hunt at Finsbury Park and the Bear Gardens in Southwick. There had long been scavengers of butchers' scraps and offal in London. Since Roman times, dogs and cats, both stray and domesticated, had carried away a certain amount of waste, while the 'Tantomy pigs' must have consumed a fair quantity as well, although they had been phased out by the end of the fifteenth century. Moreover, as a foreign traveller in the mid-sixteenth century noted, London 'was remarkable for the number of kites which were quite tame and wandered through the streets as if they owned them'.[25] Kites had been known and encouraged as scavengers for centuries, but there was a downside. They had a reputation for stealing laundry from clothes lines – in *The Winter's Tale*, Shakespeare mentions that 'when the kite builds, look to lesser linen'.[26] Some argue that the kite mentioned at that time was the black kite, *Milvus migrans*, like those today that are to be seen scouring the rubbish tips in their native habitat on the Mediterranean littoral, and over much of mainland Europe. But it is now thought more likely that the kite referred to was the red kite, *Milvus milvus*. Whatever their species, kites were protected by Royal decree and, such was their usefulness as scavengers, it was deemed a capital offence to kill one. Pepys mentions them in his diaries, but by that time, the middle of the seventeenth century, they were so numerous that there was a bounty of one shilling a head for killing them. From then on, like many birds of prey, they were relentlessly persecuted as vermin and hunted to near-extinction.

Situated in Finsbury Fields on the outskirts of London, the kennels of the Common Hunt of the City of London were another obvious place for the disposal of offal. There is no known record of this hunt, although one of the same name is mentioned two centuries later. It was known as 'The Epping Forest Lemon Pyes' and was primarily established for tradesmen to hunt carted deer. Its predecessor's exact quarry is not known, but as deer were still the preserve of the Monarch and nobility it is likely that they hunted hares and the occasional badger. What is known is that the Court of Aldermen sanctioned a new gate out of the City to the 'Doghouse'[27] or kennels so that the offal could more easily be transported.

Since the very early thirteenth century, the Royal Family had kept wild animals in the menagerie at the Tower of London, for both sport and pleasure. In 1235, Henry III received a wedding present of three leopards from the Holy Roman Emperor, Frederick II, and more diplomatic gifts of exotic animals were to follow, all welcome additions to his collection. The King of France sent an elephant that died, while the King of Norway bequeathed a polar bear. The bear was highly entertaining, and attracted vast crowds who came to watch it fishing in the Thames. Such was its popularity, the Lieutenant of the Tower considered that the City should pay for its upkeep, and the Sheriff of London was charged 4d per day for its keep and for the price of a chain and collar. Notwithstanding the rivalry between the Tower of London and the City, there is nothing to suggest that butchers' offal was ever sent to the Tower of London to feed the carnivores in the menagerie, but it would seem likely that some of the offal was disposed of as animal feed. The Eastcheap butchers' 'podyng-house' and wharf, after all, were close by, and, by the sixteenth century, it is well documented that a proportion of the offal from the St Nicholas Shambles was being transported across the Thames to feed the Royal bears. By this time, they had been removed from the menagerie at the Tower and were kept for sport at the Paris Gardens in Southwark, close to Shakespeare's Globe and the Rose Theatre.

Both bear- and bull-baiting had long been popular with all classes of society, from Royalty to the lowest in the realm. Elizabeth I was seen at the Paris Gardens, but more often staged these animal contests for her guests at Whitehall. Henry Machyn, a furnisher of funeral trappings and a great diarist, recorded in 1561 that he 'was at Whyt-hall grett baytyng of the bull and bere for the im-bassadurs of Franse . . . and wyche the Queen's grace was ther, and her counsel and mony nobull men'.[28] James I was also fond of bear-bating, and 'vast crowds assembled to see the King's bears fight with greyhounds. This afforded great amusement'.[29] The wretched bear (at that time, the brown bear *Ursus arctos* was common throughout mainland Europe, particularly in the Pyrenees) was chained to a stake, either by a hind leg or by the neck, and set upon by large mastiffs and apparently greyhounds, although they would seem to have been too light for the task in hand. The bear's teeth were ground down so they had to fight with their paws. Robert Laneham wrote in 1575 that bear-baiting:

> . . .was a sport very pleasant to see, to see the bear, with his pink eyes, tearing after his enemies approach; the nimbleness and wait of the dog to take his advantage and the force and experience of the bear again to avoid his assaults: if he were bitten in one place how he would pinch in another to get free; that if he were taken once, then by what shift with biting, with clawing, with roaring, with tossing and tumbling he would work and wind himself from them; and when he was loose to shake his ears twice or thrice with the blood and the slaver hanging about his physiognomy.[30]

Sunday was the usual day for the 'sport', when bets were taken on whether hounds or the bear would come off best. Some of the bears at the Paris Gardens survived long enough to become legends: one, Sackerson, was immortalised in Shakespeare's *The Merry Wives of Windsor*; others were great favourites with such names as Harry Hunks, Great Ned and George Stone. Two or three hundred spectators would turn up to watch, even more for an important match, paying $1/2$d a head for the privilege.

However ugly and distasteful the scene, the Butchers certainly reaped the benefit of the Paris Gardens as part of the offal collected in the two Company-owned barrowhouses was, for decades, taken across the Thames to feed the bears. During the Commonwealth, bear- and bull-bating was outlawed, not so much on the grounds of cruelty to the animals but that 'such shows were thought to foster vice'.[31] Soon after the Restoration in 1664, the Paris Gardens were revived and a new slew of bears brought in for baiting. Naturally, they needed feeding as before, so the Earl of Manchester wrote to the Lord Mayor and Aldermen to request that the arrangement with the Butchers be restored. On 29 September he wrote:

> My very good Lord [Mayor] and the rest of my
> very good Friends the Court of Aldermen.
> Being informed by the Master of his Maities Game of Beares and Bulls and of others that very well remember that the Company of Butchers did formerly cause their offal in Eastcheape and Newgate Markett to bee conveyed by the Beadle of their Company unto two Barrow Houses conveniently placed by the Riverr side to receave the same for the provision and feeding of his Maties Game of Beares And that that Custome hath beene interrupted in the late Troubles when the Beares were killed. And that his Maties Game being now againe by order of the King and Councill removed to the usuall place on the Bank side at the very charges of the Master of the Game. I shall therefore earnestly recommend it to your Lordship and the rest of my very good friends the Court of Aldermen and desire you to give such order to the Master and Wardens of the Company of Butchers that their offall shall bee duely conveyed to the aforesaid houses as formerly it was for the feeding of his Maties said Game which the under officers at present are forced to provide by extraordinary and very chargeable means soe not doubting of your Care herein I rest.
> Your humble servant,
> Manchester
> Court at Whitehall

It would appear that the Company of Butchers were delighted to comply with the Lord Chamberlain's request, as there is a reference[32] to offal once again being ferried across the Thames for the bears by courtesy of the Butchers. During the Great Plague just a few months later, the bear's offal was delivered to the wharf by the Beadle between 11 pm and 3 am and sent straight over the river. At the beginning of the eighteenth century, the bear-gardens were removed to Hockley in the Hole, near Camberwell Green, the present Ray Street. Although bear-baiting died out towards the end of the eighteenth century, it was only outlawed in 1835.

At the end of the sixteenth century, when Elizabeth I's long and eventful reign was drawing to a close, it can be seen from correspondence and the accounts that the relations between the Mystery Guild of Butchers and the Lord Mayor and Aldermen had greatly improved. Gone was the rancour over offal and pricing. Instead they willingly supplied 'half a man'[33] (as did the Turners, Basket Makers and the Glaziers) for the protection of the City. Later, in 1594, the Guild of Butchers contributed an initial £18 'for setting out the last Shippes'[34] – the Fishmongers paid £339 showing the relative worth of the two Guilds – with a further levy of £3 6s later in the year. Normally, the City raised money for land troops, but in this case they came up with a total of £7,400 towards six warships and a pinnace to reinforce the English fleet. Notwithstanding the defeat of the Spanish Amada, Spain still posed a constant threat. When the Spanish built a fort at Crozon to take control of Brest and their ships were seen reconnoitring the Southern coast of Ireland, Elizabeth I saw the danger, and the Irish their opportunity. The fort was destroyed by the English, but events in Ireland escalated rapidly into what became known as the Nine Years War.

By 1593, the Ulster lords had set aside their traditional rivalries to swear loyalty to a secret confederacy under the two acknowledged leaders in Ulster, the Earl of Tyrone and Red Hugh O'Donnell, Lord of Tyrconnell. Although Tyrone outwardly supported the Crown, his show of loyalty was only a ploy to gain time while he negotiated with Philip II for help from Spain, and exhorted his kinsmen to prepare for open revolt. The next year, the English expeditionary force sent to relieve Enniskillen was defeated, and when Tyrone sacked Enniskillen, the English declared him a traitor. Tyrone had an army of 6,000 men under arms and harried the English in a succession of skirmishes, while The O'Neill corresponded with Philip II, imploring the Spanish King to support 'Catholic liberty'. The Spanish responded, and, in 1596, landed arms and munitions in County Donegal, but the invasion force that was to follow was dispersed by a great storm off Cape Finisterre. Tyrone was holding his own without Spanish intervention, and again defeated the English near Armagh in 1598.

This was all too much for Elizabeth I to bear. She began by raising money, demanding that the combined City Companies come up with a substantial contribution towards an army to put down the Irish rebellion once and for all. The Guild of Butchers rose to the occasion and loaned £60, the transaction recorded in the Wardens Accounts as 'Item owing by the Queen that was lent part of the XX [£20,000] thousand pounds, £60'.[35] Earlier in the year they had contributed £5 that was 'paid to the Chamberlayne for horsemen into Ireland'.[36]

A massive army of 20,000 men was sent to Ireland under the Queen's favourite, Robert Devereux, Earl of Essex. After a series of minor skirmishes, then a rout of the English forces near Wicklow, Essex met with Tyrone and brokered a truce, ostensibly to reorganize and re-equip his army. Essex pardoned Tyrone and the other Ulster lords and allowed them to keep their lands and titles: for this he was executed, and replaced by Sir George Carew as President of Munster with Charles

Blount, the 8th Lord Mountjoy, as his deputy. In May 1600, another expeditionary force arrived under Sir Henry Docwra. He and Mountjoy built a ring of heavily armed forts around Ulster to cut the Irish guerrillas' supply lines, and used famine as 'the chief instrument of reducing this kingdom'.[37]

Meanwhile, in September 1601, a Spanish army arrived at Kinsale, County Cork, under the command of Don Juan del Aguila. Mountjoy marched south to besiege the Kinsale before The O'Neill and Red Hugh O'Donnell's forces could join up with their allies. On Christmas Eve 1601, the Ulstermen were defeated, the Spanish surrendered, and returned home, while The O'Neill made his way back to Ulster.

Meanwhile, the Ulster lords that included Donnell O'Cahan, The O'Neill's chief vassal, threw in their lot with Docwra on condition that O'Cahan held his lands, by then somewhat reduced, at Coleraine. By early 1603, Mountjoy was empowered to offer The O'Neill yet another pardon in return for his surrender, which was eventually accepted on 24 March, the day before Elizabeth I died. When The O'Neill heard the news in Dublin later, he 'wept for rage'.[38] For the Guild of Butchers, their part in the whole affair, the loan of £60, was repaid some time in 1600. It took the largest army in Europe to defeat The O'Neill at an estimated cost of £2 million. At the Treaty of Mellifont, O'Donnell was inexplicably created Earl of Tyrconnell and granted most of County Donegal, while The O'Neill too kept his lands and title. Notwithstanding Docwra's promise to O'Cahan, the County of Coleraine was also returned to his control. It was not long before Coleraine would reappear in the annals of the Guild, or as it was by then, the Company of Butchers.

The accession of James VI of Scotland as James I of England was a turning point in the fortunes of the Guild of Butchers. They had long since sounded out the City Authorities on the possibility of being incorporated and receiving a Royal Charter, and they continued to ingratiate themselves with the City, Parliament and the Crown. But the new King was in no hurry to take up his crown. He rode south from Edinburgh, hunting the whole way, arriving in London a month later. When he reached Stamford Hill, he was met by the Lord Mayor, Sir Thomas Bennett, the Aldermen and 500 knights and citizens all in gold chains and scarlet gowns. From there he went to Whitehall, then on to the Tower of London by barge. It was an inauspicious time to arrive, for London was gripped by one of the worst outbreaks of the plague ever known. The new King called it 'God's devouring angel' as the death toll reached around 30,000. And so the Coronation, that promised to be such a glittering occasion, was very sparsely attended, by the Lord Mayor, a few of the Aldermen and the braver courtiers and citizens. The Lord Mayor's day was cancelled – the entry in the Butchers' accounts reads 'Bargemoney: none collected this year by reason of the Great Plague the Lord Maior tooke his oath at the Tower Gate, and so no barge used'.[39]

But James I and the City were not to be denied their celebrations for the Coronation. Nearly a year late, on 15 March 1604, the Royal Family progressed from the Tower to Westminster with all pomp, flanked by the City dignitaries. The road had been strewn with gravel, and the royal procession passed under seven triumphal gates along the way – those at Cheapside, Cornhill and over the Fleet River ran with claret all day.

Mindful of their impending charter, the Guild of Butchers were careful to conform, and their contribution of £2 8s towards the festivities was in line with that of the richest Companies. They also put on a lavish display of their own, spending a great deal of money on new flags and banners with decorated poles to improve their image. By that time the livery had expanded, and extra staging was required to accommodate them. To complete the picture, a vast backdrop was hired for the occasion. The Butchers were also much in evidence at the service of thanksgiving at St Paul's Cathedral to celebrate the failure of the Gunpowder Plot, spending three shillings 'for the standing at Powles'[40] or Paul's Wharf where the King and Court came ashore.

At last the time came when the Guild of Butchers could negotiate for their charter. Although various representations to the Privy Council had been made towards the end of Elizabeth I's reign, nothing had come of it. But with a new King, chronically short of money, all forms of possible revenue were examined, particularly if the source was a City institution, for both past and future sovereigns viewed the Livery Companies as a ready supply of cash to be squeezed in time of need. A Royal Charter would give the Butchers the stability and standing they craved, and bring them into line with the majority of the other Companies. It also meant that they were legally allowed to own property that produced a net income of more than £30 per annum. The Butchers ranked then (as now) twenty-fourth in precedence, but at that time they were amongst the last of their contemporaries to be incorporated. Fifty-four companies, many of them junior to the Butchers, already held their Charters; some of them had done so for centuries, like the Weavers for 450 years or the Fishmongers approaching 350, while others, like the Fruiterers, had obtained their Charter just seven months before.

As a result of their petition to the Privy Council on 16 September 1605, by Letters Patent the Freemen of the Society or Mystery of Butchers of the City of London were finally incorporated with the grant of their Royal Charter. With a Sovereign so eager for funds, it is surprising that 'no fine or fee, large or small' was paid to the Crown – the Feltmakers had dispersed around £500 for their Letters Patent the year before. There were, however, some ancillary fees in connection with the actual grant. The charter itself is a truly impressive article, on vellum, about three feet square. It would have originally been rolled up and kept in an oblong box, specially prepared with a large, round box to take the Great Seal of wax that is attached to the vellum with a thin rope of silver thread. The whole is highly ornate. James I is portrayed in robes of state with a crown, holding the orb and sceptre, and seated on a throne. Interspersed with the Royal Arms and those of Henry, Prince of Wales, are rows of finely-painted flowers – the thistle of Scotland, the rose of England. There are pansies, cherries and a flower similar to a zinnia. There are also insects – exquisite beetles, a form of ladybird and dragon flies – and birds too, a robin and a fanciful finch. The text itself is in Latin; the calligraphy is perfect. Unfortunately, a portion of the centre of the script is badly worn, but for a document that is over four hundred years old it is in remarkably good condition.[41]

With the Charter (a document bestowing certain rights by Royal Decree, such as the right to hold a market or charge a toll fee on a bridge) the Butchers became a Corporate body in law. In its strictest terms, a corporation (from the Latin *corpus* – body) is a legal entity, being a body of people authorised – in this case by the Crown – to act as an individual. Thus, the new Company was one empowered to act in the name of the Master, Wardens and Commonalty of the Art or Mystery of Butchers of the City of London. The Charter specified at great length the aims of the new Company, principally to make ordinances for the better governance of their trade, both for the freemen and non-free alike. Their area of control was limited to a radius of exactly one mile. But the main benefit of this Charter was that, being granted by the Crown, the Ordinances created by the new Company of Butchers came under the jurisdiction of the English judicial system. Thus, any miscreant, whether free or not, could be dealt with by the Courts if need be. The same went for the Company fines and forfeiture.

A little over a year later, the Company of Butchers presented their Charter to the Lord Mayor and Aldermen, where the Court of Aldermen scrutinised every clause. A fee of 40/- was paid 'for inrolling the Letters Patent of our incorporation in Guildhall'.[42] They were then charged to come up with the Ordinances of their new Company. It is likely that these rules had already been drawn up at the same time as the Charter, as the Ordinances were submitted very soon after to the Court of Aldermen to be vetted. These were then sent to the Lord Chancellor and the Chief Justices for their approval. It took them just eight weeks to come back with a few minor alterations, but the Butchers' Company Ordinances were engrossed and returned with the seals of Lord Ellesmere, the Lord Chancellor, and Sir Thomas Flemynge, the Chief Justice of the Pleas, and returned with their account for £59 9s 6d. At the end of the year, the new Company of Butchers had just seven shillings to its name.

To attend any of the Court of the Company of Butchers' ceremonies today is to reflect on those original Ordinances of 1606, although most of the Ordinances and practices had been in place for centuries. There are sixty-eight items, all lengthy, not to say wordy, that for the first time spelt out the aims and formation of the Company. The early Ordinances deal with the appointments of the officers – as a Company, the Butchers now had a Master as opposed to a Senior Warden. The elections of the Master and five Wardens were dealt with at length. It was to be an annual event, the Master and each Warden taking the oath of office and allegiance to the Crown by 'laying his hand upon the Bible or newe Testament'.[43] Another part of the Wardens' oath was to account for 'every suche goodes plate jewels money and other thinges'.[44] Again, the Ordinances merely reiterated what had been common practice before, except that previously the Wardens need only to have been freemen, whereas after the Charter they were required to be liverymen. Anyone refusing the appointment of Warden was fined £5 – the sum today is just 5 guineas.

As today, there are 'in the livery of the same mysterye fifteene persons to be the Assistantes to the Master and Wardens'.[45] Their election was also spelled out, whereby the Master, Wardens and Assistants on

> the said generall eleccion daye in decent and commlye manner and in their liveryes to such church as shalbe assigned by the saide newe Maister and Wardens then and there to heare a sermon and there shall continue and abide during the tyme of the sermon and after the sermon ended shall likewise attend the saide newe Maister and Wardens in decent and comlye manner and in their liveryes from the churche to the hall of the said Maister Wardens and Comminaltye.[46]

Some parts of the Company's Ordinances were abandoned as being unworkable or unfair. It was prescribed that two liverymen were elected by the Master and Wardens to provide the dinner on the day the Lord Mayor took his oath at Tower Gate. Although the Company contributed twenty shillings towards the dinner, it was a heavy burden on the chosen two, particularly when the numbers of liverymen increased. Some found the fine preferable to providing the feast, even when it rose to more than the £10 stipulated in the Ordinance. Other clauses, such as the election of the Clerk, were vital to the smooth running of the Company. For this:

> as often as neede shall require elect and choose one honest wise discrete and fitt person to be Clerke to the said Maister Wardens and Commonalty of the said art of mystery to give them advise and counsel in their affairs and busines and to kepe their Courtes and to enter and register their accomptes and generallye to doe and execute all that and whatsoever which to the Office of the Clarke [and to] ... Execute youre saide office so nere as you cann as a good and faithful Clarke ought to do soe helpe you God.[47]

Likewise, provision was made for the appointment of a Beadle, whose main function appears to be have been to:

> summon all and every such person and persons as the saide Maister and Wardens of any of them at any time shall commande to be summoned according to the ordinancyes . . . without sparing with any person for favour affeccion lucre [dishonest money] gayne hatred or malice . . .[48]

With the Royal Charter, the Company of Butchers had greater powers than before, not least the right of entry to all markets, shops, slaughterhouses and the like of both freemen and foreigners alike, whether they be:

> priviledged exempt and not exempt and into all and every other place and places whatsoever within the saide Citty of London and suburbs thereof and within one myle of the same Citty of London where any fleshe shalbe killd or putt to sale . . . and there shall or may view search and see all and all manner of fleshe . . . [to] . . . be wholesome and fitt to be put to sale[49]

An appropriate fine was payable by any who 'doth resist disobey vex truble reprove or molest' the Master. Again, the question of apprentices was dealt with, much as before, with a minimum of seven years being served with a master who himself had served a full apprenticeship, all within one mile of the City. Foul language even found its way on to the statute book with specified fines for 'revile misuse or abuse with any evil or undecent speeches or words of reproach'.[50] Abuse of the Master and Wardens attracted a greater fine. There were specific items on the butchering of lambs and hogs, and on trading 'in the tyme of Divine Service' on a Sunday, when it was also not permissible to drive 'oxen sheepe calves lambes or swyne'. Butchering was, however, permitted after evening prayers. Dress was also extremely important. The butcher's apron, together with the steel hanging from his belt, became the hallmarks of his trade. But aprons were also a sign of work, and so the freemen of the Company and their servants were expressly forbidden to 'stande or goe abroade in any open streete or lane within the Citty of London or one myle of the same Citty upon any Sonday or other festival day with any aprone about hym'.[51] The rules governing dress in the presence of the Court were equally stringent, 'where every person or persons being or that hereafter shall be in the livery of the Guild of Butchers whensoever he shall weare his livery gowne and whood, shall weare therewith a rounde Capp of wooll and not a hatt'.[52] The Wardens' Accounts are full of fines for these dress infringements. A contemporary inventory of the butcher John Powle's wardrobe has survived. His 'apparayle' consisted of:

3 bands [collars]
a gowne
2 cloakes
a pair of breeches
2 pair of stockens and a hatt   Sum   £3. 4. 0.[53]

Despite his obvious grandeur, Butcher Powle would have discarded his fine outer garments when working, exactly as Shakespeare wrote of it in *Henry IV Part I* when Dick, one of the Men of Kent, points out that they 'work in their shirt too; as myself, for example, that am a butcher'.[54]

The crown was hardly on the head of James I before the pardons of the Earl of Tyrone (The O'Neill), and the new Earl of Tyrconnell were ratified. Yet despite the pardons, the two found English rule unacceptable. Ulster was divided up into nine counties – Antrim, Armagh, Cavan, Coleraine, Donegal, Down, Fermanagh, Monahan, and Tyrone, which in turn were further divided up into baronies. By 1607, The O'Neill, Tyrconnell and Maguire, rather than being arrested for plotting again with Spain for yet another Irish uprising, left for France with their families. Their sudden departure (that became known as 'The Flight of the Earls'), was for the Crown a double blessing. The prime sources of insurrection had gone, and although The O'Neill had already been attainted for high treason and stripped of his titles in August 1608, all of their lands were then 'confiscated for a supposed intention to rebel'.[55]

But the Flight of the Earls also created problems of its own. Bereft of their lords and their lands, Ulster became a 'hostile and terrifying place',[56] especially around Coleraine and the ruined town of Derry. James I was determined to stamp his authority on this rebellious corner of his realm. 'And now that all Ulster, or the most part, has fallen into His Majesty's power, he intends to order it so as it may redound to his honour and profit'.[57] To this end, he turned not to military occupation, expensive and totally ineffective in the past, but in part to the Livery Companies of the City of London, with their ready finance and expertise. His intention was create a permanent settlement where the 'rising generations be trained up to useful industrie, and civilitie, learning, religion and loyalties'.[58]

It was not the best time to fund such a venture, as the City Livery Companies were already wrestling with another opportunity – the Virginia Company. It is unlikely that that the fledgling Butchers' Company was actively involved in North America, but there is an entry in the Wardens' Account for 1619–20: 'Item paid to the Collectors of the Virginia Company, 4/4d', a contribution to a fund that sent vagrant children and 'idle fellows' to the New World. Unlike the opportunities in America, the settlement of Ulster was a hazardous and distinctly unattractive proposition for the City, and it needed 'the potent combination of threat and seduction to persuade them otherwise'.[59] But the City was loth to upset the King without good reason. Not mentioning the fact that an alien presence would be fiercely opposed by the dispossessed Irish, James I submitted his pamphlet *Motives and Reasons to induce the City of London to undertake the Plantation of the North of Ireland* in which he spelt out the advantages of investing in this 'promised land', with its fine pasture and forests, its rivers and lakes rich in fish. The City was unconvinced, even after the report of 'four wise, grave and discreet citizens' who had been sent to view the area reserved for the City Companies. The remaining Ulster counties, that is parts of Donegal, Tyrone, Armagh, Fermanagh, and Cavan, that had been divided into baronies, were granted to the Scots and English who settled them with their own people. Other lands were awarded to the Church, and others to the 'Servitors' who were rewarded with land for past military service.

But James I had his way, and the City raised an initial £20,000 to develop the project, then a further £40,000 was called in by 1613 to implement it. The land allocated for the City of London was divided into twelve 'Proportions'. The fifty-five Livery Companies were levied by means of Precepts (writs) and organised into 'Associations', each under the overall control of one of the 'Great Twelve'[60] Livery Companies. Each Company was liable for a total of around £5,000, the Grocers and the Merchant Tailors raising the whole amount themselves. The other Companies looked to their associates to make up their portion, the Butchers' Company throwing in their lot with the Clothworkers with a contribution of £230. This was a massive sum for them to find from the Liverymen themselves – at that time the Company's income was averaging £60. The Master contributed £5, others £2, and out of the total of £68 17s 6d from one hundred liverymen, some of the contributions were only 2/6d. The Merchant Tailors had no such problem and were oversubscribed by £1,186 which was added to the Clothworkers portion, alongside that of the other associates: the Bowyers (£30), Fletchers (£30), Brown Bakers (£130) and Upholders (£66).

The designated lands within the County of Londonderry (the City of Derry and the surrounding county had been given the suffix 'London' in honour of the City) were then divided into twelve lots. Each association then drew a lot, a deliberate Biblical analogy to the twelve tribes of Israel dividing up the Promised Land. The Clothworkers, and by association the Butchers, received twenty-one square miles (13,450 acres) south of the town of Coleraine in what had once been 'O'Cahan country'. Although this was one of the smallest portions (the Skinners received 76½ square miles) it was, however, certainly one of the best. It was bordered by the sea and the river Bann, fully navigable to Coleraine and teeming with salmon and eels. The land was very fertile, and heavily wooded in parts. This grant of the Parishes of Killowen, Mocosoquin and Dunboe had the added attraction of being comparatively safe from Irish insurgents, being close to the town and bordered by land held by The Honourable the Irish Society. When the estate, known as the Manor of the Clothworkers, was finally conveyed to them and their associates, it was first leased for fifty-one years to the 'farmer', Sir Robert McClelland, on payment of £250 per annum, three years being paid in advance. The term *farmer* here is not agricultural, but really a *fermator* or *fermier*, the man who collects the taxes and rents. McClelland paid the Company from these rents and was responsible for part of the infrastructure – enclosing the land, and building 'English houses, fortified manor houses, and bawns [fortified enclosures]'[61] and the like. Some farmers were disreputable, others more conscientious like George Canning of the Manor of Ironmonger whose direct descendant became Prime Minister. The Clothworkers'/Butchers' farmer, Sir Robert McClelland, served them well and rose to the Scottish Barony of Kirkcudbright.

In common with most of the other Ulster Proportions, the projected return of 5 percent from the farmer on the Clothworkers' association's investment failed to materialize. There were many, the likes of the Brown Bakers, fearing further calls on their meagre capital for the rebuilding of Derry, the expansion of Coleraine, and the fortress of Culmore, who forfeited their original disbursement. However, the Bowyers and the Fletchers, who by then had fallen on hard times, managed to sell their share to the Ironmongers, but at a loss. The only returns to be seen in the Wardens' Accounts came many years later: one in 1628 when the Clothworkers passed on £20 13 4d, with a further £26 19 11d in 1632.

In the main the Ulster Plantations were not a success for any of the Livery Companies. The Crown had misled them. When the English settlers failed to materialize, the Companies left the Irish tenants in place in breach of their original grant. As early as 1612, the King was losing patience, complaining that although the Companies 'pretend to great expenditure. . .there is little outward appearance [of it].'[62] He further accused them of being more interested in profiteering than in fulfilling their settlement commitments, as the forests were cut down and the timber exported. Nor was it easy for the farm labourers on the estates, where they worked 'wth the Swords in one hande and the Axe in th'other', such was their fear of attack.

It would appear that the Company of Butchers had written off their investment in Ulster, for they were certainly not reminded of it by regular dividends. Unexpectedly in 1674 the sum of £29 17s 10d arrived from the Clothworkers for their share of the revenue from their Manor. This payment triggered an investigation by the Court of the Butchers' Company, and it was decided that they would cut their losses and sell their portion back to the Clothworkers' Company for £130. The money was duly received, the Deed of Release[63] detailing all the properties, rights and dues, including the fisheries, being signed by Thomas Clarke, a Warden of the

Butchers' Company. But the matter did not end there, for two hundred and fifty years later the subject of the Ulster Plantations was to be rekindled.

In 1827, a bill was introduced into the House of Commons to regulate the salmon fisheries of the Irish Society and the Clothworkers, riparian owners of the north and south banks of the river Bann. After a 'long and arduous contest, the promoters of the Fishery Bill were obliged to abandon the measure'.[64] The findings were widely reported and this could well have reminded the Butchers of their interest in their former estates in Ireland. The Clerk wrote to the Clothworkers requesting the arrears from their portion of the Association. The Clothworkers dismissed the claim out of hand, but the Butchers persisted. In July 1829, counsel's opinion was sought. After careful examination of the remaining documents in their possession and in absence of all others, it was decided to abandon the claim. The Clothworkers were clearly worried by the claim, as it prompted a close examination of their Deed Poll of Confirmation, and of the structure of their Association. It was not until 1917 that the actual Deed of Release was found. The Butchers, in their haste to divest themselves of their share of the Manor of the Clothworkers, were eventually to lose out on what became a lucrative investment. In 1769, the Manor was let by public auction for 61 years at an annual rent of £600 with a premium of £28,000. The Butchers' Company share would have been around £1,300 with an income of £30 a year. Had they stayed in to the very end, around 1870 when the Clothworkers sold their estate for £150,000, the Butchers share would have been in excess of £6,000.

While the Company of Butchers was wrestling with their overseas property and the Irish question, there was better news at home. Between 1620 and 1630 the Company came into possession of several properties in London. The first was the scalding house used by the butchers of Eastcheap for centuries. It was known as 'Vanners Hall' after John Vannere a butcher who managed the scalding house in the 1350s. The conveyance dated 29 June 1620 describes 'the two messuages [house with outbuildings and land] and tenements and stables in the Parish of St George'[65] that was bounded by Pudding Lane and Botolph's Lane. It was bought from the heirs of Robert Harding, a Salter, who in turn had purchased it from the Wardens of the Fraternity and Guild of Corpus Christi in the Church of Allhallows, Bread Street in 1551. 'Le Scaldynghowse' was tenanted by John Partriche, who had fallen foul of the butchers of Eastcheap in 1507 by doubling his charges to 1d per hog. The butchers were 'sore grieved' and held out against the new charges. When some of the Wardens of Eastcheap were committed to Newgate Goal by the Court of Aldermen for disobedience, the Lord Mayor, Sir Laurence Aylmer, was called in to abjudicate. The Lord Mayor came up with an admirable solution. Both parties should cease their actions immediately, and 'every person of the Fellowship of Butchers occupying any house in Eastcheap [was] to pay yearly to Patriche for the scalding of their hogs 2s 8d for every board that they occupy whether they scald or not'.[66] There were fifty-eight boards, enough for 'every person of the Fellowship' who was guaranteed house-room, fire and water twice a week. The bristle and bladders were to remain the property of Partriche, but he had to pay the Beadle to take away offal. The final *douceur* for the butchers was that, on Christmas day, Partriche 'in the morning shall give at his own cost a breakfast to the servants and apprentices of the Fellowship of Butchers of Eastcheap for a pleasure after the manner and use accustomed'.[67] It would appear that the Guild of Butchers themselves held the lease from Alderman Robert Harding by the end of the century. By that time, however, Harding had died and in his will he left two annuities of £3 6s 8d to be paid to both the Fishmongers and the Butchers. The monies, or kind, were to be distributed to the poor. The scalding house, with its annuities, was taken over by Harding's son Simon who gave a life interest to his wife Ursula with the remainder going to other relatives. It was this interest that the Butchers were able to buy for £140, the money coming by way of loans from eight members of the Livery. Further money was raised to repair the buildings, both the scalding house and the surrounding stables and haylofts, and which, when fully let, produced an income of upwards of £35 per annum. There is mention of another building, 'the Helmett', owned by the Company and leased jointly by four butchers at £15 per annum. It was described as a 'messuage in East Chepe *alias* Candlewick Street'. The tenants changed frequently, at one stage one paying £5 to assign the lease to anyone except a 'brazier, pewterer, smith or baker'[68] because of the fire risk of their trades. There is no mention of the Helmett in the Wardens' Accounts when they resume in 1671 (after the Great Fire of London), which means that it was sold at some time prior to that date – most likely to pay for the new Butchers' Hall in 1668.

The increased fortunes of the Company of Butchers were due in part to the foresight of Robert Clements, four times Master between 1619 and 1631. As a sitting tenant he purchased a messuage in St Leonard's Parish, known as the 'sign of the Deathes Head'[69] with two other tenements for £340. His own yard abutted that of the Company's scalding house. When first Master in 1619, Clements 'for the love and affection which he beareth the Company and for the better advancement of the same and supportation of their public charges', assigned the remainder of one of his tenements that was occupied by William Hall and Christopher Child to the Butchers after his and his wife's death. Hall and Child, both butchers by trade, conveyed the property to the Butchers and their successors in perpetuity. Clements went further to demonstrate the 'love and affection he bore to the Company of Butchers of which he had long been a member' by leasing the Company two further messuages in the Parish of St Leonard for a peppercorn rent for ninety-nine years, then a further ninety-nine years after that to be paid at Common Hall if demanded. The tenant of one, George Stretton (another butcher), was willing to pay a premium of £588 for a thirty-three-year lease of what appears to have been a shop (complete with racks, hooks, stall boards and scales) with accommodation over. This consisted of a fine hall on the first floor, well appointed with wainscote, wall hangings and settles, and a kitchen, with two further chambers above. Rent was also payable, £16 to the Company and £8 to Clements and his wife Priscilla. His generosity knew no bounds, as the same year, 1632, he gave the Company £100 as a form of premium of his own house, and contributed a further £60 from of the premium of the other house.

The Company also acquired what appears to have been a public house, once known as 'le Starr', then 'le Sunne', in Eastcheap. It had formerly been 'The Crossed Keys' when, before the dissolution, it had belonged to the Monastery of St Bartholomew. The property then devolved on William Redmer, sometime Warden of the Guild of Butchers, and by 1612 Richard Stretton took a thirty-one-year lease from William Fisher. The Company was keen to buy the property as it completed the block on the corner of Eastcheap and their property between Pudding Lane and Botolph Street. They were already negotiating to buy when Fisher died, but after a little trouble with the title the 'Art or Mystery of Butchers, their successors and assigns for ever'[70] managed to secure the house from a beneficiary of the will. The rental income from that corner was £75 per annum. The fortunes of the Company of Butchers were forever fluctuating, but at least at this time, with their contiguous block of houses, they had a firm, financial base. It was truly unfortunate that these houses had to be sold. Their increased standing also brought responsibilities of its own, and it was found necessary to appoint a Renter Warden, the equivalent of a treasurer, ostensibly to oversee the collection of dues from the Company's rental portfolio. It was considered an onerous task, and one the Company generally found difficult to fulfil. But just as the Butchers were consolidating their position, the demands on the Company's funds became exhaustive. The first major expenditure was the renewal of the lease of their Hall that had expired in 1628. It was renewed for a further twenty-one years at the same rent with a 'fine' or premium of £66 13s 4d.

On top of their heavy expenses, income also fell. Fines immediately after the Charter were healthy, around £40 per annum, but as the years passed, the suburban non-free butchers flouted the Wardens' authority, and ignored their fines and directives. When such an affront became insupportable, the Master and Wardens 'made humble petition' to Charles I for a revised charter. In the petition, they complained that under the present charter

all men of the Art or Mystery [of Butchers] aforesaid dwelling without the said City and within one mile thereof and using the said art or Mystery cannot be proceeded against for their delinquencies in selling unwholesome and corrupt flesh, fraudulently, basely and deceitfully, or exposing the same for sale to the grave damage and hurt to our subjects . . .[71]

The Master and Wardens pointed out that the grant of Letters Patent should be legally binding for those 'said persons without the said City and within one mile of the same' and bound by the same laws, even though they were not 'incorporated in the Society or made members of the said body corporate and politic'. They further petitioned that all those 'persons . . . within the space of two miles of the said City' should also come under their jurisdiction to prevent 'flesh being fraudulently and basely butchered and deceitfully dressed'.[72] The practice was common among unscrupulous butchers, such as Meredith Jones who was fined 7/6d in 1635 for '2 lambs bought at Smithfield barres both stufte [stuffed], 1 blown calf and dressing meate on ye Saboth day'[73] where a calf or sheep was made to look plumper than it was by having air forced into the carcass. The Charter was duly granted on 31 July 1637. Where the original Charter was granted free of charge, £177 1s 8d was paid for the new Charter, spread over two years, with various *douceurs* to 'my Lord Keeper's gent' of marrow bones, pullets and tongues at a cost of 40/2d with the 'expenses at the eating of them'.[74]

At that time the Lord Keeper, literally the 'one charged with the physical custody of the Great Seal of England', was Lord Coventry, a senior judge. It was through his legal opinion in October 1634 that Charles I was able, without the consent of Parliament, to collect ship money, a tax or levy that was to become one of the causes of the English Civil War. It has long been the right (and practice) of the Kings of England to require the maritime towns and counties to provide ships for their defence in time of war; as Coventry claimed, 'the wooden walls being the best walls of this kingdom'. This liability was later commuted to a monetary payment. Charles I, his chronic shortage of money made worse by the costs of war abroad, was constantly at loggerheads with Parliament over their refusal to grant him further funds. Armed with Coventry's legal judgement, in October 1634 the King directed the justices of London and other sea ports to provide a certain number of ships (or their equivalent in money), giving them the right to assess the inhabitants for payment of the tax according to their worth. This was an unprecedented act in time of peace, and was later to be extended to inshore towns and counties. The City of London claimed exemption under their charter, but as no exemption on constitutional grounds could be found, all owners of property were assessed. The Butchers' Company contribution was 30 shillings on their hall, with a further £3 payable the next year, while the Beadle was assessed at 10 shillings. There appeared to be no levy on the other Company properties in Pudding Lane, possibly as the income (£3 6s 8d) was used for charitable purposes. Surprisingly, the Butchers were one of the few livery companies who actually paid the levy.

And so this conflict between King and Parliament took the country towards civil war. The King began by raising money, starting with a demand to the City for a loan of £120,000, later reduced to £50,000. The Butchers, mindful of their new charter and position within the City of London, sold most of their plate in order to raise the money – £150 that was 'paid into His Majesty's Exchequer soe much leant by this Company to His King's Majestie as by the precepts from the right honourable the Lord Maior was required'.[75] Despite the Royal drain on the resources of the Company, the Butchers gave a dinner in honour of the King's visit to the City, after which, they were amongst other livery companies that escorted him back to his palace at Whitehall.

But loyalty to the Crown was not to last. At the election of the Common Council, the Parliamentarian faction won the day, while the Lord Mayor and the Court of Aldermen sided with the King. The City was in an angry mood, and on 27 December 1641 there were clashes between the Army and the London apprentices, as they marched on Westminster. These apprentices with their close-cropped bullet heads, doubtless with Butchers' apprentices amongst them, were the first to be known as 'Roundheads'.

The City staunchly supported the Parliamentarian cause, and by October the Committee for Militia ordered the defence of London. Trenches were dug and ramparts thrown up around the City, and, as the Venetian Ambassador noted, the citizens 'do not cease to provide with energy for the defence of London. There is no street, however little frequented, that is not barricaded with heavy chains, and every post is guarded by numerous squadrons'.[76] The Butchers without doubt gave their labour too, for they had already contributed £300 to the overall loan to Parliament of £150,000 that had been raised from the combined Livery Companies, the Butchers share being passed unanimously 'by consent of the whole board'.[77] The loan, however, was not outstanding for long, and half was repaid a year later with interest, with another £50 in 1644 with £4 interest. Later that year, as staunch supporters of Parliament, the Butchers gave a dinner in their honour at the Bear, a tavern in Southwark at the other end of Bridge Foot, the site of London Bridge.

While the country plunged into the turmoil of Civil War, the Butchers' Company, rarely free of conflict, were engaged in a struggle of their own – the perennial problem of curbing the non-free, or country, butchers who continued to infiltrate into the designated flesh markets. As early as 1611, the Wardens had complained that all manner of meat was being sold outside Leadenhall, Cheapside, Newgate and Gracechurch Street. In a typical half-cock solution, the country butchers were allowed to sell their beef, mutton and lamb only within Leadenhall Market and only on a Saturday. However, veal and pork could be legally sold in any of the other markets, every day except Friday. As usual, and despite the Company's new powers within their Charter, the country butchers took no notice of the regulations. In

1620, the Company petitioned the Court of Aldermen for the order to be enforced, but, while examining the situation, the Court merely inquired why the non-free butchers were restricted to selling just veal and mutton in the markets. The City authorities did act, usually in a desultory fashion, confiscating the meat of the offenders, invariably from a private dwelling house. On occasion, the house belonged to the City, like those just outside Cripplegate that were being used as 'flesh shambles'.[78] The City authorities did close those down, Cripplegate being deemed not 'suitable' for selling meat. Sometimes the Lord Mayor acted without consulting the Butchers. In 1638, Sir Robert Ducye extended the right for the non-free butchers to sell lamb as well as veal and pork but failed to notify the Wardens of the Butchers' Company of his decision. When the Wardens seized a dozen lambs, they were sued, and lost and had to return them to the country butchers. That same year, the Wardens were taken to the Star Chamber by a consortium of country butchers, who complained that they were being forced out of Leadenhall, Cheapside and Newgate by lack of space, and that the boards that should have been provided for them had been removed. There was also a charge of assault. Again, the Butchers lost the suit, as it was found that they had influenced the Yeoman of the Channel, John Fisher, who had paid the Court of Aldermen 40 shillings for the privilege of supplying the boards for the non-free butchers. The country butchers were supported by the inhabitants of Cheapside, who doubtless found their meat cheaper.

Matters came to a head in 1645. From a petition of the Commonalty of Butchers it can be seen that both free and non-free butchers were selling all kinds of meat, including beef, in Cheapside, Newgate and Leadenhall Markets. The following year, the matter was finally resolved. By an Act of Common Council it was ordained that beef could be sold only in Leadenhall Market, but by both free and non-free butchers alike. The hours were also extended from seven in the morning to five in the afternoon in summer, eight to three o'clock in winter. With the breaks being given to the country butchers, the advantages of being a freeman of the Company of Butchers were steadily being eroded.

But still the same old abuses were rife, and by 1654, at yet another inquiry instigated by the Butchers' Company, the Court of Aldermen found that it was poor management, and the corruption and negligence of the clerks of the markets which were at fault. The clerks were summarily dismissed and replaced with the Master's appointees, who came under his and the Wardens' control. In 1657 the Butchers' Company petitioned Parliament to ratify their position and curb the malpractices in the markets. But as the markets provided the City authorities with a certain income – 4d a day for a 5 feet by 4 feet board – they were loth to lose their control, and so prevaricated. The question dragged on until 1661, when the Butchers yet again petitioned the Court, stating that matters were completely out of hand. Beef was sold in all markets, trading continued until midnight, and the illegal hawkers, often selling putrid or stolen meat, went unpunished. Again the City Committee set up to look into the question, sidestepped the issue, blaming the Butchers themselves for their lack of authority. They did suggest that the Lord Mayor himself should ride through the markets where his very presence would be enough 'for the quickening of the officers and the terror of the offenders'.[79] The net result was an Act of Parliament the next year when the practices of the 1646 Act were reinstated, except that beef could also be sold in Cheapside and the Monday market at Leadenhall was suspended as it meant butchering on a Sunday. The seventeenth century butcher clearly did not hang his meat.

The underlying reason for the antagonism and complaints of the free and non-free butchers and the City authorities was in reality more to do with the simple economics of supply and demand, rather than the monopoly on the sale of meat. The courtier-historian Peter Heylin protested that London 'is grown at last too big for the Kingdom'. By 1650, with 375,000 inhabitants, it was the second city of Europe behind Paris (which it had overtaken by 1700 with half a million). The City walls had long ceased to contain the population as it spread eastwards to what became the industrial heartland and shipping centre, while Westminster developed from a collection of palaces and an abbey, all set in fine parks and farmland, into an entity in its own right. With this great expansion of the City came the migrants, the poorer artisans and immigrants who settled to the east, the courtiers and politicians gravitating towards the new West End. This great influx of all classes over the first half of the century meant that there was an even greater demand for meat, particularly during the Commonwealth. But with this great demand there was more than enough trade for both the free and the non-free butcher. However, as there was often a decade or more between the representations made by the Butchers' Company against the non-free butchers throughout the seventeenth century, it can be assumed that the free and the non-free rubbed along well enough in the intervening years. Whatever the animosity between the two, they were both soon to lose their markets and their clients through the Great Plague, and their premises to the Great Fire the following year.

After the austerity of the Commonwealth, the Restoration of Charles II in 1660 heralded a new era of delight − not least for new mode of 'Meats and Drinks after the French fashion' for those who could afford a French chef. The news of the King's return was greeted with wild enthusiasm in London, where the mob paraded great rumps of beef, which were later roasted and devoured.

In Cheapside there were a great many bonfires, and the Bow Bells and all the bells in the all the churches . . . were ringing. But the common joy that was everywhere to be seen, the number of bonfires! . . . and all along burning, and roasting, and drinking for rumps there being rumps carried upon sticks, and carried up and down. The butchers at the May-Pole in the Strand rang a peal with their knives, when they were going to sacrifice their rump.[80]

And all that was before the King had even set foot in England. Later, the diarist John Evelyn recorded the arrival of Charles II in London on 29 May 1660:

a Triumph of above 20000 horse and foote, brandishing their swords and shouting with unexpressible joy: the wayes strawed with flowers, the bells ringing, the streets hung with Tapissery, fountains running with wine: . . . the windows and balconies all set with Ladys, Trumpets, Music and [myriads] of people flocking the street and was a far as Rochester, so they were 7 hours in passing the Citty, even from 2 in the afternoon 'til nine at night.[81]

The Mayor and Aldermen in the procession were followed by 'six hundred of the several companies of London on horseback, in black velvet coats with gold chains, each having footmen in different liveries, with streamers etc.'[82] As the Wardens' Accounts between 1646 and 1686 were destroyed, there is no record of the exact part the Butchers played in these celebrations. It can, however, be safely assumed that they would have had their staging, suitably decorated, in their usual place on the route (in order of precedence), with a feast at their Hall afterwards. Such celebration would have been as much out of loyalty to the new sovereign, as to rival, or even outdo, their fellow Livery Companies.

Livery, proudly worn by freemen and grandees' servants alike, gave the wearer a sense of corporate or family identity and belonging. Rivalry between such bodies was inevitable; the hatred between the Montagues and the Capulets in Shakespeare's *Romeo and Juliet* being a prime example. For the Butchers, it was the Weavers' Company who were their principal antagonists, as Samuel Pepys observed in a 'great discourse of the fray' in Moorfields in July 1664:

. . . how the butchers at first did beat the weavers (between whom there hath ever an old competition for mastery), but at last the weavers rallied and beat them. At first the butchers knocked down all for weavers that had green or blue aprons, till they were fain to pull them off and put them in their breeches. At last the butchers were fain to pull off their sleeves, that they might not be known, and were soundly beaten out of the field, and some deeply wounded and bruised; till at last the weavers went out triumphing, calling £100 for a butcher.[83]

The sleeves or cuffs Pepys referred to had by that time become another distinguishing mark of the butcher, along with a short apron with a pocket and the steel strung around his waist. His breeches and doublet were of the fashion of the day, but the 'rounde cap of wooll' was peculiar to the butcher. Fines were payable for wearing an apron away from the premises, particularly on holidays, or in church, but the offence was gauged to be even more serious if the steel, a potential weapon with its pointed end, was also worn.

Within five years of the Restoration, terrible times struck the inhabitants of London. One in six of their number died, and the following year the very fabric of the City was largely destroyed. The godly saw the Great Plague of 1665 and the Great Fire the year after as divine judgements on the excesses of the Restoration, Old Rowley's new reign of pleasure. But, in reality, the plague had been a constant resident of the City since the Black Death, claiming the lives of tens of thousands of people over the years – 17,500 in 1563, 18,000 in 1593 and over 30,000 in 1603, the year of James I's accession, with another 40,000 in 1625. As the pamphleteer Thomas Dekker put it: 'Imagine then that Death . . . hath pitched his tents (being nothing but a heap of winding sheets tackt together) in the Sinfully polluted Suburbs'.[84] In this case, the suburb, or slum, was St Giles, just below modern Oxford Street. As before, the plague germs were a disease of rats which spread to man through the bite of their fleas; once it had taken hold, the bacillus could be further spread by the common human flea. The infected bite caused a painful bubo or swelling in the lymph gland, which drained the limbs – in the majority of cases the groin since most bites were on the leg. Internal haemorrhaging followed, with death generally following within five days.

It was widely held that both dogs and cats spread the plague, and the Lord Mayor ordered them all to be destroyed. Daniel Defoe, the author of *Journal of the Plague Years*, estimated that 40,000 dogs and 200,000 cats were killed, so removing the only natural enemies of the rats who carried the plague fleas. This in turn only increased the spread of the disease. Defoe, best known as the author of *Robinson Crusoe*, was the son of James Foe, sometime Warden of the Butchers' Company, and was admitted as a freeman of the Company in 1688 by 'virtue of his Father's Copy'. It appears that he had little interest in the Company, as he paid to be 'discharged from all offices of this Company for the future'.[85] Nor did he ever trade as a butcher. Notwithstanding his lack of involvement with the Butchers, he has been honoured with three stained glass windows over the years. In fact Defoe was only five years old at the time of the Great Plague, so his account is entirely hearsay.

The plague respected no one, although the rich and the professional classes moved out to the country when it took a serious hold on the City. With their flight, the butchers lost their most valuable customers, and many succumbed to the plague themselves. The country butchers did not enter London – a certificate of health was needed to pass through the City Gates – which at least left the markets free of their competition. It had long been held that the plague was spread through the air – Pepys recounts how victims would breathe on healthy passers-by out of spite. Just as letters from the capital were suspect, variously scraped, heated, soaked, aired, and pressed flat to 'eliminate pestilential matter', so the butchers insisted that their money, possibly contaminated, was thrown into a bowl of vinegar. In return, the customers, fearing his meat tainted by the butcher's hand, would serve themselves. By the time the King thought it safe to return to London in February 1666, an estimated 80,000 Londoners had perished.

But Providence had still not been placated, thanks to Thomas Farrinor, a baker who lived with his family and servants in a house with 'five hearths and one oven' in Pudding Lane, at the other end of the street from the Butchers' properties. Farrinor, baker to the King, apparently failed to dampen his oven one evening and, in the early hours of Sunday, 2 September 1666, his house caught fire. Four days later, four fifths of the medieval City of London was totally destroyed. When questioned later by Sir Robert Vyner, jeweller and banker to the King, the baker and his family all swore that 'their Oven was drawn by 10 a-clock at night'; as Farrinor went down to light a candle at midnight 'there was not so much fire in the bakehouse as to light a match for a candle'.[86] Another theory is that the fire started as some small cakes were left in the oven overnight. Two hours later, the family was choking with smoke, from which all but a maid managed to escape. The fire, fanned by a stiff east wind (as Sir Robert Vyner was to say, 'God with his great bellows blows upon it'),[87] swiftly carried the sparks to the neighboring Star Inn on Fish Street Hill. Fires were common and unremarkable. After an hour, the Lord Mayor, Sir Thomas Bludworth, was woken, but dismissed it with 'Pish! A woman might piss it out!' But London, in the grip of a drought, was tinder dry. By the next morning, three hundred houses were on fire and a third of London Bridge alight.

It was not long before the fire had spread the whole way along Thames Street, fuelled by the stocks of pitch, oil, tallow and spirits in the warehouses, and the hay, and straw, and timber, on the wharves beside the River. The fire had taken a firm hold and two churches were soon engulfed, followed by the Fishmongers' Hall, the first of many. Pandemonium, as Pepys observed, spread through the City, with:

Everybody endeavoring to remove their goods, and flinging into the River or bringing them into lighters that lay off. Poor people staying in their houses as long as till the very fire touched them, and then running into boats . . . And among other things, the poor pigeons I perceive were loath to leave their houses, but hovered about the windows and balconies till some of them burned their wings, and fell down.[88]

By the Monday morning, as John Evelyn observed from the comparative safety of Southwark, the 'whole south part of the Citty [was] burning from Cheape Side to the Thames, and all along Cornhill. Tower-streete, Fen-church-streete, Gracious-streete [Gracechurch Street] and so along to Bairnard Castle and was now taking hold of St Pauleschurch to which the scaffolds contributed exceedingly'.[89] By Tuesday morning, the third, the great church itself was truly alight. The heat was so intense that the stones 'flew like grenados, the lead mealting down the streetes in a streame and the very pavements of them glowing with fiery rednesse, so as no horse, nor man, was able to tread on them'.[90] By then, the Master and Wardens of the Butchers' Company (records of their names perished in the Fire) would have long feared for their hall, for it was only a matter of time before it too would be consumed by the fire. They would certainly have arranged for the Company's plate and other valuables to be carried away through the crowded streets, no doubt co-opting their own Liverymen and servants with their barrows. It is possible that the Butchers' plate was removed through the Cripplegate to either Smithfield or possibly Moorfields.

Then, at around seven in the evening on Tuesday 4 September 1666, the Hall of the Butchers' Company caught fire and was burned to the ground.

By the next morning, the wind that had fanned the flames was dying down, and the firebreaks, long resisted, finally proved effective. The Great Fire of London had petered out by midday 5 September, the fifth day. It was said that it had stopped on the corner of Cock and Gilspur Streets, the spot now marked by the statue of the Fat Boy (sometimes known as the Golden Boy). The fire had consumed four hundred acres within the City walls and 63 outside, but remarkably only six recorded deaths. Thirteen thousand, two hundred houses were razed to the ground, along with eighty-nine parish churches, the Guildhall and the Royal Exchange, the Customs House and various prisons, gates and bridges. Along with forty-three other livery companies, the Butchers had lost not only their hall, but their flesh markets as well. As with the majority of Londoners over the centuries, however, when faced with disaster, the Butchers took stock of their position, retrenched, and moved forward to a new era.

4 The Third Hall
1668–1829

BY EARLY AFTERNOON on Wednesday 5 September 1666, the pall of smoke that could be seen from as far away as Oxford, fifty miles away, had cleared, as the Great Fire of London finally burned itself out. Like Samuel Pepys, whose 'feet were ready to burn, walking through the town among the hot coles',[1] the inhabitants of the City crept back from the vast refugee camps at Moorfields and Islington, gingerly picking their way through still-smouldering piles of timber and mountains of ash. At first they were disorientated, there being few familiar landmarks to identify what had once been their thriving ward. Among them the Master and Wardens of the Butchers' Company edged their way from their lodgings outside the City walls to the place that had once been their Hall. It can only have been a depressing sight as they stood there amongst its charred remains, a heap of blackened timbers, a few broken chimney bricks and dressed stones, whitened through the intense heat. They had lost the very core of their Company, their recent records and the entire inventory that they could not carry away in the face of the fire. Like the rest of the Company, their houses, along with their livelihoods, had been wiped out in those four days, as their shops, stalls and markets had all perished. But the Butchers were not alone in their plight.

Within days of the fire, there was intense activity throughout the City. The Courts of Common Council and Aldermen set up and met at Gresham College. For the restoration of the City, it was essential that revenue should be collected as soon as possible, and temporary quarters were found for the customs, excise, hearth tax and post offices. Christopher Wren produced a grand master plan, with a new St Paul's and Royal Exchange as focal points of the City laid out to grand, wide streets. His friend, Robert Hooke, the City Surveyor, and John Evelyn came up with similar plans. But Wren's grandiose scheme required money and time, of which the City had neither. Had they been adopted, London would have looked very different today, with such delights as a great piazza on Fleet Street and wide embankments beside the Fleet.

The quickest solution was for the burned-out owners or leaseholders to rebuild their properties themselves; but, to 'prevent architectural bedlam and ensure safety',[2] a series of Parliamentary acts were passed in a hurry. It was decided that on all the principal streets, the houses had to be four storeys high, three storeys in side streets, while in backstreets or alleys the building could be just two storeys high. Some streets, like Cheapside, Poultry and Cornhill, were considerably widened, and through the Sewage and Pavement Act pavements were raised and roads cambered, replacing the old streets with their central 'kennels' or drainage ditches. With the threat of fire, the use of wood was restricted. Windows and doors, previously flush with the outside wall, had to be set back at least four inches. Wooden barge boards on the eaves were prohibited.

But London had to eat, even if the majority within the City were dispossessed. The freemen butchers re-established themselves, as did the country butchers, setting up temporary stalls wherever they could. For the City authorities, the Great Fire did have one benefit in that all the troublesome markets, in particular the flesh markets, were removed from the streets. They were quick to capitalise on their destruction and one of their first acts was to erect new purpose-built markets. They began with Leadenhall, the largest of its kind in Europe, to accommodate the street meat market of Eastcheap, and those of Cornhill and Gracechurch Street, within its four massive courtyards. Newgate Market, rebuilt on the present Paternoster Square, followed soon after when the stalls in St Nicholas Shambles and the surrounding shops were swept away as Newgate Street was enlarged and widened. The market remained there until 1869, when it was replaced by Smithfield. Along with prisons, wharves and warehouses, the markets were funded by the City authorities from a levy of one shilling on every ton of coal – this was increased to three shillings a ton to fund Wren's rebuilding of St Paul's Cathedral and the London churches.

While other Livery Companies, such as the Carpenters, were either thankful that their halls had been spared or delayed rebuilding, the Butchers immediately set about restoring their premises. Their lease from St Bartholomew's Hospital had still five years to run. Normally, the lease would have been extended at the same rent for a further forty years to encourage the lessee to build. However, it would appear that the Hospital governors had other plans for the site of Butchers' Hall as they had already agreed to let the land to another, even before they had received the surrender of the Butchers' lease. They did, however, waive the arrears payable for the preceding two years, as the 'Company was in very great povertie'.[3] Instead, the Master and Wardens decided to build on the site of the slaughterhouse and properties they owned in Pudding Lane. The decision was purely financial (and brave), as clearly it made sense to build on their own site rather than pay a premium and ground rent on the Hospital's land. Also, building sites after the Great Fire were hardly at a premium, and they would have found it difficult to find a new tenant willing to build. Consequently, in June 1668, they applied to the City authorities to build a new hall, the foundations being laid out by their surveyor, the celebrated Robert Hooke.

Just as the Butchers had railed against competition from the non-free butchers, so the Companies of Bricklayers, Stonemasons and Builders saw to it that they held their respective monopolies within the City. Restrictions were soon relaxed with the amount of work in hand, and the Butchers employed an outside contractor, a bricklayer and builder called John Beaseby, to undertake the work. Although not a member of the Guild of Tylers and Bricklayers, he was nonetheless bound by an Act of Parliament to employ skilled labour. But two months into the contract, the Master was complaining to the Lord Mayor that Beaseby's bricklayers were unskilled, whereupon two City Surveyors were sent to give their opinion. The outcome was presumably favourable as Beaseby finished the contract. But the Butchers were also in contention in another quarter. Pudding Lane, being a side street, demanded a three-storey building. As the building works progressed, the Lord Mayor received another complaint, this time against the Butchers for infringing the right to light of the Globe Tavern. The surveyors found for the plaintiffs, and pronounced that there were 'no means of maintaining those lights except by demolishing the Hall'.[4] As the north wall, overlooking Eastcheap, was already forty feet high, a compromise was reached. The kitchens at the rear of the building were restricted to a height of one storey, and a fine of £150 imposed by the Court of Aldermen was payable to the aggrieved owners for the nuisance caused by the new hall. This was a serious blow to the Company's funds, as they had borrowed the whole amount for the rebuilding from their Members. It was to be years before they were fully paid out. Even by 1688, the Company still owed £500. A surviving list, probably just of the Court of Assistants, shows twenty-eight names with the amount each could afford written against them. The sums vary between £4 and £1, and this exercise only produced £54. Notwithstanding the added setback of the heavy fine, the Butchers were the first livery company to complete their new hall, followed soon after by the Salters. The Clothworkers made substantial repairs to their hall, which they reoccupied within a few months after the fire.

Despite the Butchers' difficulties with the funding of the new hall, the result was grand, spacious and practical. The Master and Wardens who orchestrated the building programme and its finance were indeed farsighted, for it was to serve the Butchers' Company well for one hundred and sixty years until it too was burned to the ground in 1829. Although lacking a contemporary account, a passable depiction of the hall and its furnishings can be drawn from an account (Strype's edition of Stow) written fifty years later.

'The Hall of the Company of Butchers' with a 'large edifice of brick' was described as 'a pretty handsome small building with a freestone paved court before it, and hath a back passage into Pudding Lane'.[5] Several sources have it with just two floors, but it is more likely to have had at least three if the account of the front wall being 'forty feet high' is accurate. Furthermore, with only two floors it is unlikely that they would have infringed their neighbours' right to light. The entrance was grand. Approached by two stone steps, it was flanked by a pair of large Ionic columns with garlands spread between the volutes. Iron railings were added later, a gift from George Lowing, Master in 1738. The hall on the ground floor was well appointed, with no expense spared. The walls were 'wainscoted to about five feet in height all round', with a stucco ceiling 'beautifully worked'[6]. An iron stove was set in the fireplace. It appears that the hangings for the Company's stand were on display along with the hearse pall. Later, the reception hall housed the Master's chair, standing beneath a bust of William Beckford, Alderman and later Lord Mayor in 1762. The kitchen led off the hall, with an iron range and an open fire to take the 'two stands, three trevitts, six iron spits'.[7] The kitchen inventory – which included ninety-three pewter plates and twenty dishes (as well as a large chamber pot and two small ones) – shows how seriously the Butchers' Company took their entertaining.

'A noble staircase' led to the Court Room on the first floor. Lit by a series of brass wall sconces, this had a fine ceiling 'finished in stucco, beautifully worked'. The walls were panelled to full height with the chimney-piece, carved with foliage and fruit, a part of it. Above the mantel there was a framed picture of St Peter's vision, surmounted by a broken pediment with the carved and painted arms of the Company. An iron stove, more likely a basket to burn sea-coal, was set in the fireplace. The Court Room was suitably furnished with the Master's chair, emblazoned with the Royal Arms, together with a set of two dozen chairs for the rest of the Court. It is likely that the parlour was above and not beside the Court Room as it is known that the kitchen was a single-storey addition at the back. The furnishings included 'a curious and massy [weighty] oak table of considerable solidarity, the four legs of which vases of elegant form and workmanship'.[8] From the description of these bulbous legs, this was a Tudor table, certainly no later than 1640 when that style went out of fashion. This implies that at least this table was amongst the pieces of furniture rescued from the old hall before it was destroyed by fire. There was also the Barr Room from which drinks were served, and a 'Musick Room'.

To give further credence to the theory that the Hall had three storeys, both the Clerk and one of the two Beadles lived in. The Beadle's and the Clerk's occupancy were 'subject to a condition that he and all other persons that shall hereafter inhabit in the said Hall shall find and provide mops and brooms, and clean the Hall at their own charges'.[9] The fate of the Beadle is unknown after certain representations were made against him to the Court by a Mr Maydew. He was fined 20 shillings for asserting vociferously 'that the Court of Assistants did employ a rogue for their clerk, and they were a parcel of rogues for so doing'.[10]

The Butchers' Hall, the first to be rebuilt after the Great Fire, marked them as a prescient company, one with a confidence in the future of their Company and, in particular, in their trade. Nor was their confidence misplaced, for it was a time of changing fortunes and agricultural innovations. The Restoration of Charles II coincided with greatly improved farming practices. A new landed gentry had sprung up, mainly through the fortunes of the merchant adventurers, such as the shareholders of the East India Company founded in 1600. As a result, 'land purchases doubled and rents trebled'[11] throughout the century. The overall effect was that more land came under the direct control of the landowner, who was receptive to new ideas and, more importantly, had the capital to develop them. The imbalance between the production of stock, for both wool and meat, and corn during Tudor times was largely reversed when the high price of corn encouraged farmers to switch out of livestock production. Books on agriculture were published throughout the century, most notably Gervase Markham's *Farewell to Husbandry or, The Inriching of all sorts of Barren and Sterril grounds in one Kingdome, to be as fruitful in all manner of Graine, Pulse and Grasse as the best grounds whatsoever*. Although Markham's treatise deals mostly with husbandry and soil improvement through sanding, liming, marling and manuring, for the first time it was considered worthwhile to improve pastures and not just to rely on natural meadows. This naturally benefited the stock. Another great advance was made towards the end of the century when two new crops, 'great clover' and turnips, were introduced into England. Although turnips were known in the kitchen garden, they were not considered an agricultural crop until they followed the Dutch, largely through Sir Richard Weston in his *Discourse of the Husbandrie used in Brabant and Flanders* of 1650. The effect was not immediate, as it took several decades before the practice of folding sheep on a field of roots became widespread. But, where it was used, it greatly improved the quality of the meat of both sheep and cattle, now bred more for the table and than for work, although the agriculturalist Lord Somerville still thought that draught oxen became stunted if not worked hard between four and six years. Cattle were better fed during the summer months on the new pastures and, more importantly, they could also be fattened throughout the winter. At first, sheep were folded on the roots, a narrow strip at a time. Then the Dutch practice of storing the turnips in a clamp, either of dry soil or sand, was adopted, the roots being fed to the stock with no wastage – 'better fed than spread' was the cry in Suffolk, where 'Great Turnip bullocks'[12] were produced. These improved practices were only aimed at fattening stock within easy distance of the urban markets, the most lucrative being London where the demand was insatiable. The store cattle driven by drovers to these fattening grounds needed to be lean for the long journeys:

Beasts are driven to London for sale; and, where the distance from the metropolis is very considerable, they are liable to many calamities or accidents on the road, besides their diminution in point of weight; which, even under the eye of the most attentive drivers, is necessarily incurred, and is often great.[13]

This general demand for meat, not just in London, increased the need to move large quantities of livestock from where they were produced to those urban areas. Drovers had been providing meat for London for centuries, but throughout the seventeenth and eighteenth centuries their numbers increased as more and more livestock were required to be brought from distances further and further from the capital. Originally, the stock were moved on sheep and cattle tracks, the only routes between farm and village, village and town, and town and city, but after the Turnpike Act of 1663, arterial roads linking cities were being constructed. Through their great expense, proper roads were a long time coming. The drovers' routes were well tried and tested as vast numbers of cattle were brought in, mostly from the north and west to the south and east. Often there were several changes of ownership along the way, as with cattle from say from north Wales that were driven to the border market towns, such as Shrewsbury and Leominster, where they were bought by Midland graziers who fattened them before their eventual push to London. Large numbers of cattle came from the north of England, particularly Cumbria, as well as from Scotland, where it was estimated that 20,000 cattle a year were driven across Bowes Moor from the Highlands (including the Isle of Skye and the West Coast, principally Argyll). A similar number from the Borders, Dumfries, Galloway and Wigtownshire, also passed through Carlisle on their way south. As many as 40,000 cattle were shipped annually from Ireland, then driven to the fattening grounds of Somerset and points east. Obviously, the closer to London the lean stock was fattened, the less condition the fat cattle lost on their way to the London markets.

The drovers lived a hard, although potentially financially rewarding, life. Cattle were driven slowly, around twelve to fifteen miles a day. At that pace they could snatch a little grazing along the roadside. The nights were spent either in the open, one drover always on watch, or at an inn along the way. The inn keepers usually had well-watered fields and fodder for the drove, also access to a blacksmith to shoe the cattle. Known as 'cues' or 'kews', cattle shoes were strips of iron, somewhat lighter than a horseshoe, forged in the shape of a comma or a crescent. Being cloven-hoofed, each beast needed eight shoes, although often only the outer sides were shod. Dogs were a vital part of the droving for both sheep and cattle. Those used for driving cattle were called Cur Dogs – that were

quick in their actions, courageous and intelligent. They are faithful and attached (though often ill-treated by the drovers, who have not the kind heart of the shepherd). Drovers' dogs are most sagacious; on the approach of a vehicle a passage is made for it through the biggest flock or herd without any signal from the drover.[14]

The cur cog was contemporarily described as being black and white with a smooth, short coat, half-pricked ears and short tail. They were larger and more ferocious than the well-trained, 'docile and sagacious' sheep dogs, known as collie dogs after the black-faced breed of sheep called 'Collies'. At the end of a cattle drive, drovers would often send their cur dogs home by themselves, even to the Highlands. These dogs would retrace their outward-bound route, 'stopping to be fed at the same inns or farms where the drove had rested'[15], the drovers paying for their food the next year when they passed back.

A different breed of dog was used to drive the great flocks of anything up a thousand turkeys and geese from East Anglia to London. The drovers would start by dipping the birds' feet in tar, then set out in August for the hundred-mile journey to Smithfield and Leadenhall Markets to arrive in time for Christmas. Turkeys had been the traditional Christmas fare in England for a century, ever since Cortez and the Conquistadors discovered the domesticated turkey kept by the Aztecs and brought them back to Spain from the New World. Pigs, too, were driven to London from the neighbouring counties. There are accounts in the seventeenth century of drovers taking pigs from Suffolk to Surrey, Sussex and Hampshire to fatten them on beech mast before they were driven to Smithfield 'well and sufficiently fed for bacon'.[16] Driving pigs was particularly difficult, as 'the pig is sluggish, obstinate, not very social and has no desire for seeing foreign parts. Think of him in a multitude, forced to travel, and wondering what the devil it is that drives him! Judge by this the talent of his drover'.[17]

Another reason that the Company of Butchers had such confidence in their trade after the Great Fire was the changing pattern of society, and the resulting increase in the wealth of the merchant class. When many of the dispossessed refugees left London for the country, their places were quickly taken by others seeking a new life. Thousands of builders moved into the City – in just two years, most of the burned-out houses had been cleared and twelve hundred rebuilt, with another sixteen hundred the year after. The aristocracy and the landed gentry, who by then included the newly rich, brought their families and a large retinue of servants to London for the winter, either to their own houses around Westminster and the new 'West End', or to houses rented for what became known as the season. An integral part of the season was dining, and as the French commentator Henri Misson noted: 'the English eat a great deal at Dinner; they rest a while, and to it again, till they have quite stuff'd their Paunch. Their Supper is moderate: Gluttons at noon and abstinent at Night'[18] And the Butchers, with their ready supply of fresh meat, were there to 'stuff their paunches' from their new markets and newly-built shops.

By 1668, the rift between the Company of Butchers and the country butchers flared up again. Immediately after the Great Fire the free and non-free butchers traded on the same basis, from the same makeshift stalls wherever they could find a pitch. But when the free butchers were moved to the new markets of Leadenhall and Newgate, the Company complained to the Court of Aldermen that country butchers were still operating wherever they pleased on the streets, mostly around Leadenhall Street and Bishopsgate. The Aldermen found against the country butchers and ordered them into Leadenhall Market, presumably more from the revenue that they would generate in the new market, rather than out of a desire to protect the Butchers' trading rights. Notwithstanding this half-hearted support from the Aldermen, the Master and Wardens could see their control of the meat trade being further eroded, and petitioned the Court to be released of their duties within the new markets. Their authority was further undermined by an Act passed by the Common Council. To the free butcher in London in 1672, the advantages of membership of the Butchers' Company can only have been questionable. Apart from the good fellowship and the use of the new hall, he paid his quarterage and was bound by the stringent rules of Company, and was fined if he transgressed. But when it came to trading, he was no better placed than any butcher outside the two-mile radius of the City, who could rent a stall in any of the new markets.

Quite apart from this unfair competition against its Liverymen, the Company of Butchers, in common with all other livery companies, had a major problem of their own. It was not of their making but one caused by the conflict between the City of London and Charles II, precipitated largely by the Earl of Shaftesbury. As President of the Privy Council, Shaftesbury had pressed for the Exclusion Bill to keep the Roman Catholic James, Duke of York, from the throne, Charles II having no legitimate heir. When Shaftesbury openly supported the claims of the Duke of Monmouth, the King's illegitimate son, in 1679 he was dismissed from his post. He persisted with the Exclusion Bill from outside Parliament as he was still technically leader of the Whig Party. With the Whigs in the majority and opposed to the Catholic succession, Charles II dissolved Parliament in 1681. The Whigs were discredited and the King was left in complete control of the Government. Shaftesbury's position was at best precarious. In July 1682, he was indicted for fomenting rebellion, which was partially true. But the City was staunchly for the Whigs, and as they elected the London Sheriffs from within their ranks they saw to it that the Middlesex jury that would hear the indictment was made up solely of their own. When the accusation was finally brought against Shaftesbury the grand jury threw it out. So long as the City remained in the Whig camp, Shaftesbury was unassailable.

As a result, the King set about destroying Whig authority within the City of London. In 1682, an action was brought in the Court of King's Bench against the self-governing Corporation of the City by means of a writ of *Quo Warranto* (from the Latin, 'by what warrant', first used by Edward I to restore his power eroded after the First Crusade). The City was accused of abusing its privileges. Although the case for the Crown was in all respects weak, judgment went against the City and its Charter was forfeited in June 1683. The King then offered to restore the Charter to the City, but on his own terms that included the clause that he should have the power of veto over the appointment all of its principal officers. The City agreed, then reneged, whereupon the King appointed his own Lord Mayor and Aldermen from his own supporters.

The knock-on effect from the loss of the City's Charter was that the Butchers' Company, along with all other City Livery Companies, were also ordered to submit to the Crown and surrender their Charters and with them their privileges. For the Master and Wardens of the Butchers' Company, the loss of their Charter, combined with the erosion of their powers, was disastrous. But it was agreed that they would be better off with a Charter than without one, and a petition to the King to renew it was drawn up. At last the summons came, and on 7 April 1684 the Master, Edward Newins, Past Master Francis Follansby and three Assistants travelled to Whitehall for an audience with the King to present their petition. Three months later, the Court met to discuss how they would pay for the new Charter, which was likely to be expensive. To tide them over, the Assistants all agreed on an immediate loan of forty shillings each, until the exact cost of the Charter was known. But Charles II died in February 1685, and surprisingly soon after, on 6 November that same year, James II granted the Company of Butchers their new Charter. There is no record of what was paid to the Crown for the privilege. There was, however, a modest fee of £6 13s 4d paid to the Hanaper Office (a department of Chancery that received fees for sealing and enrolling documents, named after a 'hanaper' or hamper, a wicker basket that held the papers).

The Charter, drawn on vellum is dull by comparison with the James I Charter, although the text is written in gold. The content of the James II Charter differed little from that of Charles I in 1637, with very similar Ordinances throughout. The Master, Wardens and Assistants were named, to be replaced by their heirs and successors as before, but the fundamental difference between the two charters (apart from the fee) was that they, along with the Clerk, could now be removed at the 'King's pleasure' through an Order of the Privy Council. Furthermore, the officers of the Company of Butchers were required to swear the Oath of Allegiance to the Crown, and to prove that they were members of the Church of England by receiving Holy Communion within six months of taking office. The only material benefit from the new Charter was that the annual value of the land that the Company was permitted to hold was increased from £30 to £100.

The Company of Butchers being incorporated once again by Royal Charter, the next step was to petition the Court of Aldermen to be recognized as a Livery Company within the City. On 12 January 1686, the right to wear the same blue and white livery was restored to the Butchers, along with their original position of twenty-fourth in order of seniority, on the strict proviso that the livery did not exceed twice the number of the combined Master, Wardens and Assistants, and that the liverymen were all 'of unquestionable loyalty'.[19] Loyalty was hard to define in the religious maelstrom of 1686, with a Catholic James II who had promised, but not delivered, religious tolerance – at his Coronation in Edinburgh he deliberately omitted the oath to defend the Protestant religion. It took the Master and Wardens a full nine months to come up with a suitable list of liverymen. Presumably to ingratiate the Company with the Privy Council, Past Master Edward Newins, along with eighteen Assistants, affirmed their allegiance to the Stuart cause by signing a declaration declaring that the oath for reformation and defence of the Scottish Presbyterian Church, known as the Solemn League and Covenant, was illegal. Three names that had originally appeared on the James II Charter were even left off the list. But, despite this declaration, the list of liverymen was still not acceptable to the Council, who removed another two names, Samuel Trowell of Islington and James Garrett of St Olave's Street, for some unspecified reason.

But the upheavals for the Butchers' Company in connection with the James II Charter did not end there. Under the King's protection, Catholics were favoured for most major offices in the Kingdom, including the City. Fearful of a backlash from the Church of England, the King attempted to counter their potential opposition by passing, in April 1687, the Declaration of Indulgence formally ending all discrimination against both Catholics and Non-conformists. It also abolished the requirement to swear an oath to the Church of England before advancement to military, or civil, office, which naturally included all Court positions in Livery Companies. The same applies to the present day. For the Company of Butchers, the result was immediate, and by Order of Council 'certain of the Assistants and Liverymen' (fourteen Assistants, including Trowell and Garret, and twenty-three liverymen) 'were restored to their former condition'.[20]

For the Company of Butchers, with their members drawn from all faiths, the Declaration should have eliminated all causes of possible conflict with the City Authorities and the Crown. But it was not to be. By an 'Order in Council from his Majesty', at a meeting of the Privy Council on 10 February 1688, 'Master John Jowkes, two of the Wardens [Samuel Wakelyn and Thomas Taylor], and seven of the Assistants were removed from their office'.[21] The election to replace them was held soon after, and John Sergeant was duly elected as Master. Why Jowkes was dismissed is not known, (it took very little to upset the King), but it is likely that he was 'a Tory of a too pronounced a character'[22] and a staunch supporter of the Church of England. His replacement John Sergeant came from Non-conformist

. HRH The Princess Royal by Michael Noakes. She is wearing the gold and enamel brooch of the Butchers' Company Arms given to The Queen Mother. The portrait was presented to the Company by Michael Katz in memory of his wife, Ilse.

2a. The Boar's Head Ceremony 2004, the 50th anniversary of the revival of the 13th century custom and the 400th of the granting of the first Royal Charter. Soldiers of the Royal Logistic Corp carried the fanciful head. The Master, Colin Cullimore, stands on their right with the Clerk, Anthony Morrow.

2b. Stained glass window in the Great Hall depicting a medieval Court. They are wearing knitted woollen bonnets, the traditional headdress of butchers.

3. The James I Charter granted in 1605. The text is in Latin, part of which is badly worn. When it had to be consulted for a constitution change, the scholar read an X-rayed version.

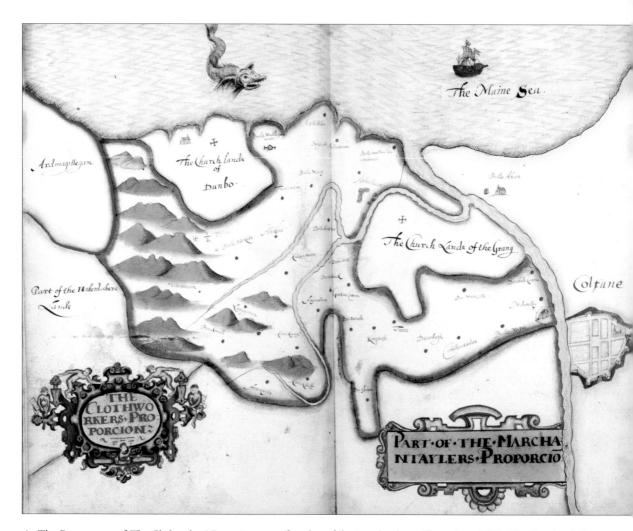

4a. The Raven map of *The Clothworkers' Proporcion,* one of twelve of the Londonderry Plantations, 1622. The Butchers' Company joined the Clothworkers in this Irish venture in 1613, only to sell out at a loss 60 years later.

4b. The new Smithfield Market shortly after it opened in 1868. With its cast iron and glass construction, underground railway acce and hydraulic system, it became the model for meat markets world wide.

stock in Lincolnshire and, in common with an estimated nine hundred Dissenters appointed to the various Courts of all Livery Companies that year, he was elected principally for his beliefs that were acceptable to the City and to the Crown. Even with the religious tolerance in the last throes of James II's reign, office of any kind could be a dangerous. For the Butchers, only twelve Assistants could be found who were willing to take up their appointments, and of the restored Liverymen three failed to appear when summoned, while two still refused to take the oath when elected to office. All were fined, although two of them paid a further fine to be excused all other office.

When news came of an imminent invasion by the Protestant Prince William of Orange, James II became even more conciliatory towards the City. By Order in Council their original rights and privileges were restored in October 1688 in a bid to gain their support. Those who had been disenfranchised were immediately reinstated. When William landed at Torbay and marched slowly towards London, the King tried to rally the City behind him but failed. Realizing his plight, he fled from London on 12 November. In what was described as 'the unexpected revolution', the bloodless change of regime was complete when James was dethroned and the Crown offered jointly to William and Mary. As for the Company of Butchers, they too had their 1638 Charter restored, with all its rights and privileges. Ironically, it was Samuel Wakelyn of Eastcheap, one of the two Wardens removed by Charles II, who was elected Master of the restored Company. The end of Charles II's reign and the brief reign of James II had been a rather expensive and disruptive interlude for the Butchers.

Throughout the reign of William and Mary, London continued to expand in all directions. With the new rich and ever-burgeoning population, trade, especially the meat trade, prospered, for London was a city of plenty:

> For pleasure, or luxury, London is a magazine where all is at hand, and scarce anything wanting that money can purchase. Here is to be had, not only what Europe affords, but what is fetched by navigation from the remotest parts of the habitable world.[23]

The new purpose-built markets were the envy of Europe. César de Saussure, a Swiss visitor and astute commentator, who reported London life in a series of letters home, wrote that:

> Nowhere can you see finer markets than in London, especially those of Leadenhall, of Stocks Market, and several others; they are vast, covered and shut in, and in them you can find every kind of butcher's meat, the finest in all the world, and kept with the greatest cleanliness. England is celebrated, and justly so, for her

excellent meats, especially beef and veal, mutton being rather coarse, often tasting of tallow, but full of juice. In these markets an abundance of every kind of salt and freshwater fish is to be found; also vegetables and poultry of every description.[24]

For the household and servants' hall alike, meat was the most important part of their diet, . 'I have always heard they were great flesh eaters', Henri Misson, a Frenchman living in London, wrote, 'and I found it to be true.'[25] For those who could afford it, beef was the preferred meat, for 'English beef is reported to excel that of all other countries in the world'. Furthermore, meat was eaten in great quantities by all classes. Where the aristocracy often had French chefs and ate in the French manner, by contrast

> the middling sort of people, ... have ten or twelve sorts of common meats, which infallibly take turns at their tables, and two dishes are their dinners; a pudding, for instance, and a piece of roast beef: another time they will have a piece of boil'd beef, and then they salt it some days beforehand, and besiege it with five or six heaps of cabbage, carrots, turnips, or some other herbs or roots, well pepper'd and salted, and swimming with butter.

Alternatively, for the less well off, Sunday was the day 'to feast as nobly as possible, [where] it is common practice . . . to have a huge piece of roast-beef, of which stuff till they can swallow no more, and eat the rest cold, without any other victuals the other six days of the week'. César de Saussure observed that the beef came to the table weighing 'according to the number of those who are to partake of it, ten, twelve, or fifteen pounds, though I have even seen it weigh twenty'.[26] To prepare for these dinners (formerly eaten at one o'clock in the afternoon, then later and later as fashions changed) one of the kitchen staff in a grand London house, or a housewife, would rise even earlier than normal three days a week, Monday, Wednesday and Friday, to arrive at Leadenhall Market (or indeed any of the other new markets springing up in London) by six o'clock. As they entered the market, a bell would sound to start the day's trading. If beef was to be on the menu, they would make their way to the hundred or so stalls in the Beef Hall, where both free and non-free butchers alike were trading. The joints of beef were well displayed on a large board (eight or six feet by four feet for which the butcher paid 2/6d or 2/- respectively), or hung up on hooks around the stall. For everything else connected with the butchery trade, principally mutton, veal and poultry, housewife and servant alike would go to the larger Green Yard. There was plenty of choice among the hundred and forty butchers' stalls in the Green Yard. There was fierce competition too between the stallholders, and no butcher was allowed to take more than two stalls.

Servant and housewife would have paid cash, the goods being handed over unwrapped and placed in their large wicker baskets. Although by the end of the seventeenth century copper coinage was in circulation, it is possible that the change would still have been given in trade tokens. During the Commonwealth, the previous Stuart coinage struck from the Royal Mint was replaced by a new denomination called the Rump, named after the Rump Parliament, the remnant of the Long Parliament. Clearly the Rump coinage would take some time to phase out after the Restoration, and even a year later 'the calling in of the money inscribed *The Commonwealth* must be suspended awhile: there are great quantities of it, and the Mint is not yet supplied'.[27] By 1663, the Royal Mint had struck a new coinage consisting of a guinea (when first coined 'in the name and for the use of the Company of Royal Adventurers of England trading with Africa'[28], it had an emblem of a little elephant on the obverse and was made from gold from Guinea, hence its nomenclature), a half-guinea, a crown and a half-crown in both gold and silver, a silver shilling and a sixpence, along with smaller coinage that was in such short supply and so minute as to be impractical to use. Small denominations had always been a problem for tradesmen, and one that had not been addressed by the new coinage. So the traders took the matter into their own hands and, starting around 1650, produced their own coinage to give out as small change. They were called trade tokens.

These tokens were mostly of copper or brass (as in a *brass-farthing*). They were struck either round, square or hexagonal (heart-shaped is also known), about the size of the present 5p piece. Their value was either a half-penny or a farthing, although one-penny tokens were not unknown, particularly from coffee houses. The tokens were of course illegal, but as the king's head was not represented, and they were not passed off as currency of the realm, their use was accepted. The idea was that traders would give out their own tokens as change to customers, who in turn could pay for purchases using tokens received from a variety of different traders. Once a trader had collected enough of another trader's tokens he could exchange them for silver coinage or for a promissory note. For the system to work effectively, the tokens would have to be confined to a very local area for the exchanges to take place. During the twenty-two years that tokens were in circulation in those well-defined areas throughout the country (including Ireland), an estimated 14,000 tradesmen and women issued their own tokens, of which over 3,500 were in London and the suburbs. Of these, the tokens of forty butchers have survived, nine of which are from London. While some of the country butchers' tokens have the symbols of their trade – a crossed knife and cleaver, a slaughterman's axe, and the like – stamped on the token, most have the arms of the Company of Butchers whether the issuer were free or, as it turned out, mostly not. The use of the Company arms would certainly have given authority to the tokens. Most surviving Butchers' tokens are for a half-penny, as meat purchases tended to be more expensive than those from say a baker or grocer. One surviving butcher's token was issued by Thomas Taylor, the same who as Warden of the Butchers' Company was removed from office by Charles II. Taylor traded from a shop in Beech Lane (now Street) in the Barbican, most likely with a stall in nearby Newgate Market as well. Other surviving butchers' tokens include those issued by Isaac Peckett of Smithfield, Andrew Porter from St James's Market, and Nathaniel Higgins, with a beef stall in Green Yard, Leadenhall Market.

When the market bell rang again on the stroke of 10 o'clock Nathaniel Higgins of Green Yard, along with his neighbours, would have effectively changed from a retail to a wholesale butcher as other retail butchers, free and non-free alike, came to buy for their shops elsewhere in the City and the suburbs. Hawkers would also be there to buy their meat, cut up and sell on the streets. As de Saussure observed, 'quantities of small vendors go through the streets, especially in the morning, calling out their wares for sale; thus, if you prefer it, you need not leave your house to buy your provisions'. As they could not set up stalls in the street, everything was sold from trays around their necks or from baskets. Hawkers were banned from selling around the markets when the City Authorities passed an Act that prohibited 'the sale of goods of shops and warehouses of Freemen of the City'.[29]

Hawkers had always been the bane of the free butcher, for not only were they taking their trade away, but they also had the reputation of selling tainted or stolen meat. In the Company's Ordinances (number 28) of 1607, hawkers were specifically outlawed within two miles of the City. If any were caught, the Company was empowered to seize their meat and donate it to the Bethlehem Hospital for the Insane (the site of the present Imperial War Museum) or the prisoners of Newgate Prison. A fine of ten shillings was also extracted. Naturally, such an Ordinance was difficult to police, so the Court of the Butchers' Company, 'considering the great discredit and damage to the Company by the idle and lewd people who sold corrupt flesh by way of hawking',[30] appointed two of their number to arrest all hawkers within the City and seize their goods. The cost of ending 'the sales of rotten, corrupt and unwholesome meat in covert and secret manner in streets, lanes, inns and chambers, escaping all search, to the deceit of the public' was met by the Freemen, who donated nine pence a quarter each. This donation only ended nearly a century later.

In Leadenhall Market the bell was rung for the third and final time at the end of the day, 8 o'clock in the evening in the summer (later extended to 10) but 5 o'clock in winter.

The nature of the Company of Butchers, along with all the others, changed after the Great Fire. Before, the City Authorities had insisted that all trades and professions occupy the same areas. After the Fire, free butchers set up wherever they pleased, either in their own shops within the City or outside in the suburbs, or in one of the many new markets that were springing up throughout an ever-expanding London. In the return of Liverymen of 1686, over half of them operated outside the City giving their addresses as such places as St James's Market, by Haymarket, noted for the quality of its veal, or Hungerford Market in the Strand. This elegant building with its rows of colonnades and flight of steps down to the Thames, possibly designed by Wren, was built by Sir Edward Hungerford on the site of his burned-out house. The success of this market lay its proximity to the new development of the fashionable West End; it was later demolished to make way for the present Charing Cross Station. Honey Lane Market, another built after the Great Fire, was demolished in 1835 to make way for the City of London School.

Another site was Clare Market, close by Lincoln's Inn Fields, now long demolished and the site of the present Kingsway. In 1720, Stowe described Clare market as 'very considerable' and 'well served with both meat and fish; in addition to the butchers in the shambles, it was much frequented by country butchers and higglers. The market days were Wednesday and Saturday'.[31] There were 'about 26 butchers in and about Clare Market', in what was one of the poorest districts in London. Nearby was a tripe-house, and in

> a yard distinct from the more public portion of the market, is the place the Jews slaughter their cattle, according to a ceremony prescribed by the laws of their religion; here greater attention is paid to cleanliness.[32]

Other Liverymen worked out of Clerkenwell and the nearby market of Saffron Hill, named from the saffron that was traditionally sold there. Saffron was much sought after, particularly during the Great Plague when it was thought to be a remedy, even reviving the dead. Further afield some Liverymen set up their stalls across the river in Southwark to cater for the growing population there, and to the east in Whitechapel, traditionally the home of labourers and immigrants, and soon to be known as the East End. It had the reputation of 'a place of thieves' kitchens and ragged public houses charged with the unmistakable overpowering damp and mouldy odour attendant upon street crime'.[33] Fifty years later, Dick Turpin, the highwayman, was apprenticed to a butcher in Whitechapel. The butcher's name is not known, but the fact that Turpin was apprenticed surely means that his master was a Liveryman. Dick Turpin was perhaps not alone, for there was always supposed to be a 'pronounced association between butchers and highway robbers'.[34] Nor was the alternative 'profession' out of character, for traditionally butchers have always been known for their 'boisterous, individualistic and sometimes violent nature'. Indeed, in a survey of those hanged in London in the eighteenth century, those born in London tended to hang in their early twenties, and 'the main trades that reached the scaffold, were butchers, weavers and shoe-makers'.[35] Conversely, butchers were generally recognized as leaders of their particular communities. On occasion, butchers even set the cultural tone, as in the theatres around Clare Market, where they were 'the arbiters of the galleries, the leaders of the theatrical rows, the musicians at actresses' marriages, the chief mourners at players' funerals'.[36] But more often their role was one of disorder. In one violent affray in the late seventeenth century 'the Butchers have begun the way to all the rest, for within this toe [two] days they did all rise upon the excise man'.[37] Despite their Ordinances to the contrary, the Company of Butchers had lost control of the large number of non-free butchers, and their censures were soon to be a distant memory.

Matters were conducted with a great deal more decorum within the Company. A cook had always been employed by the Butchers, primarily to cater for the various feasts, the most important being that held for Election Day on the Monday previous to St Luke's Day (18 October). For many of the Livery, Election Day was a day to dread, as it could mean that they were elected to the Court as Assistants, with an attendant fine if the honour was refused, or, worse still, that any number of them could be called upon to act as stewards. This was a particularly onerous task as it meant that they had to cater, and pay for, the banquet given by the Company for the Livery on Lord Mayor's Day. Defaulters could be fined, as much as £20, although the fines were usually means-tested. Usually three or four stewards were appointed, occasionally five 'by reason of the dearness of the victuals'.[38] On one particular occasion in 1693, the Liveryman John Oliver was excused from serving as a steward on account of his 'being poor'. The meeting at which this was decided was held not in the Butchers' Hall but at Mr. Godall's coffee-house, which implies that the Hall was let, the Company's funds still being in a precarious state.

Notwithstanding their parlous state, the Butchers were not to be thwarted in their feasting. Wives were often included and friends invited. There was, however, a fine of five shillings apiece 'if persons that shall bring any other friend more than their wives, or more than one friend instead of their wives'.[39] Nor were the diners allowed to take any uneaten food home with them. Dress code was also strictly observed, and he 'that doth not attend and appear in his gown to walk with the Master on the Lord Mayor's Day, shall not be admitted to dine'.[40] For some reason, wives 'and any other woman' were excluded from all banquets at the turn of the eighteenth century.

For the Company of Butchers, the banquets did not always go smoothly, as shown by the account of the one held in 1709 after the inauguration of Sir Samuel Garrard as Lord Mayor. The Beadle, as was his job, had summoned the Liverymen with the following letter:

Sir,

You are hereby summoned, by Order of the Master and Wardens of your Company, to be and appear in your Livery Gown and Hood, at Butchers' Hall, on Saturday the 29th day of this Instant October, 1709, being the Lord Mayor's Day, at Nine o'clock in the Forenoon, thence to walk with your Company to their Stand, and thence to return to your Hall to Dinner. You are not to bring your Wife, or any other person with you. If you do not walk with the Master in your Livery, you will not be admitted into the Hall to Dine with the rest of your Brethren.

Signed by the Upper and Under Beadle.

The day was doomed from the start. Two Liverymen, Richard Miles and Charles Whapshot, had been chosen to act as stewards at the Election Day meeting. A few days later, 20 October, Miles refused the office and on the same day the Master and Wardens took him before the Court of Aldermen. Miles presented his case, which was deemed inadequate, and was ordered to perform his duties as per the oath he took to the Company with its prescribed byelaws, to which he unwillingly agreed. Two days later, the Wardens delivered the list of ingredients required for the feast. :

9 dishes of pullets, oysters, bacon, and sausages, three in a dish,
9 dishes of geese, two in each dish,
9 dishes of mince pies, two in each dish,
9 large tarts of pippins and quinces,
3 sirloins of beef and 3 middle ribs,
10 quarts of oysters,
15 lb bacon
9 lb of sausages,
6 dozen red wine, 4 dozen white wine, 1½ dozen canary,
2 three-firkin barrels of ale, 1 barrel of beer,
bread, cheese, etc

The provisions for the feast were duly bought by the two wretched stewards and delivered to the cook at Butchers' Hall. On the morning of the Lord Mayor's Day, the Master and the rest of the Livery turned up expecting to find the wine to take to their stand for the day. Miles and Whapshot informed them that breakfast was not included in the deal and certainly not the wine for the stand. The Master, Samuel Tomlinson, went off to the Queen's Arms in St Paul's Churchyard (later to be frequented by the likes of John Wilkes, and famous for political debate) and bought the wine to be consumed on the stand during the day.

Meanwhile the cook, Thomas Bentley, a veteran of twenty-four years at the

Butchers' Hall, was appalled at the stinking meat provided by the stewards and by the lack of butter for basting. When he pointed out that the meat was putrid, Miles and Whapshot rounded on him, calling the Master and Wardens 'rogues, rascals and villains'.[41] To the charge that the meat was unfit for the Livery to consume, Whapshot replied 'Damn them, they never eat any other'.[42] The Company returned to Butchers' Hall as expected at five o'clock, only to find the gates into the courtyard at Pudding Lane firmly locked. The disgruntled Livery went off to a nearby tavern to dine, along with the standard-bearers who had lodged the Company flags in the house next door, leaving the Master and Wardens to deal with the errant stewards. In a later testimony, some members of the Livery reported that they heard Miles and Whapshot call the Company 'nothing but a parcel of broken dogs' and say 'God damn them they shall none of them come in'. It would appear that much of the wine bought for the banquet had been drunk by the stewards by that time.

The affront to their dignity and the slur on the Company was too much for the Court to bear. The case was taken by the Master and Wardens to the Court of Aldermen on the grounds that such behaviour impinged on the honour of the City. Witnesses were questioned; and affidavits were sworn before the Lord Mayor. Miles and Whapshot were called upon to give their version of the affair. Council for the Company conferred with the lawyers for the Court of Aldermen for legal precedents as to the punishment the stewards should receive. The whole was an expensive affair, with all manner of fees payable. In the end, the Aldermen decided that it was an internal matter and they had wasted enough time on it already, and took no further action. But the Butchers would not leave it alone. They believed that they had suffered damage at the hands of Miles and Wapshot, and sued them in the Queen's Bench. The acrimony increased when Miles accused the Master of giving two of the witnesses a bribe of £50 each to testify against him, whereupon the Court passed a resolution that, if either of the stewards brought a counter-action against any of the Livery, it would be defended at the Company's expense. Like so many legal actions, it just petered out, but the Company was saddled with an enormous legal bill of £140. Eventually, it was paid with two promissory notes, the Company coffers, as usual, being empty.

The result of the whole sorry affair was that the Company picked up half the cost of the dinner for the Lord Mayor's Day. To make sure that there was never a repeat of the Miles and Whapshot débâcle, the Renter Warden was ordered to

have a Bill of Fare of provisions appointed on the Lord Mayor's Day, to be found by the stewards for that day both at breakfast and dinner, in order to be inspected by the said Renter Warden, to see if it is in accordance to the Bill of Fare delivered, and the Renter Warden shall have a key, and the steward of the wine to take an account what wine is brought in for the service of the day, whether the same is in accordance with the bill of fare, and if any Renter Warden disobeys this order he shall be discharged.[43]

Other changes in the Butchers' dining practices came when women were admitted again, although 'from that, and after this time [1713] no more dancing to be in the Hall on Lord Mayor's Day'.

The love of pageantry has always been a feature of City life and the Livery Companies, not least for the feast that usually accompanied a big event. As soon as the news of the Peace of Ryswick (where Louis XIV finally recognized William III's title to the British throne) reached the Lord Mayor in London in September 1697, he immediately set about organizing a suitable reception. At last 'after long and impatient expectation' the King came back in November, and the Court of the Butchers was convened to discuss

the King's return through the City from Flanders, by virtue of a precept from the Lord Mayor, the Livery being ordered to attend the King's return tomorrow at the stand in Cheapside by 9 in the morning and they are to appear at the Hall by 8 o'clock.[44]

It was one of the finest pageants the City had ever staged, combining the best of all previous royal visits. The Butchers' Company took their stand, 'well apparelled and with all the ornaments of their Company before them'.[45] No expense had been spared, with new gowns for the magistrates and new banners for the Companies. The Mayor, Aldermen and Sheriffs rode out 'in their formalities' as far as Southwark, where they met the King, 'and where the usual ceremony took place of surrendering the civic sword into his majesty's hands, to be immediately returned to the lord mayor'.[46] Since at least the fourteenth century, the Mayor has surrendered his sword (sometimes the mace as well) to the Sovereign at the boundary of the City. This is to show 'the over-lordship of the Sovereign', and is symbolic of the fact that that the Mayor holds the City on behalf of the Sovereign. This particular ceremony began with Charles I's entry into the City in 1641, and is still carried out today whenever the Queen officially enters the City. After William III had returned the Lord Mayor's sword, the procession formed up and the King was escorted the length of the City accompanied by musicians playing kettledrums and trumpets, the entire route being lined with the men of six regiments, past 'houses rendered bright with hangings of tapestry'.[47]

Since its foundation, as a livestock market Smithfield has always been the very artery of the London meat trade. The pens were the final goal of many a drover who delivered fat cattle and cows, sheep and pigs as well as horses. As a consequence, first the Guild and then the Company of Butchers have always been there to protect the interests of their members and to see that the Market was managed to their advantage. Regulations governing the funding of the Market soon developed – in the thirteenth century there was a levy of 1d for each head of cattle or a dozen sheep sold. There were strict laws, rigorously enforced, over the resale of the same cattle in the market. Members of the Butchers' Guild were penalised for late payment, or for slaughtering a beast before the drover had been paid. To protect the London trade the practice of regrating was forbidden, that was buying stock at the fairs in say Essex and the surrounding countryside to sell on, 'by which resale prices were raised to the grievous hurt of the citizens'.[48] By 1548 an Act was passed to prevent forestalling where stock could only be sold in a market and any infringement was reported by the Wardens to the Lord Mayor. So when two Leicestershire graziers, James Mortymer and William Alman, in the mid-sixteenth century bought two hundred sheep at Smithfield and were caught reselling them, they were ordered to surrender forty of them (valued at five shillings each), keeping the rest on the surety that they would never to the same again.

In the early days, Smithfield Market favoured the free butcher with friendly market hours. They could buy at seven in the morning on Wednesdays and Fridays until ten o'clock, later extended to eleven o'clock, leaving the non-free butcher just one hour to buy what was left. As the population of London and the suburbs continued to grow, Monday was added as a market day to cope with the insatiable demand for meat. The restricted hours were blamed for the increased price of meat – always risky in a volatile market with a shifting economy – to 'the impoverishment of poor housekeepers'.[49] As a result, the non-free butchers went off to Barnet Market for their supplies. This upset Smithfield, and it was agreed that the non-free butchers could, after all, trade after eight o'clock in the morning. The Company of Butchers then retaliated by saying that as the non-free butchers continued to frequent Barnet, there was no need to accommodate them at Smithfield – their own freemen being heavily fined if caught trading at Barnet. The Master and Wardens persuaded the City authorities to revert to the eleven o'clock opening for the non-free butchers, which was enacted, but shortly after, as a compromise, the hour for the non-free butchers was put back to nine o'clock. There was then a move, promoted by the Company of Butchers and Smithfield, to outlaw Barnet Market altogether.

Not unnaturally the traders of Chipping Barnet (Chipping means market) and their clients were upset at the proposal, and in a petition to the Privy Council they accused the London butchers of ruining their trade. The petition also made mention of the fact that many of the grander freemen butchers were also graziers, who either owned or leased all the best pasture land, meadows and marshes within a five-mile radius of London to quarter their stock. It was believed that they could regulate the supplies to Smithfield, and so manipulate the price of meat at will to the detriment of the non-free butchers. In 1631, the Attorney General looked into the complaint, studying the 'Butchers' books of common acts' (a diary) to see it they were in any way responsible for the 'overthrow or hinder' of Barnet Market. After close examination, he recommended that the Butchers' Company should be investigated, and found that the fluctuations in the price of meat was indeed due to the closure of Barnet Market, and the actions of the grazier-butchers. Certainly some of the grazier-butchers had made fortunes from their operations, buying cattle far beyond the needs of their own butchers' shops. Richard Hodgkins, who was Master in 1673, leased marshland in Barking with a grass-keep rent of a staggering £326 per annum, a marsh at West Ham costing £70 per annum, with more land at Plaistow and Woolwich. He died a very rich man, his funeral alone costing £75.

Whether the Butchers were censured or not for the closure of Barnet Market is uncertain – those minute books have not survived, but presumably the findings went in their favour as the new Royal Charter was granted by Charles I just six years later. In any event, Barnet Market reopened and in its time became one of the biggest markets in the Country. But, because of the Attorney General's findings in the Barnet Market affair, an Act was passed in Parliament in 1707 that outlawed the sale of fat cattle and sheep by one butcher to another, as:

> that by the Carcase or Wholesale Butchers trading they hinder a thousand or more butchers coming to the markets of Smithfield, etc., and so that the grazing part of England for sheep or lambs is subject to about sixty or wholesale butchers which do govern the markets.[50]

The Company of Butchers 'humbly offered to the Honourable House of Commons [reasons] against appealing against a clause in the Act made the last Session of Parliament for preventing one butcher selling fat cattle or sheep to another to sell again either dead or alive'. They maintained

> that by the quantities of land held by the carcase and wholesale butchers in the counties of Middlesex and Essex, lying about seven or eight miles from the City of London, where they keep great quantities of sheep and lambs continually, they subject the graziers to their own prices. But if the fair trader, the butcher, were to buy alive, and not dead, the graziers would have a quicker dispatch by reason the butcher is always desirous of going to keep his shop or stall, whereas the carcase or wholesale men have no dependence on retail customers; which make them delay the time in the market at Smithfield to lower the price of sheep, etc.[51]

Parliament was not swayed by the rich carcase butchers' demand to have the clause repealed, although towards the end of the eighteenth century the whole method of marketing meat was to change. With the advent of the carcase butcher, the traditional hostility between the free and the non-free butcher had come to an end, when they as retailers united against the middleman who was cutting into their profits.

Whatever the route to the butchers' stall, the carcase that was bought by the butcher in the eighteenth century was vastly superior to anything that had gone before. At the beginning of the century, an average carcase weight for a fat ox was 667 lb, with an estimated live weight of 1,212 lb. In fact weights were usually expressed in stones, the standard since the reign of Edward III being 14lb, although there was also a 16lb stone known as either a Scotch Stone or a Dutch Stone. In the South West, Wales and the North West, the Score (20lb) was used. In London and the Home Counties 'the Smithfield' Stone was just 8 lb, and applied to both meat and fish. The advantage of the Smithfield Stone for expressing carcase weight was that for every 8lb of carcase there would have been 14lb of the beef animal's live weight, the same proportion as the killing yield of 57 percent. The Smithfield Stone was only phased out in 1939.

The improved weight and quality of the stock produced in the first half of the eighteenth century exactly mirrored the improved conditions of the country, where 'for the first fifty years of the century, fortune smiled on most of the people of England'.[52] It was a time of exceptional harvests, when the number of wet summers or droughts 'could be counted on one hand'. As a result corn was plentiful and cheap and, along with it, all the staple foods. Although the wages of the labourers and less skilled workers had barely risen, their money went further with the fall in price of food. Meat that had been 5d. or 6d. a pound could now be bought for 2d. or 3d., well within their means, although for the smaller tenant farmer who produced the stock the lower prices often spelled ruin. There was work to be had in the country; industry was burgeoning in the towns and cities. For the butchery trade life was difficult, with smaller and smaller margins despite this ever-increasing market. Nor were matters any better with their Company, as through reasons of incompetence by the Master and the Clerk, the Butchers' Company was in a sorry state, both financially and constitutionally.

The knock-on effect of the Great Fire on the Company was to be felt for a century or more. The rents from the properties in Pudding Lane and Eastcheap ceased, and a paltry £2 per annum ground rent was received from the tenant who bore the cost of rebuilding on the other four sites. Furthermore, some of the Company's obligations ceased with the introduction of advanced facilities in the new markets, and the new Commissioners of Sewers now coped with the butchers' waste. This made the barrowhouses, the lanes leading to the River Thames, and their pudding houses on the wharfs all superfluous. The standing at Queenhithe was let on a long lease to a William Bucknall for a mere £1 per annum. The issue of the other lane, leading to the former Eastcheap butchers' barrowhouse and standing at Fresh Wharf, was rather more complicated. Unknown to the Butchers, the lane had also been let by the City Corporation to Thomas Hopkins from 1657 for sixty-one years, while the Corporation was at the same time still collecting (as they had since the fifteenth century) rent of 13s 4d. per annum from the 'Wardens of the Butchers for Rithers Lane where the barrow house is kept for Eastcheap'.[53] Later, the Butchers let the site and the lane for development to Sarah Hopkins, presumably a close relation of Thomas, at a rent of £1 per annum. There the matter rested, probably with Sarah Hopkins paying her ground rent to the Butchers as well as to the Corporation. The matter lay unresolved for the term of the Hopkins lease, but when the lease was due for renewal in 1719, an action for encroachment was brought against the City Corporation by the Butchers' Company, who in turn were indicted by the Mayor and Commonalty. The Company's case rested on the fact that they had been granted a lease for Katherine Lane in perpetuity (see page 20) and that, since 1402, they had duly been paying rent for the privilege. Although the Corporation acknowledged that the annual rent of 13s 4d had been paid, the nature of the rent was not known – that is, whether it was 'a rack rent, a free rent, or a rent of inheritance'[54] as they maintained that there was no record of the original grant. The Lord Chancellor considered the facts, including the written entry of the original grant in the Corporation's own Letter Book, and after a very long deliberation found for the Company of Butchers, and awarded them costs.

As early as 1724 (the year when Nathaniel Edwards preferred to donate a silver loving cup rather than serve as Master) it was recorded in the sketchy minutes of the Court that the Ordinances of the restored Charter of 1637 of the Company had been examined and found wanting for their current needs. But nothing was done, possibly because of the dire financial straits of the Company. Income, gained mostly through the fines of those elected to the Livery and the crippling office of Steward, rarely covered expenditure. Debts were piling up. Through their Ordinance (see page 65) they were entitled to collect quarterage from all non-free butchers trading within two miles of the City, but the right had rarely been exercised. On occasion, it had been paid voluntarily. In an effort to balance the books, seventeen collectors were employed to extract 'Foreign Quarterage' from the non-free butchers of the markets at Newgate, Honey Lane and Cripplegate, while others went to Whitechapel, East Smithfield and Wapping. Some went to collect from Temple Bar, and the markets of Clare, Brook, Bloomsbury, Southwark and St James, even Westminster and Spitalfields. Although this extra money helped, the Company continued to borrow from their own and outside sources. When these loans, along with many others, were called in and there was no money to pay them, the Company accepted Captain Thomas Frend's proposal for a life annuity of £50 per annum in return for £500 loan secured against the Butchers' Hall. The money thus raised went some of the way to discharging their debts, but the Company's deficit continued to rise. When Frend's annuity could not be paid, the Clerk was ordered to pawn 'a large silver cup, a beaker, a large spoon, and five small spoons'.[55] They were desperate times, compounded by the mismanagement of the Company.

Matters came to a head when the election day of 1743 passed without a Common Hall, in clear breach of the Company's main Ordinances. The day should have been arranged by the Clerk, John Leadbeater, in conjunction with the Master and Wardens. Instead, the immediate Past Master, George Carter, stepped into the breach and declared himself Master. This stirred the apathetic Livery into action. They applied to the King's Bench for a writ of mandamus (a judicial writ issued as a command to an inferior court) for Carter, the Wardens and the Court to hold the elections forthwith. Finally, a month later, the elections were held and Thomas Shadd, one of three candidates, was voted in as Master by a large majority, along with five Wardens. The fifteen Assistants were chosen and sworn in soon after. The first action of the Master, Wardens and Court was to dismiss the Clerk, John Leadbeater, who was accused of

> having for several months last past greatly misbehaved himself in not doing the office of his said office, not attending any of the Courts holden by the said Company for a great while, and for divers and other misdemeanors committed by him, and in that year as well in the preceding and subsequent years.[56]

Leadbeater was further accused of 'reproachful and scandalous speeches against several Members of the Court in particular and of the Livery in general' and that he 'allowed other misdemeanors to be done to the prejudice of the Company.'[57] Although he had agreed that he held his position at the 'pleasure of the Court', and had signed a declaration promising that, were he found wanting, he would 'peaceably surrender and resign', Leadbeater did not go quietly. He obtained a mandamus for his restoration, citing the fact that, as the Company had failed to hold a Common Hall for elections, in clear breach of the Company's Ordinances, their Charter was forfeit. The Company did not argue the case and granted him an annuity of £12 a year for life – mercifully for them only another seven years – rather than reinstate him.

But that was not the end of the affair. There was the inevitable rivalry between the former Court and the new, elected from those members of the Livery who had instigated the Quo Warranto proceedings. In addition, the 'Master elect declined to serve'. Instead a series of committees met throughout 1744–45 to discuss what was best for their defunct Company. The next year, proceedings were started to negotiate for a new Charter, and the Company's lawyer, John Myles, prepared a draft. This was mulled over by the whole Company, and significantly it was 'the divers persons members of the Art or Mystery' rather than the Master elect, Thomas Rolfe, Wardens and Assistants, who agreed the draft. The final petition for the restoration of their Charter was presented to the Privy Council. It was a difficult time for the Company. As the Company was no longer obliged to hold elections the former Master, Wardens and Court remained in office, but the next year, when Samuel Saunders was elected Master, he too refused to take up office for fear of legal reprisals. In the elections held in January 1749, Thomas Shadd was again elected Master, along with five new Wardens and thirteen Assistants (later made up to fifteen), and those, with their successors, were named in the new Charter 'granted to the Company by King George II on 10th October, 1749'.[58] To the great relief of all, it was read to the assembled Company a fortnight later. There was no fee payable to the Crown, but Myles charged £850 for acting as lawyer and Clerk. The Company was restored to its former position, with no loss of seniority.

It was to be another three years before the fresh Ordinances (much on the lines of those that went with the 1637 Charter) were ratified. What they did contain, however, was a clause incorporating the Freemen of the Company of Butchers and stating that 'every other person not being already free of the City and using the art, trade or mystery of a butcher within the City of London or liberties thereof [within two miles] shall take on himself the freedom and be made free of the Butchers' Company'.[59] Although the payment of foreign quarterage was better assured, the Company was still not satisfied that their authority over other factions within the City, as specified in their new Charter, was to their complete advantage. In a petition to the Common Council it was pointed out that there were those butchers practising their 'art or mystery' who were free, but their freedom was of another Company, to the obvious detriment of the Butchers' Company. The Act was finally passed, confirming that

> no person therefore using the said trade shall be admitted by the Chamberlain to the Freedom of the City of or in any other Company than the said Company of Butchers. Provided that anyone entitled to the freedom of any other Company by patrimony or service and who ought to be to the provisions of this Act to be made free of the Butchers' Company on payment of such fees and no more as are usually paid on admission of the child or apprentice of a Freeman of the same Company.[60]

In other words, anyone practising as a butcher who was free of another Company had to be admitted to the Butchers' Company, but at a fee no greater than the one they had been paying. Those butchers who flouted the new Ordinance were liable to a fine of £5 in the Mayor's Court in the name of the Chamberlain, the fine going half to the Company, the other to the London Workhouse. The passage of the Butchers' Act was considerably eased by the fact that the Bakers, Cooks and Scriveners had obtained a similar order the year previously, while other Companies were soon to follow suit. However, it was not long before the Act was challenged.

William Cope was a butcher trading out of Newgate Market. He had been apprenticed to his uncle, but failed to apply for his freedom to the Butchers' Company when his seven years were up. Disaffected with the Company, he obtained a mandamus from the King's Bench directing the Chamberlain to admit him as a freeman of the Clothworkers' Company, where another uncle was a freeman. The Butchers put it to the Common Council that their authority was being challenged and the validity of their Act questioned. As they were heavily in debt, yet again, the onus was put on the Common Council, and the case defended (and won) at their expense. It was a great victory for the Company, one that was celebrated for many years at an anniversary dinner.

Armed with their new Charter and authority, the Butchers once again made their presence felt. Purveyors of bad meat were punished and fined, the offending meat being burned or thrown into the River Thames. Two butchers from Newgate Market were imprisoned for a similar offence in the space of one month, while another, Richard Whitehead, was prosecuted 'for threatening the Beadle [saying] that if he ever met him in his shop he would cut his hands off, and if that would not do, he would take off a quarter'.[61]

Whereas the first half of the eighteenth century was marked by good harvests and a time of inexpensive food, the second half experienced quite the reverse. With the advent of the industrial revolution, the predominantly rural economy changed steadily through the end of the eighteenth century and the beginning of the nineteenth to one centred on the towns and cities. The population continued to move from the country, where most food was home-grown, to the towns and cities (particularly London), creating an ever-rising need for supplies. With bad harvests and increased demand, food prices rose steadily. This situation in turn induced farmers and landowners to increase both their land holdings and numbers of stock, and so more and more land was enclosed. During the twelve-year reign of Queen Anne at the beginning of the century, a mere 15,000 acres had been enclosed through two Acts of Parliament. By the end of the century, more than three million acres had been taken over by the larger farmers and landowners, to the detriment of those farmers and smallholders who relied on their grazing rights. Farming practices were changing; even the great agronomist Arthur Young thought that there was no room for the small farmer, whom he dubbed 'a poor, wretched set of people' with 'universally bad' husbandry. Furthermore the trend that had started at the beginning of the century, when the meat value of cattle and sheep had far outstripped their other economic values (as draught animals or for their wool or milk) had continued apace. This gave the landowners and farmers the incentive to produce better-quality animals through selective breeding and improvements in stock husbandry. Nor did these improvements come a moment too soon. A Monsieur Gosset, a French visitor to London at the end of the century, complained that the meat, which had previously enjoyed a great reputation abroad, was now not as good as that sold in Paris. Tobias Smollett in his *The Expedition of Humphry Clinker*, has Mathew Bramble disgusted at the mutton sold in St James's Market '. . . which, in fact, is neither lamb nor mutton, but something betwixt the two, gorged in the rank fens of Lincoln and Essex, pale, coarse and frousy'.[62] In his *Honours of the Table for the use of Young People* the Reverend Dr Trusler advises his readers 'to refrain from smelling to the meat whilst on the fork'.

The great pioneer, among many, in the improvement of stock, and the acknowledged founder of modern breeding was Robert Bakewell, a Leicestershire farmer. After leaving school, Bakewell travelled throughout the whole country and in Europe, studying agricultural methods, but, when his father died in 1760, he returned home to take over the tenancy of the 440-acre family farm at Dishley, just north of Loughborough. He began by laying a quarter down to arable crops with the rest set aside for grass. He used the manure from his stock on his arable land (even wintering his neighbours' cattle for free). He pioneered grassland management, flooding his pastures from irrigation canals he built, and established experimental plots to test different manure and flooding methods. His amazing stocking rate of sixty horses, four hundred sheep and 160 cattle on three hundred acres were evidence of his success. At the outset, his aim was to 'produce 2 lbs of mutton where there was only 1 before'. To achieve this Bakewell established certain criteria by concentrating on the proportions of the best cuts of the animal, the texture of the flesh, and its potential to fatten. He began by 'in-and-in' breeding. By keeping the sexes of livestock apart – formerly they had run together to produce a totally random animal – he could control the breeding by selection, and exaggerate those traits he felt desirable by inbreeding.

His first success was in turning the old Lincolnshire breed of sheep into what he called the New Leicester. Not only were they big and delicately boned with a good-quality fleece, he had bred them with the fatty forequarters, demanded by the butchers, the fat shoulder of mutton being the preference of the day. Bakewell's success brought him fame and fortune. In 1786 he leased twenty rams to farmers to improve their stock, which netted 1,000 guineas. Soon after, just three rams brought in 1,200 guineas. The Dishley Society, with a strict code of conduct, was formed to maintain the purity of the breed and to protect his monopoly, but shortly after his death in 1795, tastes changed and the New Leicester died out as a breed.

Bakewell was no less successful with cattle. In his travels, he had noted that the Longhorn was by far the most efficient meat producer, eating less and gaining weight faster than any other breed. Applying the same principle as with sheep, he accentuated their best characteristics that 'enabled him to "grow" more meat, more efficiently'.[63] The result was a desirable breed of cattle that were fat and meaty with heavy hindquarters, but like his New Leicester sheep, the Dishley Longhorn was overtaken by the increasingly fashionable Shorthorn. Although few breeds today are directly descended from Bakewell's stock, his memory lives on through his methods of selection that have since become accepted practice world-wide.

Bakewell's successes spawned a host of other notable breeders. Charles Collins, with his brother George, improved their native Shorthorns of Holderness with Dutch imports for both beef and dairy cattle – the famous Durham Ox, said to have had a liveweight of 3,024 lbs, was bred by them and exhibited throughout the country. At the same time, Thomas Booth was concentrating on producing the best Shorthorns for beef, while Thomas Bates developed the dairy Shorthorns. Between them, they pioneered the major breed of cattle throughout the world during the nineteenth century. Other breeds followed. Herefords, with their distinctive white face, throat and belly, markings that were only developed at the end of the eighteenth century, were improved by Benjamin Tomkins. The same selected breeding practice led Hugh Watson of Keillor in Forfarshire to transform the local cattle, known as 'doddies' or humblies', into what became Aberdeen Angus. They were greatly prized then, as now, by the butcher and stock farmer alike for their 'potential for early maturity [and] were quick to fatten . . . [they] were short of leg with a compact form that was well fleshed with fine grained meat'.[64] Other improved breeds appeared at this time – Devons and Sussex, Lincoln Reds and Red Polls. The Welsh black and Galloway, along with West Highland cattle, were much sought after as store cattle. Sheep also improved with breeds like the Southdown, when demand dictated that a well-proportioned carcase was of more importance than its fleece. Pigs imported from China in the 1770s did much to transform the scrawny native animal, once thought fit only for peasant fare, to desirable pork. The Chinese pig was 'small in limb, round in body, short in the head, wide in the cheek and high in the chine, and above all, fattened readily'.[65] Conversely, the British pig was described as 'long in the limb, narrow in the back which is somewhat curved, low in the shoulders and large in the bone; in a word, uniting all those characteristics which are now deemed most objectionable, and totally devoid of any approach to symmetry'.[66] The most common breed was the Berkshire, but even before crossing with the Chinese pig (and later the Neapolitan) it could reach vast proportions – one killed in 1774 in Congleton in Cheshire weighed 1,410 lbs liveweight, with a dressed carcase weight of 1,215 lbs.

The great farming innovations in the sphere of crop rotation, pioneered by the likes of 'Turnip' Townshend, had taken hold by the turn of the eighteenth century. His work was continued and advanced by his Norfolk neighbour, Thomas Coke, later created first Earl of Leicester. This revolutionary farmer worked on crop rotation and improved such breeds as the Southdown sheep, South Devon cattle and Suffolk pigs. Through his writings and monthly magazine, *Annals of Agriculture*, Arthur Young's contribution cannot be underestimated. But these great improvements to the breed and the animal were not just the diversions of the aristocracy or the landed gentry, but proved of real value to the farmer, and the butcher, as well as to the consumer, whether householder, tanner, clothworker or tallow chandler. Apart from the fifth quarter (the value of the horn, tallow and hide, but less and less the wool) the improvers of all the breeds sought to accommodate the constantly changing public taste. They strove to produce well-finished animals with quality carcases 'with a plentiful layer of subcutaneous [under the skin] fat covering the outside and fat within the carcase. Marbling fat within the carcase was highly esteemed as good quality'.[67] One notable sheep breeder, George Cully, produced a carcase with seven inches of fat where two to three inches would have been the norm. This preoccupation with producing well-fatted animals, where 'the best sign of good flesh is that of being marbled, of having the fat and the lean finely veined, or intermixed when the animals are killed'[68] gave rise to the term 'fatstock' for beasts ready for slaughter. The taste for animals that produced excessive quantity of fat lasted throughout the nineteenth century, as evidenced by the ubiquitous surviving portraits of cattle, sheep and pigs of the day.

Hard on the heels of these great improvements came the founding of the Smithfield Cattle and Sheep Society, formed in 1798, under its first president, Francis Russell, 5th Duke of Bedford, together with twenty-eight other 'leading agricultural improvers'. Arthur Young was the first honorary secretary. The first fatstock show was held a year later, and has been held annually (except during the two World Wars and the foot and mouth epidemics) to the present day. The competition element amongst the entrants assured a meeting of minds and ideas to continue the general improvements to the breeds. Naturally, the Company of Butchers kept a close watch on the Society's activities and there was much cross pollination over the years, featuring the likes of W. Fred Bonser 'who had filled the Chairs of both the [Royal Smithfield] Club and the Butchers' Company'.[69] Thomas Bonser was a butcher at Newgate Market, was born the year the Smithfield Club was founded.

At the turn of the nineteenth century practices in the market were also changing. The sheer volume of meat that was consumed daily turned the craft of the sole trader butcher, little changed since medieval times, into a vast, organised industry that throughout the century led to the rise of the powerful international companies. So confident were the breeders of their product that for the first time they sold by liveweight, rather than leaving the butcher to assess the worth of a standing beast. There were various tables, such as Lord Somerville's 'The Farmer's, Grazier's and Butcher's Ready Reckoner', published at that time to help in working out the weight from the measurements:

by measuring the girth, just behind the shoulder blade, with a cord, and ascertaining the number of feet and inches it is in circumference, by a foot rule, taking one fourth of it; and also by measuring from the fore part of the shoulder to the setting on the tail, and ascertaining the number of feet and inches the animal is in length, and multiplying one with the other, and allowing 42 lb for every cubic foot of flesh, the precise weight of the beast (sinking the offal) [disregarding the offal weight] may be known. The allowance given for a half-fatted ox, must be a deduction of one stone in twenty from that of a fat ox.[70]

Although the stock that ended up on the butchers' stalls in Newgate and Leadenhall Markets (or indeed in any of the thirteen other London markets where meat was sold) was greatly superior to that of the previous century, and better marketed, the drove was still the only method of bringing the beasts from the farmer and grazier to London. Numbers escalated; in 1734, 76,210 cattle and 514,700 sheep arrived at Smithfield, but just sixty years later, numbers had risen to 109,064 cattle and 717,990 sheep. Store cattle continued to be brought in vast numbers from all over the country. Such was the demand for store cattle from the graziers in the Home Counties who supplied Smithfield, that it was economical to drive cattle from as far away as Sutherland, particularly after the Highland Clearances, Ireland, and the reaches of Wales. One particular description of a drove from Anglesey survives, when a thousand cattle were made to swim across the Menai Straights and driven to Abergele Fair in Denbighshire, where they were sold. There, as with all the smaller markets, the farmer or drover sold to the local butcher or to a grazier or dealer, local markets tending to be cheaper. From there, the dealer's drover then took them to his land in the Welland Valley, outside Market Harborough in Leicestershire. When the timing was right, the fat cattle were driven direct to Smithfield for their market days of Monday and Friday, where they were taken on by a salesman. This was the acceptable face of the Market. The salesman not only acted on commission on behalf of the grazier or the farmer, but also of the dealers. Their services were indispensable, for they could gauge the strengths and weaknesses of the market, the value of the cattle and sheep, and who would be their likely buyers. They also had contacts with graziers who could take unsold stock to keep until the price moved favourably. Their commission naturally was reflected in the increased price of meat.

Other cattle from the drove went to the restored Barnet Fair, where they were sold on again to another dealer, who took them down one of the new turnpike roads to any of the holding pens or 'lairs' at places closer to London like Kentish Town, Knightsbridge, Paddington, Bayswater, Islington, Holloway, Newington and Mile End, to arrive between noon and five o'clock on a Thursday, ready for market the next day at Smithfield, or to be held over for the Monday market. It was there that the carcase butchers picked over the stock, buying the best for themselves, which, since the laws against forestalling had been repealed in the reign of Queen Anne was not in itself an illegal act. The carcase butcher was in competition with the jobber, a dealer who bought out of one market and sold on at another, usually Smithfield. There were also badgers, itinerant dealers who travelled the markets looking for a deal. The result was that, by the turn of the nineteenth century, the ordinary cutting butcher was almost exclusively in the hands of the carcase butcher.

The Company of Butchers had long been unhappy about the rise of the carcase butcher. The Act of Parliament of 1707 (that outlawed the sale of fat cattle and sheep by one butcher to another), like so many passed in the meat trade, worked well enough at the outset, but was slowly weakened over the years. By 1786, both free and non-free butchers had had enough. They met at the Nag's Head Tavern in Leadenhall Street, determined to curb the activity of the carcase butcher who manipulated their trade at will, by forestalling as many as 500 cattle in a day. This left the Market short, which in turn inflated the price to the wretched cutting butcher. In addition, jobbers would not sell if the price was not to their liking, whereas left to the salesman and free market forces the stock would have been sold to the highest bidder. The resolutions of the Nag's Head Committee were put to a Committee in the House of Lords but although their Lordships agreed that the rise in the price of meat could be attributed to the actions of the carcase butcher and the jobber, the petition failed, along with the motion that the laws against forestalling should be revived. The wealthy carcase butchers, described at the time as 'a set of men making a bold attempt to obstruct the consummation of an Act so eminently tending to the good and comfort of the public',[71] were now a powerful arm of the trade, and their influence was beginning to be felt in the Company of Butchers. There was even a move to have Smithfield's Friday market put back a day, but as that would mean altering all the other market days of all the markets around London this was abandoned as being too complicated.

Although the majority of meat sold in London was still going through Smithfield market, with the rise of the wholesale butcher came the 'country killed' carcases, that is those beasts slaughtered outside London and brought in to either Leadenhall or Newgate. They were normally transported on horse-drawn wagons, were they should be:

cleanly and carefully packed, as well as to preserve it from dust and dirt, as to defend it from heat in summer, and frost in winter . . . there should be fresh cloths to lay the meat upon at market. Flannel or woollen-cloth is frequently used to defend bodies from the warm air of summer, as well as the cold air of winter. Cloth, however, at any rate, must, be put next to the meat, and the woollen kept particularly clean. When butchers send calves to London in winter, they sometimes wet the cloths, especially if the meat be not very white, as they think it makes it whiter, and prevents it losing weight.[72]

Not surprisingly, there were several attempts by local residents to remove Smithfield Market to a more suitable site. Later, in 1809 when the question of removal was brought up again, the Company was one of the strongest opponents of the Bill before Parliament. A petition, signed by 177 farmer graziers, 99 salesmen and butchers and, surprisingly, only 30 residents alleged that:

> the ancient market place at Smithfield is much too small to contain the live cattle necessary for the supply of the immensely increased population of the metropolis and its environs; . . . that the cattle often bruise and lame, and sometimes trample upon and kill each other, by being confined for hours together in a crowded state in the market; and some of them are maimed and or bruised in a shocking manner by the wagons, carts, or drays driven through Smithfield during market hours; . . . that the buyers cannot go between or among the beasts in their very crowded state at market, to examine them, without danger of sustaining serious bodily injury.[73]

Although that Bill failed, the residents had a point.

The night before and in the early hours of market days, cattle and sheep were driven through all the surrounding streets. Charles Dickens wrote of the scene in *Oliver Twist*:

> It was market morning. The ground was covered nearly ankle deep with filth and mire; and a thick steam perpetually rising from the reeking bodies of the cattle, and mingling with the fog, which seemed to rest upon the chimney tops, hung heavily above . . . Countrymen, butchers, drovers, hawkers, boys, thieves, idlers, and vagabonds of every low grade, were mingled together in a dense mass: the whistling of drovers, the barking of dogs, the bellowing and plunging of beasts, the bleating of sheep, and the grunting and squealing of pigs; the cries of hawkers, the shouts, oaths, amid quarrelling on all sides, the ringing of bells, and the roar of voices that issued from every public house; the crowding, pushing, driving, beating, whooping and yelling; the hideous and discordant din that resounded from every corner of the market; and the unwashed, unshaven, squalid, and dirty figures constantly running to and fro, and bursting in and out of the throng, rendered it a stunning and bewildering scene which quite confused the senses.[74]

It was a dangerous time too to be abroad in the streets. Anyone who ventured out was in real danger of being knocked down and gored, or trampled on by any of the 'poor, frightened and half-mad cattle'. In 1818, a meeting was organised by the Company in the Butchers' Hall, where they and the trade met to discuss 'the most effectual means of preventing the evil arising from bullock hunting'.[75] The practice, known as 'bull hanks', was common when the more unsavoury drovers would run the most dangerous steer ahead of the herd to cause maximum commotion, often robbing passers-by in the confusion. If it was foggy 'the glaring lights of the drover-boys' torches added to the wild confusion, whilst it did not dispel much of the gloom'.[76] The next day the streets would be full of the dung of the animals from the night before. And that was twice a week, every week of the year. If that were not enough, there were all the associated trades connected with the sale of livestock in the Smithfield area 'surrounded [as it was] with slaughter-houses, triperies, bone-boiling houses, gut-scraperies',[77] and fat renderers, all to the further distress of the residents.

Clearly, the question of Smithfield Market would not go away. If it could not be removed, then it might be enlarged and improved, paid for from the revenue raised through increased tolls. In 1812, a deputation from the Butchers' Company was summoned to Guildhall to advise on the scheme, but nothing came of the plan and the Market went on as before. Instead, the Company busied themselves with having carriages banned during all market days, for

serious accidents were frequently occasioned by the passing of carriages through the market when it was thronged with cattle, and not a market day passed on a Monday without some injury being done to the cattle by carriages driving against them, and the violence the drovers used to the cattle to make way for carriages occasioned a great deal of cruelty, which might be avoided.[78]

Even in the first quarter of the eighteenth century, the Company of Butchers were concerned with the image of the butcher and their trade. Butchers were described as those 'whose employment, bloody and cruel; which practices, actions and motions of the human body, by repeated strokes of violence . . . never fail to stamp the signatures of brutality and inhumanity'.[79] Butchers were barred from serving on a jury when 'sitting on the life of a fellow subject', as by the nature of their trade, they were thought to be 'less feeling and humane than other classes of men'.[80] Guidelines were set out by the Company on limiting the cruelty to livestock, especially on the drove. In the eighteenth century drovers were fined or imprisoned with hard labour for 'negligence or ill usage . . . by improper driving',[81] while prosecutions were brought for cruelty by the Society for the Suppression of Vice. One such prosecution was brought against a butcher who was 'sentenced to three months imprisonment, for cruelty, maiming and torturing a sheep; the court deeply regretting that they were not authorised to inflict the additional punishment of

whipping'.[82] Much in the Company recommendations was more to do with producing the best possible carcase, than with the health and welfare of the livestock.

Partially due to the arrival of the carcase butcher into the ranks of the Company
of Butchers, the fortunes of the Company took a definite upturn. Their Hall was
much in demand; they even allowed it to be used by the local Militia, 'the Volunteer
Corps of this Ward' to store their weapons in the lower hall. They did, however,
draw the line at them 'using the Hall for public meetings and for cleaning arms, as
being beyond the liberty which had been granted them'.[83] The Militia were slung
out and replaced by a Sunday school of 'about 150 children'. This was later extended
to allow the older children to be taught to write on Monday nights. By 1827, the
Company found that their Hall was too small for their purposes and decided to
enlarge it. Tenders were received and a contractor's estimate of £995 accepted.
Before the work started, the Company removed their pictures to the Clerk's house
that they had leased in Brabant Court, in Philpot Lane, where they also held their
Court meetings. Work progressed, and many alterations to the fabric of the building
were added to the original specification, doubling the cost. The Court produced
£425, while the Livery came up with another £525. The internal works were
finished, and the pictures and furniture returned to the Hall. Twenty-two days later,
on the morning of 24 April 1826, the Hall caught fire. An entry appeared in *The
Times* the next day:

> Yesterday morning between two and three o'clock the embers of a recent fire in
> St Botolph's-lane burst out afresh, and communicating with the premises of Mr
> Lowell immediately adjoining the large committee room of the Butchers' hall in
> Pudding-lane, totally destroyed it, together with a very fine and valuable collec-
> tion of paintings valued at nearly 2000l.[84]

The Times also reported that a great many pickpockets operated 'in the most daring
nature' among the vast crowd of 'city folk' who had come to see the burning
buildings. As dawn broke the next morning, the burned-out shell of the Butchers'
Hall made for a sorry sight, an inglorious end to a once-fine building that had
witnessed one hundred and sixty years of the turbulent history of the Company of
Butchers.

a. The Borthwick Screen, engraved by John Hutton, was presented to the Company by Thomas Borthwick & Co, principally as a memorial to Algernon Borthwick. It depicts the four seasons with the flora and fauna of New Zealand and Australia, the countries of their main operations.

b. The Vestey Tapestry designed by Lucien Fleury and made by the Aubusson factory in Paris. It shows various aspects of the Vestey Empire and examples of their munificence, such as the tower of Liverpool Cathedral.

6a. The cover and spine of the new Golden Book that replaced the original stolen in the silver robbery. The book contains the names of all dignitaries who visited the Hall, along with Masters, Deputy Masters, Clerks and benefactors.

6b. The Prince Arthur Cup. This golf trophy competed for by all Livery Companies was inaugurated in honour of the Duke of Connaught, Freeman of Coachmakers' and Coach Harness Makers' Company. The Butchers' team were the first to win it in 1927, again two years later, and the third time in 2004.

6c. Ch'ien Lung Chinese Export Porcelain plate and tea bowl, circa 1780. The initials G M F C are those of the original owner. The name of Edward Fisher, admitted to the Freedom of the Company in 1775, is on the dish (from the same factory) and was presented to the Company by the Hon. Sam Vestey.

The drawings for the stained glass window destined for the reception hall by Mel Howse, a Freeman of the Worshipful Company of inter-Stainers. It 'conveys the meeting of minds with a common goal, a forum for the exchanging of experiences especially whilst tertaining. The shaking of hands repeated across the table conveys the continuous process of development within the industry'.

8. The 'Millennium Window' in the Great Hall donated by John Baker, MBE. The top stained glass panel shows 'the beasts of the field', an allusion to the Company's motto, the next shows their arms, while the bottom panel represents The Butchers and Drovers' Charitable Institution. The actual artwork was later adopted as the Charity's logo.

5 The Fourth Hall

1829–1883

T HEY HAD BEEN there before, only it was one hundred and sixty-three years later that the Master and Wardens of the Company of Butchers stood before their burned-out Hall. They had that same desperate feeling as their predecessors had experienced after the Great Fire of London, as they too gazed at the empty shell of the building they had only finished renovating three weeks before. The walls were still standing, but that was all, for such was the intense heat of the fire the fabric of the building had been reduced to ash. It was appalling bad luck. The Hall had survived the fire in the neighbouring house the day before, but in the early hours of the morning, the embers had flared up again and taken hold, spreading to the Committee Room. It was worse luck that all the furniture and pictures had come back not three weeks before from the Clerk's house ready for the feast to celebrate the splendid, new enlarged Hall.

But the Master, William Collins, and the Wardens were not men to mourn their loss. Richard Hicks, an Assistant, was appointed as the Company Surveyor that very day. He called in a Mr Woodward who declared: 'that he had carefully examined the Hall with a view to consider the possibility of repairing it but he was of the opinion it could not from its greatly injured state be safely repaired and he considered it absolutely necessary for it to be replaced'.[1] Just twelve days after the fire, the Butchers received a draft of £2,000 from the Protector Insurance Company in full settlement for their Hall. With the money in the bank, there was no time to lose. Richard Hicks was again charged with coming up with plans and a specification for 'a good and substantial hall well calculated to meet the comforts of the livery' on the same site; and again he went with his design to Woodward for him to draw up the plans. The detailed plans were then presented to the Court at a meeting held in the tavern, the George and Vulture, on 14 May, a mere eighteen days after the fire. It was approved on the spot, and tenders were invited to be in by a month later. There were nine contractors who tendered, with estimates that ranged from £3,831 from a Mr Featham, to £2,095 from a Mr Lindfield, whose tender was accepted.

Lindfield subsequently withdrew, having accepted another commission, and the contract for the new hall was finally awarded to Hugh Welsh Cooper of Gray's Inn on his quotation of £2,275, the second lowest. Work began on clearing the site almost immediately.

The payment for the contents, only £501 15s, came in July. In *The Times* it was reported that eighty paintings to the value of £2,000 had been destroyed in the fire, which seems unlikely considering the payout. Also, in Thomas Allan's work, *The History and Antiquities of London* published in 1828, only six portraits were mentioned. *The Times* also mentioned a portrait 'of Mr William Mellish, formerly the principal [Master in 1803] of the Society of Butchers for which the committee had paid 300 guineas'.[2] That was a staggering sum for a portrait at that date, and if *The Times* was correct, it would have put it in the league of an artist like Sir Thomas Lawrence, at that time even Reynolds and Beechey were not charging half such an exorbitant figure. If the report was true Mellish must have presented his portrait himself; he came from a rich grazier–butcher family in Chingford, Essex, and owned a private pack of greyhounds.

At the end of August 1829, just four months after the fire that had wiped out their newly restored Hall, the Company met on the cleared site in Pudding Lane. With all the dignity of the occasion, William Collins, the Master, cleared his throat to attract the attention of the large crowd who had gathered to witness the ceremony. He was joined by James Horwood, the long-serving Deputy Master. They each took a builder's trowel from the Beadle, then symbolically tapped a large pale sandstone block, the foundation stone of the new Butchers' Hall, that had been inscribed:

> THIS STONE WAS LAID THE
> 29th August 1829
> WILLIAM COLLINS Esq[re] Mast[r]

The Master then declared: 'May this Hall be substantially built, and may it never experience the fate of its predecessors.'[3] A great cheer went up from the whole Company as they witnessed the beginning of the resurrection of their new hall, the phoenix rising from the ashes.

The dispossessed Butchers used the George and Vulture Tavern for their meetings, but for the 1830 election meeting they were back in their new Hall. The whole Company was rightly delighted with the grandeur of the building and the extra space housed in two high storeys. The address was 5½ Eastcheap, the entrance being between number 5 and number 6, occupied by the Paris Chocolate Company, both houses being owned by the Company. Two covered ways led from Eastcheap and Pudding Lane into a generous courtyard, then a fine double staircase leading to the raised ground floor. For the first time, the Clerk had a decent place to work, with a large office and a fine mahogany desk. A lobby led into the Court Room, handsomely appointed with a marble chimneypiece and floor-length sash windows. In the semi-basement were the kitchen and scullery and various storerooms. By the Clerk's office, a flight of stairs led up to the good-sized dining hall, almost forty-six feet long by twenty-six feet wide, high enough for a music gallery at the far end. It was a graceful room with three pier glasses and tables under the three high sash windows. There were also four plaster pilasters, later to be decoratively painted to resemble Siena marble, with chryselephantine Corinthian capitals. No expense appears to have been spared. The doors were of heavy mahogany, with fine brass door furniture. At the other end of the building was another staircase leading to the Beadle's apartment, complete with parlour and kitchen. There are only two pictorial records of the Hall, one appears in a handbill in the corner of a portrait of the Master William Collins, the other in drawings of the entrance by Shepherd in around 1855.

Thomas Hosmer Shepherd was an architectural artist working in London under his patron, Frederick Crace, the Commissioner of Sewers. Crace was concerned at the rate at which old London was disappearing with new developments, and commissioned Shepherd to record as much as possible. Among the thousands of watercolours and sketches that have survived, two depict the fine Eastcheap entrance to Butchers' Hall.

All the furniture, some of which had even survived from before the Great Fire of London, was completely destroyed and had to be replaced. For this, the Company went to the leading cabinet makers of the day who made all the pieces specifically for the Hall. Other items were donated over the years, such as the Master's chair, a gift from William Collins. The chandelier for the Court Room came from James Horwood, Master in 1793 and Collins's Deputy Master, while William Mellish came up with seven sconces and his brother Peter, Sheriff of London and Middlesex and Master in 1800, donated a large gilt mirror that went over the marble chimney-piece in the Dining Hall. In an inventory of the Company's possessions in 1929, four portraits of these major donors are mentioned. These four paintings also appear in a photograph of the Banqueting Hall, all in identical frames of a later date to the portraits. In 1829 James Horwood was sent off at 'his earliest convenience' to have his portrait painted by an artist of his choice 'to replace the one destroyed by the fire'[4]. They later arranged for a portrait of Peter Mellish to be copied by an artist called Shepperson, the canvas to 'correspond in size with that of Mr Horwood's [portrait].'[5] Shepperson was paid 10 guineas for his work, but had to return as 'Mellish's arms were not correctly painted'. William Mellish's portrait was also replaced for £50, this time by Frederick Yates Hurlstone, while the same sum was paid to Mr Wood for his portrait of William Collins. The final portrait of the quartet was of Richard Hicks, the Assistant responsible for the design and the rebuilding of the hall, for which Hurlstone was again paid £50. The artist wanted to exhibit his portraits at an exhibition, but the Court denied him. The portraits were sold sometime in the 1950s, one of them, the portrait of William Collins, turning up in an auction in New York twenty years later. It is this portrait that has the sketch of the only known representation of the fourth Butchers' Hall.

The new Hall was undoubtedly grand, appropriate to the standing of the Butchers' Company. But, as ever, they began life in their new Hall in debt. Not only was the estimate for rebuilding £300 over what they received from the insurance company, but costs had escalated by nearly £600 over the original contract price. As it happened, the Company was soon forced to sell their two properties in Eastcheap (number 6 leased to Joseph Worrell for a mere £35 per annum, and number 7 leased to Thomas Lewis for £40). Such was the expansion of the suburbs south of the river, especially Southwark, that the City Corporation had applied to Parliament for permission to compulsorily purchase various properties in Eastcheap and else-where to improve the access to London Bridge. The compulsory sale was completed by the end of 1833, and the compensation of £1,550 went some way to covering the Company's debts. Other moneys came from voluntary contributions from the Livery to make ends meet. The outgoings on their various properties, Land Tax, Poor Rate, Watch Rate, Water Rate, Tithes, Sewer Rate, and Billingsgate Ward School amounted to nearly £150 with net rents of only £62. The balance and all the other expenses had to be met by the Livery themselves. By that time their annual fines were virtually their only source of income, their control over the non-free butchers of London having slowly ebbed away. The impact of the Industrial Revolution was to dominate the century, and it was not to be to the lasting benefit of the Butchers.

In the first half of the nineteenth century, the population of London grew by 73 percent. Free and non-free butchers alike benefited from the extra money the greater population had to spend on food, with their larger families and a longer life-expectancy, but the Company of Butchers itself lost out. Butcher's shops sprang up all over the new suburbs, contributing to the inexorable rise of the carcase butcher. As the number of butchers increased within the City and the two-mile radius, it became more and more difficult for the Company to monitor their trade, or to insist that they be 'free' of the City. The Minute books are full of 'Summonses' of non-free butchers, but generally the entries are accompanied by 'did not appear'. The Master and Wardens appealed to the Lord Chamberlain for clarification of their Charter and their powers to demand non-free quarterage. Eventually the Chamberlain replied that 'on consideration . . . we are of the opinion that the

Butchers' Company being an ancient corporation are entitled under the Act of Common Council to proceed for penalty against any person carrying on the Trade of Butcher without being free of the Company'.[6]

But even with the ruling of the Lord Chamberlain, the Butchers realised the impossibility of effectively collecting quarterage from the non-free butchers, other than the little that had been paid voluntarily in the past. In a last-ditch attempt in December 1842, the Company discussed reinstating their authority and prosecuting 'those persons carrying on the trade of a butcher in the City without being free of the Company'[7], but they decided that, despite the Lord Chamberlain's ruling, they had lost the unequal struggle. In March 1851, the last two non-free butchers to be prosecuted, Green and Hyrons, did appear before the Court, accused of trading without being free, but refused to pay their fines. By an Act of Common Council dated 1856, the obligation to be free in order to trade as a butcher, within or without the two miles of the City, was finally removed. With the passing of that Act, the primary role of the Company of Butchers changed forever. Furthermore, the London Markets had long been appointing their own commissioners and inspectors, in consultation with, but totally independent of, the Company. After nearly 900 years of administering their trade, the Company of Butchers remained an important advisory body and a charitable institution, roles that they still fulfil today.

An indication of this sphere of influence was provided when, in April 1835, the Company was approached by Lord Ebrington over his Bill to standardise the stone weight. Hitherto, the standard stone had been 14 lbs with many local variations, including the 8 lb Smithfield Stone (see page 94). The Company advised Ebrington that 'the stone weight must remain at 14lbs but that parties selling were not compelled to sell at so much a stone but the trade were at liberty to sell at 8lbs or any other quantity they pleased, only the stone to be 14lbs.'[8] The Company was later asked to support the 'Members and Friends of the Association for Promoting Rational Humanity towards the Animal Creation',[9] but although the Court expressed their sympathy towards them and their aims, they left the proposal 'on the table' and it was never referred to again. However, the Company of Butchers was at its most determined when the livelihood of its members was threatened, and no more so than with their campaign to preserve Smithfield as a livestock market.

The fight began at the turn of the century and continued with various petitions to the City Authorities or Parliament, such as the banning of 'wagons, drays and carriages' during market hours, or the erection of chains to separate livestock from pedestrians. In 1833, a Bill was presented to Parliament for the entrepreneur John Perkins to erect a livestock market at Islington. A rival market, better placed, would have been the death knell for Smithfield, and the Butchers' Company sprang into action. They immediately organised a meeting of the trade in their Hall, all of whom were unanimous in their condemnation of the Islington proposal. A petition was sent to the Common Council requesting their support in having the Bill defeated. Later, the Company sent their own strongly-worded petition to the House of Commons on the grounds that 'if pursued, [it would] interfere with the Chartered right of the Citizens of London, be injurious to the rights and privileges of your petitioners sanctioned.'[10] The Company, through Richard Hicks, further argued that 'if such an Act be granted it will be highly injurious not only to themselves and all other parties connected with Smithfield Market but to the public in general'.[11] Smithfield, Hicks maintained, was best suited to the Metropolis being well served by roads to all corners of London, particularly as all wheeled traffic was banned until 12 noon on Mondays.

In July 1834, the Bill was narrowly defeated by eighteen votes to sixteen, its failure attributable to the Company's direct intervention. On the back of the Bill came the move to enlarge Smithfield Market. Again, the Company was at the forefront of the campaign, and a resolution was sent to the City Lands Committee, who in turn endorsed their proposals to the Common Council.

But Perkins was not to be thwarted and, ever-persistent, had another Bill set before Parliament for his Islington market. This time it was approved with the proviso that, should the City suffer financially through the market, they were to be compensated. The anti-Smithfield lobby were delighted. The press, seeing the competition from Islington closing Smithfield Market, sarcastically wrote that 'the citizens will be deprived of the wholesome excitement occasioned by the sight of half-strangled oxen dying of thirst, the bellowing of bullocks, and yelling of drovers; the salubrious smells arising from the City cellar-hole slaughter-dens; and many other delights which the said citizens have hitherto enjoyed in full swing'.[12]

The development of the Islington market went ahead on a fifteen-acre site by Balls Pond, Islington (between the present Essex Road and Regents Canal). It was said to have cost £100,000. Surrounded by a ten-foot-high brick wall, it could accommodate 7,000 head of cattle, 40,000 sheep and 500 calves with 1,000 pigs. The Market opened in April 1836 and closed just nine months later,

> such was the influence of custom in the name of Smithfield, and the associations attached to an old spot, that salesmen still continued through crowded streets to drive their cattle to the favourite locality of the London butchers.[13]

It came as no surprise that only a handful of buyers and salesmen deserted Smithfield, for in those nine months Smithfield, with 230,000 cattle, had sold nearly ten times as many as Islington. The Butchers could hardly contain their delight 'that the several salesmen who had signed a resolution to support Islington Market had all returned to Smithfield.'[14] With Islington out of the way, the Common Council were 'determined to enlarge Smithfield Market',[15] their campaign orchestrated and supported by the

Company. Although Smithfield was safe for the time being, the constant debate whether to remove or enlarge raged for the next twenty years. The City Corporation owned the market, along with Leadenhall and Newgate, the two main centres for dead meat, and they feared for the great revenues they brought in. But opposition was mounting. Max Schlesinger, a German visitor to London in 1853 wrote:

> to the north there is the provoking, broad, impertinent extent of old Smithfield, the notorious cattle-market of London, the greatest cattle-market in the world, the dirtiest of all the dirty spots which disgrace the fair face of the capital of England.
>
> This immense open place, or more properly speaking, this immense conglomeration of a great many small open places, with its broad open street market, is covered all over with wooden compartments and pens, such as are usual on the sheep-farms of the continent.
>
> Each of these pens is large enough to accommodate . . . an ox and a certain number of cattle, pigs, or sheep . . . The appearance of that quarter of the town is curious but not agreeable. Surrounded by dirty streets, lanes, courts, and alleys, the haunts of poverty and crime, Smithfield is infested not only with fierce and savage cattle, but also with the still fiercer and more savage tribes of drivers and butchers. On market-days the passengers are in danger of being run over, trampled down, or tossed up by the drivers or 'beasts'; at night, rapine and murder prowl in the lanes and alleys in the vicinity; and the police have more trouble with this part of the town than with the whole of Brompton, Kensington, and Bayswater. The crowding of cattle in the centre of the town is an inexhaustible source of accidents. Men are run down, women are tossed, children are trampled to death. But these men, women, and children, belong to the lower classes. Persons of rank or wealth do not generally come to Smithfield early in the morning, if indeed, they ever come there at all. The child is buried on the following Sunday, when its parents are free from work; the man is taken to the apothecary's shop close by, where the needful is done to his wound; the woman applies to some female quack for a plaister [plaster], and if she is in good luck she gets another plaister in the shape of a glass of gin from the owner of the cattle. The press takes notice of the accidents, people read the paragraph and are shocked; and the whole affair is forgotten even before the next market day.
>
> For years Smithfield has been denounced by the press and in Parliament. The Tories came in and went out; so did the Whigs. But neither of the two great political parties could be induced to set their faces against the nuisance. The autonomy of the city, moreover, deprecated anything like government intervention, for Smithfield is a rich source of revenue; the market dues, the public-house rents, and the traffic generally, represent a heavy sum. In the last year only,

the Lords and Commons of England have pronounced the doom of Smithfield. The cattle market is to be abolished. But when? That is the question – for its protectors are sure to come forward with claims of indemnity, and other means of temporisation; and the choice of a fitting locality, on the outskirts of the town, will most likely take some years. For we ought not to forget that in England everything moves slowly, with the exception of machinery and steam.

Smithfield and its history are instances of the many dark sides of self-government. For self-government has its dark sides, commendable though it be as the basis of free institutions. It is to the self-government of every community, of every parish, and of every association, that England is indebted for her justly envied industrial, political, and commercial, greatness. But self-government is the cause of many great and useful undertakings proceeding but slowly; and, in many instances, succumbing to the assaults of hostile and vested interests. The government, indeed, attempts to combat all nuisances by mooting and fostering a variety of agitations. In Germany, it wants but a line from a minister to eradicate small evils, or introduce signal improvements. In England the same matters must be dealt with in a tender and cautious manner; it takes a score or so of years of agitation, until parliament yielding to public opinion, passes its vote for the improvement, or against the nuisance. Great joy there would be in London, if Smithfield, as Sodom of old, were consumed with fire; but the whole of London would have been urged to resistance if the government had presumed, on its own responsibility, to interfere with Smithfield.[16]

As Schlesinger predicted, the market remained as it ever was. As a stop-gap, it was decided to enlarge it and a further acre and a quarter was purchased by the City Corporation (at a cost of £40,000). The enlarged Smithfield could, at any one time, accommodate 4,000 cattle, 25,000 sheep and lambs, 1,000 pigs and 300 calves. However strong their influence, the Company of Butchers, always on the defensive, were tested again in 1848 when the New Smithfield Market and Abattoirs' Company (little more than a reconstituted Islington Cattle Market and Abattoirs' Company) made a fresh approach to Parliament to redevelop the site of Smithfield Market. As soon as it appeared on the House of Commons order paper, the Butchers' Company once again sprang into action and, through seven Members of Parliament who spoke on their behalf, violently opposed the scheme. With their extra land and larger market, they argued that the necessity to replace the market had past. This time, their initial lobby was unsuccessful, and the Smithfield Market Removal Bill became the subject of a House of Commons Select Committee under the chairman-ship of Edward Caldwell. Evidence was heard from all interested parties, both for and against, let by the Company of Butchers. Thirty-nine witnesses were questioned over six days of sessions held between 22nd May and 3rd June 1851. They included farmers, salesmen, butchers, land agents, and an architect. Over 2,500 questions were picked over, along with previous evidence taken concerning 'conditions at Smithfield, the driving of animals through the streets, injury to stock, slaughtering, the benefits or inconveniences to various parties of moving the site of the market, possible improvements or extensions, railway station proximity and use of railways'.[17] The Company of Butchers were allowed to examine and cross-examine witnesses for and against the Bill, to show that the Market served the best interests of the producers of the livestock and graziers, the salesmen and the butchers, and therefore the public at large. The matter dragged on for three more years with further debates in both Houses of Parliament. Finally, the Select Committee lost patience with the Company and refused to take further evidence from those who actually worked in the market, along with those who sold and bought there. Then, in 1851, much against the wishes of the Company, the Metropolitan Cattle Market Act was steered through the House by the City Council, so paving the way for another livestock market to be built in a more convenient place.

The area chosen for the new market was known as the Copenhagen Fields in Islington. The original house was built in 1606 to house the Danish court (hence its nomenclature) when Christian IV, King of Denmark, visited his sister, Anne, the wife of James I. By the 1750s the grounds of the house were a tea-garden, and later in the century it was used for skittles, fives, dog-fighting and bear-baiting. A cricket ground was opened in 1835, along with the first athletics track in London. The athletics proved a huge success, with as many as 16,000 people paying to watch a ten-mile championship race. But sport was to give way to progress, and the cricket ground and track were eventually compulsorily purchased for the new Metropolitan Cattle Market to replace Smithfield. The location was well chosen, being close to a railhead, with open spaces for pens and, later, enough room on the seventy-five acre-site to build slaughterhouses. The days of Smithfield as a live market were numbered when the Smithfield Market Removal Act eventually received its Royal Assent in 1852. The Market finally closed on 11 June 1855, without ceremony. At 3.15 in the afternoon, the market bell rang for the last time, and over 900 years of continuous trading came to an end. Just two days later, the Prince Consort opened what was to be called The Caledonian Market at Copenhagen Fields. The cost was over half a million pounds, and the market traded until 1939, when it reverted to a recreational ground.

The Company of Butchers expressed their regret at the passing of Smithfield in their Minutes, but bowed to the inevitable advance of progress. The old Smithfield Market was reduced to a derelict site, where 'the pens and enclosures for beasts, sheep, and pigs remain in status quo; but the rude genius of the place has departed, the bank shutters are closed, the public houses look empty and forlorn'.[18] A chair was made from some hurdles from the livestock market and presented to the

Company in recognition of their great contribution to Smithfield over the years.

But the passing of Smithfield only highlighted the inadequacy of Newgate Market, still the major dead meat market for London. The surrounding twenty slaughter-houses, some no more than a private house, were fed annually with some 200,000 animals on the hoof. They were totally inadequate to cope with the market that handled an estimated 100,000 tons of meat a year. The place was gridlocked – at one count, it was estimated that there were 2,400 horse-drawn vans and hand-carts in the surrounding streets. *The Times* took up the plight of the neighbourhood:

> Through the filthy lanes and alleys no one could pass without being butted with the dripping end of a quarter of beef or smeared by the greasy carcase of a newly slain sheep. In many of the narrow lanes there was hardly room for two persons to pass abreast.[19]

Once again, the Company of Butchers took the initiative. At a meeting of the Court in September 1856 it was recognised that Newgate was totally inadequate and should be replaced. Various sites were suggested. The existing Farringdon Market was a possibility as it could be suitably enlarged, but the road access was poor. The old Fleet Prison was also considered. The original prison was built in 1197, and had been destroyed three times – during the Peasants' Revolt in 1381, in the Great Fire, and during the Gordon Riots in 1780. By the 1750s, the Fleet Prison was mainly used for debtors and bankrupts and housed around 300 prisoners and their families. The Fleet was demolished in 1846 and the site was still available, but being just off the Farringdon Road it had the same problem of access as the Market. Victoria Street was another option, but it was thought that the new residents of Westminster and Pimlico, becoming even more gentrified, would resist a meat market. The one place that stood out above all others was the derelict Smithfield Market, the place once known as 'Ruffian's Hall'[20].

Although ideal in many respects, Smithfield posed a problem of its own. The first Royal Charter had been granted by Edward III, and renewed by Charles I in 1638. But the Charter was specifically for an open-air market, so when the Company of Butchers sought counsel's opinion, they were told that a complicated Act of Parliament would be required before a covered meat market could be built on the site. The opinion further stated that whereas the open land of the former market should remain undeveloped, the land to the north of Long Lane could be used for the new market. The Company was brought in to advise at Committee stage of the Parliamentary Bill on the suitability of Smithfield as a dead meat market. In their reply, they endorsed the plan, pointing out the site's suitability and access advantages – the 'eight approaches from the East, North, West and South and from its central position, its excellent sewerage . . . and it being on high ground'. Once again, their advice was adopted. The Metropolitan Meat and Poultry Market Act of 1860 was passed and, at a stroke, Smithfield was redeveloped into one of the finest covered markets in the world, due largely to the energies of the Worshipful Company of Butchers.

To finance the new market the City Corporation began by raising £235,000 to buy extra land (including the burial ground of St Sepulchre's church), with a further £200,000 to begin the construction. They then appointed Horace Jones (knighted in 1886), the well respected architect of such developments as Tufnell Park, and of various London buildings that included Marshall and Snelgrove, the Oxford Street store. In 1864, he was elected architect and surveyor to the City of London. Smithfield, or, as it was to become known, the Central Meat Market was his first major work in that role. He went on to reconstruct Billingsgate and Leadenhall Markets as well as the Guildhall library and museum, and drew up the plans for Tower Bridge over the Thames – after his death in 1887 his engineer, John Wolfe-Barry, changed his simple, medieval design to the Gothic construction of today.

Jones was greatly influenced by the Crystal Palace, the great cast iron and glass construction built by Joseph Paxton to house the Great Exhibition. For the roof of the new market, he used the same principle with louvered glass to great effect, so that the building was well ventilated and cool in summer. Work started in 1866 and took two years to complete. Nearly two hundred thousand tons of soil were removed to create a vast cavern, with access to the new underground railway, and powerful hydraulic lifts were installed to raise the meat from the sidings. The foundation stone of the building itself was laid in 1867, and, a little over a year later, the new market was complete. It was a triumph of design and construction, being both functional and aesthetically pleasing. It was Italianate in style, the

outside walls are a series of arcaded recesses, Portland stone Doric pilasters supporting round arches with richly carved keystones. The recesses are filled with red brickwork and fancy grillwork, elegantly coiled and twisted. At the four corners are octagonal pavilion towers, each with a dome and supporting grotesquely carved stone griffins flaunting the City coat-of-arms. The length of the building [630 feet by 246 feet wide] is relieved by a central arcade, the Grand Avenue, which divides the market in two. The entrances are impressive; huge statues, representing London, Edinburgh, Dublin and Liverpool, stand guard at each end and fiery bronze dragons glare down at the paving. Roofed by an elliptical iron arch, the Grand Avenue is shut off from the interior of the market by open ironwork screens, fourteen feet high, which carry ranks of old decorative gas lamps mounted on brackets. Access to the market is through two sets of intricate iron gates each twenty-five feet high, nineteen feet wide and weighing twenty-five tons. The hinges are prodigious.[21]

The market, with its 162 stalls, was formally opened in November 1868 by the Lord Mayor, James Lawrence, with a luncheon of boar's head and baron of beef. The Master, Wardens and the Court were among the 1,200 guests, in honour of their part in steering the project through Parliament. The band of the Grenadier Guards played, the gas lamps hissed. The toast – to the 'tolls to the Corporation, cheap meat to the people and fair profits to the salesmen' – was to come true, as from the very outset the Market was a great success. The moment Smithfield (known as the Central Meat Market) opened, Newgate Market was closed for ever by the Newgate Market Abolition Act passed in 1861, and Paternoster Square was returned to its former glory.

Yet again, the nature of the meat trade was changing, not least through the rapid spread of other methods of transporting livestock. By 1835 the drover's trade was at its peak, but his days were already numbered. As more and more land was enclosed the drovers' routes became increasingly difficult to negotiate. Their costs were mounting; fodder, formerly to be had free on the roadside, now had to be paid for, and tolls were being charged on the new turnpikes. For some time fat cattle had been shipped from the east coast of Scotland, some even being transported to London on the new canals, where sheep travelled on two-tiered barges. But it was the spread of the railways that finally brought about the demise of the drover.

The first railway to transport livestock ran from Liverpool to Manchester in 1831. But it was not long before the railways reached the newly-built Caledonian Market at Islington, and with it came an entirely new approach to the meat trade. Livestock could be transported swiftly and in comparative comfort from the ends of the country. They were also ready for slaughter, so cutting out the need for the fattening grounds around London. Often, the stock was slaughtered where it was produced, and just the carcases taken to London while still fresh.

The greatest change to the industry, as butchering had by then become the realm of the carcase or wholesale butcher, came through the wisdom of Sir Robert Peel whose Tory Party was swept back into power in 1841. Since the Napoleonic Wars, agriculture had been protected against cheap foreign imports. This was strongly opposed by the commercial and industrial classes, who resented the special status afforded the rural landowners. Convinced by the merits of free trade, Peel reintroduced income tax (seven pence in the pound) to 'obtain a freer hand for tariff reductions'.[22] By progressively removing import and export duties through a series of free trade budgets, Peel paved the way for Britain, and in particular London, to become the international centre for the trade in livestock and meat, and for the repeal of the Corn Laws in 1846. Up until 1842, all the meat sold through the London markets was home-produced – at that time 'home' included Ireland. Such was the demand for meat from the rapidly-expanding population that it far outstripped the ability of the British farmer to produce enough livestock to satisfy the trade. Another significant factor was the vast amount of feed-grain and fodder that was diverted to feed the increased number of horses employed on the farms and in industry. The ban on imported livestock (imposed as much to contain disease as to protect the livestock market) was lifted in 1842, opening up a vast new market, beginning in a small way from Europe, then the Americas. By the end of the century, 40 percent of the meat consumed in Britain came from abroad. Throughout the Parliamentary debates the Company of Butchers again played their part in advising the sub-Committees on the question of meat. Later, the French Consul even wrote to the Company for clarification on the finer points of exporting livestock from France. However, the early European meat imports were of poor quality. Where British cattle were producing an average carcase weight of 700 lbs, the European cattle were producing no more than 480 lbs.

With the importation of livestock from the Continent came the inevitable diseases. In 1848, a cargo of German sheep introduced sheep pox to the country. Worse was to come in 1865 when the SS *Tonning* landed a cargo of cattle from Revel (today's Tallinn, the capital of Estonia) which were infected with Rinderpest, a contagious viral disease of cattle, that wiped out over a quarter of a million British cattle. This prompted the Government to act, and the Cattle Diseases Prevention Act followed the next year, restricting the number of ports where livestock could enter and decreeing that stock should be slaughtered at the port of entry within ten days of landing. The Port of London was one such designated point of entry and as a direct consequence of the Act, the Foreign Cattle Market was established at Deptford in the former dockyard. The Royal Victualling Yard had supplied the Navy with all their needs over the centuries, including vast quantities of meat, salted in barrels, from their own slaughterhouse. The operation was closed down in 1868, the dockyard filled in and converted into the Foreign Cattle Market by the City Corporation. Once again Horace Jones was the architect.

As ever, the Company kept a watching brief on the trade and acted as a strong pressure group. The bond between the Butchers and the market at Smithfield had always been strong, and the market's Association frequently sought the 'assistance and protection of this Court'. When it was reported that the Government inspectors were being over-zealous 'by the refusal to allow certain cattle imported from the Continent to be sent to the markets for sale on the grounds of being diseased',[23] so acting unfairly as that was not the case, the Deputy Master was 'heard on the subject of complaint of injury done'. The Court pronounced that it was 'a subject of such importance as to justify the interference of this Court and that a memorial [petition] should be presented to the Lords of the Treasury.[24] The Government climbed down.

While the meat trade was expanding out of all recognition, the Company of Butchers too were flourishing. Judging by their wholehearted support of the Smithfield livestock market, and then of the new Central Meat Market and the Foreign

Cattle Market, it would seem likely that the predominant element of the Court, the Masters and the Wardens, at that time were rich, wholesale butchers. Through them the affairs of the Company were well managed, with an unprecedented annual surplus of income over expenditure for nearly twenty years in the 1860s and 70s. Consequently, their investment portfolio was building up too, boosted by the sale of property.

The ancient lease of the Butchers on the passage and barrowhouse at Brooks Wharf, Queenhithe had been assigned to Sir John Cust, Speaker of the House of Commons, in 1762 for a fee of £250 for a term of ninety-nine years. Cust's lease on the parcel of land, that had become appropriately known as Gut Wharf, fell in at Michaelmas 1861. By that time, the lease was truly complicated in that it comprised one half of a house in High Timber Street owned by Joseph Tatum, a strip of Brooks Wharf and some warehouses. The rent had remained fixed at £1 per annum, although the Company's surveyor had put the rental value at £150, with the freehold at £3,000. In the end, in 1858 the parcel of land was sold to John Maitland for the sum of £2,500, and the net proceeds of £2,000, after costs and repayment of a small loan, were invested in 3% Consols.

The greatest of all the bequests to the Company came from William Bayley, Master in 1834. Having spent a life that ended in 1851 trading out of Newgate Market he died a very rich man. In his will, after certain bequests, he left the residue of his estate to the Company of Butchers under the trusteeship of the Master, Wardens and Assistants in perpetuity. An initial £5,000 was handed over at the outset, then the balance, the total sum being £23,461. The whole was invested, and the income either kept for the Company as originally intended, or partly distributed to the needy. As a family, the Bayleys must have been extremely successful, as William Bayley's sister Ruth was also a major benefactor when she died in 1840. She too left everything to the Butchers – after various bequests 'all the rest of my Property whatsoever and whatever the name or discipline may be, I give and bequeath unto them the Master, Wardens and Court Assistants of the Worshipful Company of Butchers',[25] so that 'each widow or freeman that hereafter partake of the same may be allowed £15 per annum according to the discretion of the Worshipful Company of Butchers'.[26] Today, it has been amalgamated into the Worshipful Company of Butchers United Charities. In recognition of this great bequest, in 1851 the Court erected a plaque to Ruth Bayley, 'An excellent Benefactress to the Poor of this Company'.

Charity had always been a fundamental role of the Company of Butchers. From the beginning, the Guild looked after its own, funerals paid for, masses said for the departed, and widows cared for. An early testator, John Edwards, specified in 1357 that the Fraternity of Butchers from Eastcheap should ensure that his body be interred in the Chapel of St Mary in the Church of St Leonard. Then they should sell his tenement when they would receive the entail after the death of his son. The legacy was for the benefit of the poor. There are also records of payments to help scholars, such as 'Thomas Merest, a pore scholler in Cambridge',[27] who received £2 13 4d a year to pay his board and tuition at the end of the sixteenth century.

Another early benefactor to 'poor butchers, freemen of the Company and the widows of freemen'[28] was James Leverett, who in his will dated 20 August 1662 (a month before his death) left the whole of his copyhold land in the Manor of Lambeth to the Butchers. As a family, the Leveretts had been prominent butchers and members of the Company – one, Simon, was fined for the trifling offence of appearing in Smithfield without his cloak. His Arms, three running brown leverets above and below a silver chevron, were hung in the hall of the third Hall, but perished in the Great Fire. In his lifetime, James Leverett lent various sums to the Company, five bonds totalling £575 being assigned to them by his widow Mary after his death. His son Richard was paid an annuity from his father's inheritance, but later he too assigned it to the trustees of the Company for poor relief. Thomas Thompson, an Assistant, became the first copy-holder in trust for the beneficiaries of the Company, and the property was let to James Trevitt. It raised £24 per annum and four pensioners received £1 10s quarterly. At that time, without charges or liens on the property, it worked well. At the end of the seventeenth century, the grant included a tavern called the Bell, along with various effects including 'a nine-pin shed [bowling alley], a nine-pin stone, a shuffleboard table and a scorer'.[29] There was also a barber's shop, a stable and a pottery making clay pipes. Lambeth, being on the riverside, was traditionally an area known for its potteries, and along with the Fulham potteries was one of the first to produce salt-glaze ware in Britain, often referred to as 'Lambeth stoneware'. This was made by throwing a handful of salt into the kiln at its hottest point during firing. The salt then vaporised and the chloride evaporated through the chimney, leaving the sodium to combine with the silicates in the stoneware to provide a thin salt-glaze. The process was much in demand for the manufacture of sewage pipes and other sanitary ware.

By the eighteenth century the Lambeth property had become a liability, the various charges virtually wiping out any income. There was a move within the Court to dispose of it altogether, but this was resisted and the entire parcel was let to a carpenter, Richard Filewood, in 1754 on a building lease of sixty-one years, with a nominal rent. Filewood proposed to build eight houses, but only completed five, each with 'a kitchen basement, shop and parlour, two chambers above and two garrets'.[30] A large courtyard reached by a passage between the houses remained undeveloped. Later, the Court went to inspect the properties, and took with them the Beadle and a carpenter to fix the Company's Arms to the front of the houses. When Filewood objected 'most strongly',[31] the Company dropped the idea after taking legal advice. James Gilmore, a tenant of one of the houses, took over the lease at £50 per annum in 1816 when Filewood's lease fell in. The rent was invested to provide an income to help Lambeth pensioners, but the stock had to be sold after ten years to pay for repairs and for an order to evict Gilmore for non-payment of rent. By 1838, the annual distribution had halved to £102 from its peak ten years before. Notwithstanding their previous contributions to the furnishing of the new Hall, William Collins and James Horwood, along with James Boote, topped up the fund with £25 each, while Simon Payne gave £50. Their example was followed by other Liverymen.

The whole Lambeth property was rented by Messrs Williams, a pottery company, who erected a large kiln in the courtyard and took over first one of the houses, then all the others by 1853, at an increased rent of £93. More kilns were added in the courtyard. By 1875, the whole copyhold estate had been enfranchised. Although the rental value had been assessed at £150 per annum, the Company found it difficult to find a new tenant. Eventually Sir Henry Doulton made an offer for the freehold in 1893. The Doultons had been in Lambeth since the beginning of the century, Henry Doulton joining the firm at the age of fifteen. Like the early tenants of Ferry and Fore Streets, they too were making salt-glaze stoneware pipes and sanitary fittings, branching out into art pottery, ornamental and commemorative pieces, and tableware. When Doulton moved his factory to Burslem, in Staffordshire he kept on his Lambeth works, known as the Lambeth Studio after the students he hired from the Lambeth School of Art. Doulton had several potteries in the area, but, after some were compulsorily purchased to create the Albert Embankment, he was quite prepared to pay £4,000 for the Butchers' property, strategically placed as it was opposite his new factory – a far corner of the Doulton factory can be seen today in Black Prince Road, close to Lambeth Bridge. When permission was granted by the Charity Commission for the Company to sell the Lambeth property, the moneys were lodged in the account of the Official Trustee of Charitable Funds at the Bank of England. Today this endowment forms a significant part of the Worshipful Company of Butchers United Charities.

Apart from these generous bequests, much of the Poor Fund had come from the Livery itself. A poor box was traditionally placed on the table at each Court meeting of the Company, where those attending would donate part or all of their attendance fee, together with a percentage of the fines, the proportion depending on the liquidity of the Company. This practice continued well into the nineteenth century, when anything between £20 and £48 was donated annually. By 1774, the Poor Fund had grown to such a significant sum that a separate account was opened and the money invested separately, the interest being added to moneys already set aside for poor relief. At the beginning of the eighteenth century the Poor Fund was considerably enlarged by receipts from the Flaying Acts.

In conjunction with the Curriers and the Cordwainers, the Company of Butchers administered the inspection of all hides under an Act of Parliament popularly known as the Flaying Acts. All hides of cattle, pigs, sheep and lambs, and even horses, that were killed and flayed within a fifteen miles radius of the Royal Exchange had to be taken to Leadenhall Market to be examined by inspectors appointed by the three Companies. They also administered the whole scheme which was very lucrative as fees had to be paid for inspecting the hides – $\frac{1}{2}$d for the larger animals, $\frac{1}{4}$d for sheep and lambs. They were marked with an 'S' near the tail for those not damaged, 'D' on a flank for those that were. A fine of anything between $\frac{1}{2}$d and 2/6d was payable for 'wilfully neglecting or carelessly cutting or gashing the hide or skin of these animals'.[32] One quarter of the moneys received in levies and fines was paid to the Butchers for their part in supplying and overseeing the inspectors. This money added around £200 per annum to the Poor Fund, until the Flaying Acts were repealed in 1824.

Alongside these charitable functions, the Company continued with another of their prime aims, that of good fellowship. Often there was a dinner 'in lieu the Lord Mayor's Day' procession – the expense of hiring a barge was thought too great to warrant their participation. The Butchers made an exception when one of their own was elected Sheriff or Lord Mayor, as in the case of Thomas Challis, Master in 1839, Alderman of the Ward of Cripplegate and Lord Mayor in 1852. Another event that promoted great fellowship amongst the whole Company was the annual summer picnic. For this the Company, their families and guests were taken by the barge, *Maria Wood*, chartered for the day, to Teddington Lock on the Thames. Matthew Wood had served twice as Lord Mayor (1815 and 1816), and while in office he commissioned a new Lord Mayor's barge. It was named after his daughter Maria. The *Maria Wood* was replaced in the 1830s and was sold to a lighter company to be hired out on special occasions. As late as 1876, the Butchers were still hiring the *Maria Wood*, and members were 'permitted to take three guests, other to be charged at 21/- each'.[33] After she went out of service for commercial boat hire, the *Maria Wood* was painted black and used to transport prisoners from Millbank jail to the transports destined for Australia. Family legend has it that the sobriquet 'Black Maria' for a police van for transporting prisoners comes from the barge.

Another integral part of the Company, since well before 975, has been the fellowship promoted by Guild and Livery dinners. One dinner held on 7 February 1878 at the Butchers' Hall was rather less harmonious, however, for at least for two of the guests. That night, all appeared to have gone well, but a few days after the dinner, the Master, James Mathews, received a letter from a new Liveryman, Francis Horwood of Stanley Villa, in Lewisham, who wrote: 'I feel that it has fallen to my somewhat disagreeable task to have to inform you of an unwarrantable insult offered to myself on Thursday night after leaving the hall of our Company'.[34] Horwood was particularly concerned that not only was it his first dinner, but it was also the first dinner that the Master had presided over. He went on to explain that he had left the dinner and gone downstairs to the cloakroom when:

> I suddenly received a blow upon the cheek from a stranger to me (evidently intoxicated) followed sharply by language I will not put pen to paper. This low individual without any warning was about to attack me again but was prevented by 2 or 3 gentlemen closely following.

He continued with various clichés of 'letting sleeping dogs lie' and 'the more you meddle with pitch the more it sticks to your fingers', and ended by naming his attacker – James Morris Junior. The Master put the letter to the Court, where it was discussed in detail. They resolved to censure Morris for his action that was 'against all codes set out by the Art or Mystery of Butchers'. A suitable letter was then dispatched to Morris, who replied that the Court had only heard one side of the argument. He maintained that:

> . . . he came back into the hall and saw his father being pelted with pieces of orange peel while Mr Horwood took a napkin off the table and put it on my father's head as he was passing from the room. My father went down stairs and I heard Mr Horwood say 'let us follow, we will trip the old – up'. I said 'Don't take advantage of an old man, I am his son, do so to me.

Morris was suitably contrite and admitted that he should have reported the matter but instead he 'had lost control and hit him'. He offered to meet Horwood to make amends. The Court found against them both and ordered them to appear before them. When they finally met, Morris realised that he had struck the wrong man and apologised profusely to Francis Horwood. The real culprit was never identified. Francis Horwood was summoned by the Court again the next year, but this time to act for them over the question of the compulsory purchase of the Butchers' Hall by the Metropolitan District Railway.

The Metropolitan District Railway, which in time became known just as 'the District Line', was the second underground railway in the world to be built, the first, the Metropolitan Railway, opening between Paddington and Farringdon Street on 10 January 1863. It was constructed mainly by the cut-and-cover method, whereby the route was excavated and the line laid, then a brick arch built over the line and the top refilled. For ease and cheapness of construction, the lines generally followed the line of the road, but where necessary, buildings had to be removed as there was then no reliable way of tunnelling under them. Metropolitan District Railway work began on the 1860 with a line that opened between South Kensington and Westminster. It then pushed on through Blackfriars to Mansion House by 1871, with the idea of eventually completing the circle and simultaneously linking up to the East London Line at Aldgate. The route was to take them directly under the Butchers' Hall.

To counteract this threat the Court immediately set up a committee under the chairmanship of Francis Horwood with the idea of 'looking into the line proposal and the progress of the Bill [the Metropolitan and District Railways City Lines Extension Act] through both houses of Parliament'.[35] Horwood arranged for a petition to be sent to Parliament, which was read at the Committee stage on 6 March 1879. It was to no avail, and the Act received the Royal Assent just five months later on the proviso that the line from the east had reached Aldgate. The Company added another appeal to the twenty-one already lodged with the House of Lords, but again to no avail. Although the Company had lost its case to retain its Hall, at least Horwood did come away with something. After a hard-fought battle it was agreed that the Railway Company should compulsorily purchase not only 'the whole Hall and the house 35 Pudding Lane, but number 33 as well', (in the end, the whole block went). Matters dragged on, but finally the Hall and two properties in Eastcheap were valued and the sum of £23,700 was agreed, with a further £226 12s 6d for the fixtures. The Company of Butchers finally completed the sale on 25 March 1883 and vacated their fourth Hall just a week ahead of the demolition team. The centuries-old ties of the Company of Butchers with Pudding Lane were severed after nearly three hundred years. The Butchers' final request to the Metropolitan and District Railway Company was that they should be allowed to take away the foundation stone laid by Collins and Horwood just 54 years before.

6 The Fifth Hall

1883–1957

H ARRY H. V. PHILPOT, the new Clerk, had made a grave error. He had selected the Guildhall Tavern, on the very corner of the Guildhall Yard and Gresham Street, for the Court Meeting on 3 September 1883, the Company of Butchers being temporarily without a hall. But the date he had chosen coincided with a billiards challenge match between the legendary 'Master' Stanley and Louis Kilkenny 'for £500, to 1,000 points on a new table'.[1] So the Master, Wardens and Assistants had to force their way through the expectant crowd that thronged around the billiard table to get to the stairs that led to their meeting room. In the comparative quiet of the private room, the Court donned their gowns and sat down around the large mahogany table. The Clerk then opened the meeting with a report from the Committee formed 'for the purpose of considering and reporting on the building of a new hall and premises'.[2]

He read from his prepared script: 'We are of the opinion that No. 86 Bartholomew Close should be purchased at a sum not exceeding £1,000, and No. 10 Duke Street at a price not exceeding £1,000.'[3] The Committee had done a thorough job. They further recommended that their new hall on the chosen site should not cost more than £8,000 to build. They had made an exhaustive survey of the buildings in Bartholomew Close and Duke Street, and had visited the Royal Institute of British Architects for advice as to who would best serve their needs. A long list of possible architects had been drawn up, and then whittled down to just eleven candidates. Examples of their work in London had been visited, which further reduced the list to three architects, Douglas Matthews, H. Ford and Alexander Peebles. These had then been asked to submit drawings for which 'each gentleman should be paid £31 10s for his remuneration and that the plans become the property of the company'.[4] The committee's report, and the suggestion that it 'should be a red brick building', were adopted unanimously by the Court, and it was recommended that their proposals go ahead. The Court were then joined by other members of the Livery for lunch in the private dining room, before they too went to watch 'Master' Stanley handsomely win his billiards match.

The Committee were galvanised into action. The next day they made an offer on 10 Duke Street (afterwards renamed 44 Little Britain) which was accepted at £950 with an annual ground rent of £36, but their offer of £1,000 for 86 Bartholomew Close was refused. The Committee then found a problem in that their petition to the Chancery Division to hold the Duke Street property in mortmain, the legal term for 'lands or tenements to be held inalienably by an ecclesiastical or other corporation',[5] was denied them. When they cited the test case of the Worshipful Company of Carpenters who sold a property to the Great Eastern Railway in 1845, their petition was finally granted. The Building Committee met frequently over the next few months, agonising over every detail. Their suggestion of red brick was revised to red brick and stone corners, then yellow Burham brick from Kent became an option. However, when it was revealed during the course of the petition over 10 Duke Street that the moneys from the Metropolitan and District Railway could only be used for a replacement hall, the Committee recommended that the new hall should be faced in an institutional white Portland Stone. While a further offer was being made for 86 Bartholomew Close, the two properties next door, 87 and 88, came up for sale. These, being larger, with a ninety-foot frontage and of 2,540 square feet, were far more suitable than 86, and they had the added advantage of being joined to 10 Duke Street by a covered courtyard and a warehouse. The Committee did not want to lose the chance of returning to their original home, close to the old St Nicholas Shambles and their second hall, so a consortium of the richer members of the Court led by James Horwood purchased the two houses on behalf of the Company, as they thought that they would lose them if they had to wait upon the deliberations of the Chancery Division.

The consortium entered 'into an agreement whereby they were prepared to transfer the same to the company upon being reimbursed their outlay but without profit'.[6] The houses were bought and eventually sold to the Company for £5,500 (the purchase price) when the finances were finally agreed.

With the site secured in August 1883, the Committee were spurred into action to finalise the plans for the building. They began by auctioning off the existing buildings for the fixtures and fittings at The Mart, Tokenhouse Yard, a common enough practice at the end of the nineteenth century. Finally, out of the three shortlisted architects they chose Alexander Peebles and commissioned him to draw up a new set of plans for a single building to cover 87 and 88 Bartholomew Close and 10 Duke Street. A specification was sent out with the final plans, and, a year later, W.B. Nightingale's tender for £8,814 was accepted. By coincidence, Nightingale's works were in the next street to the Company's Lambeth property off the Albert Embankment. At one stage it was considered having the kitchen large enough to cater for a dining room for a hundred in the Duke Street property, and so joining it with 87 and 88 Bartholomew Close. The idea was abandoned as being too extravagant, so Alexander Peebles drew up plans for the Duke Street property and tenders ranging between £750 and £830 were duly received with the lowest accepted. Peebles' fees for the two assignments came to £1,600.

As is ever the architect's wont, Peebles suggested various additions once building had started. A heating and ventilating system was added: his suggestion that the windows in the Banqueting Hall should be of stained glass sparked off a flurry of offers, mostly from Past Masters and Masters elect. They began with an offer from Alfred Lyon, Master in 1893 and a great benefactor, who donated the window depicting Shakespeare, while another benefactor, Peter Meech (Master 1889), gave one of Cardinal Wolsey, the son of a butcher and cattle dealer from Ipswich. The three Charters to the Company were represented by their Royal grantors – James I donated by Alderman Hart, Charles I by Benjamin Venables, Master in 1874, and George II by Thomas Killby, Master the previous year (1883), who laid the foundation stone of the new Hall. His immediate predecessor, John Garton, donated a window depicting Daniel Defoe, author, errant Liveryman, and son of James Foe, active in the Company at the end of the seventeenth century (see page 70). The last window depicted Queen Victoria, and was a present from Benjamin Baker, Master in 1869 and 1870. Equally important were the stained glass windows on the main staircase, one depicting Miss Ruth Bayley relieving the poor of the Company and the other her brother William Bayley making his will bequeathing the residue of his property to the Butchers, these windows being the gift, appropriately enough, of another benefactor to the Poor Fund, Charles Game. The plaque dedicated to Ruth Bayley was placed under her window. That and the foundation stone were all that was rescued from the Pudding Lane Hall before demolition.

At last the Hall was ready for the grand opening. The Master, Alderman Hart, had originally planned a 'conversazione', then a dinner, then a lunch following Common Hall on 7 September 1885. But before he handed over to his successor Hart formally declared the Hall open, his last act as Master. The whole Company of Butchers were well pleased, and rightly so for Peebles had done a good job. For its day, the design was radical. The offices were all on the ground floor, accessible to all comers. The first floor was given over to a drawing room and a Court Room, while the Banqueting Hall occupied the whole of the second floor. It was a fine room with its panelled wainscot and moulded ceiling. The gas chandeliers, originally a gift from James Horwood, came from the Pudding Lane Hall along with the wall sconces. These were later converted to electricity in January 1899, paid for by John Hills. The rest of the furniture, pictures and Company treasures came out of store.

Firmly ensconced in their new Hall, the Company of Butchers could set about their business as before. The Hall became a popular venue to hire with an assortment of renters, particularly those charities and trade associations connected with the Central Meat Market, Smithfield. Often the meat trade asked the Company to intercede on their behalf. Sometimes they acted in tandem, as with the Foreign Meat and Foreign and Colonial Meat Bills that set out to regulate the sale of imported meat, William Bonser being the prime mover in overturning the Bill on behalf of the Company. 'While most strongly deprecating all description and misrepresentation in the quality of meat', Bonser was firmly convinced that the provisions of the two Bills before Parliament 'would be totally unworkable for the objects desired that they contravene the old established principals of English jurisprudence that every man is presumed innocent until proved to be guilty'[7] and that their operation would be 'most unjust and oppressive exposing the malicious prosecution and extortion of all persons engaged in the meat trade'. On Bonser's resolution, the Court decided to petition the 'Honourable Commons of the United Kingdom of Great Britain and Ireland in Parliament assembled'. The petitioners were described as 'well and practically acquainted with the trade of a butcher, a large proportion of their number being actively engaged in carrying on that business both in the wholesale meat market and in retail shops'. Having carefully considered both Bills, they declared that they could not possibly be carried out as 'it would in many cases be absolutely impossible, for an expert to decide whether a particular piece of meat had been cut from an animal bred and slaughtered in Great Britain or from one imported within one calendar month from a Foreign Country or one of Her Majesty's Colonies'. Thus, those 'carrying on the trade' were in danger of prosecution for selling as English that which they have honestly, although erroneously believed to be such' or vice versa. The petitioners, the Company of Butchers, 'therefore humbly pray that the said bills may not pass into law but that should your Honourable House see fit to proceed with the Bill, the same may be referred to a Select Committee and that your Petitioners may be heard before the said Committee'. The Bill only made the first reading, after which it was thrown out. The Company of Butchers, representing their members and the meat trade in general, had won the day.

During the second half of the nineteenth century, this 'Foreign' meat came exclusively from the Continent, to cope with the ever-increasing demand for meat in Britain and the shortfall of home-produced animals. This shortfall was in part occasioned by the increased numbers of horses required on the farm, by carriers and in industry, that consumed much of the feed and fodder that had previously gone to feed the livestock. Imports from Europe began modestly, but at their height in the 1880s over a million sheep and half a million cattle were transported annually. As the market for home-produced European meat increased, particularly in France, so the export trade fell off. This shortfall was immediately filled by live imports from the United States and Canada, so much so that, by the end of the century they had completely replaced the Continental imports. English pedigree stocks of Aberdeen Angus, Shorthorn and Hereford had been shipped over before the American Civil War, producing high-quality animals in great quantities. With unlimited grasslands, the North Americans were also finishing their cattle on Indian corn (maize) to produce a beast far superior to the European animals, and more suited to the British taste.

Not everyone condoned the transport of livestock across the Atlantic, often in overcrowded, and therefore dangerous, ships. The Worshipful Company of Butchers was visibly supportive of efforts, led by The Royal Society for the Prevention of Cruelty to Animals, to make the treatment of the animals a central feature of the regulations governing this transatlantic trade. Founded in 1824, primarily to curb the excesses of the drovers and the cattle markets, the RSPCA had turned its attention to the cattle ships in the 1870s. Another problem was disease. At first these North American imports were considered to be disease-free, but it was not long before contagious bovine pleural-pneumonia was discovered in a shipment from the United States, which therefore came under the Contagious Diseases (Animal) Act 1878. Canadian cattle were also found carrying the same disease in 1893 and they too became subject to the same regulations. From the 1870s, live cattle were also shipped from South America, but by the turn of the century foot and mouth disease was endemic in Argentina and Uruguay, and imports were banned altogether.

The discovery of these diseases meant that all the livestock shipments that came through London (as opposed to Glasgow or Liverpool) could only be landed at the Foreign Cattle Market at Deptford, where each beast had to be inspected and its slaughter mandatory at the dock. The market expanded rapidly to cope with this huge influx of cattle. It was a vast organisation, with twelve lairages to accommodate 5,000 cattle and 22,000 sheep, and sixty-six slaughter booths employing over two thousand staff, including the women, known as the 'Gut Girls', who cleaned offal and scraped guts. Chill rooms were also installed to cope with the escalating numbers of carcases before they could be transported by rail, mostly to the Central Meat Market at Smithfield. The Foreign Cattle Market at Deptford dealing with live imports lasted until 1913, when it was completely overtaken by the frozen meat trade.

Outside the Court Room in the present Butchers' Hall is a perfectly ordinary meat cleaver. But what makes it special and worthy of display is not that it was presented to Queen Elizabeth The Queen Mother, but the inscription on the label beside it that reads:

THIS CHOPPER WAS USED BY
MR EDWARD JEFFREYS AT BUCKINGHAM PALACE
TO CUT UP THE FIRST NEW ZEALAND LAMB CARCASE
SHIPPED TO THE UNITED KINGDOM IN THE S.S. "DUNEDIN"
AND PRESENTED TO HER MAJESTY QUEEN VICTORIA IN MAY 1882.

& 9b. A large bomb was dropped from a Zeppelin on the night 15 September 1915, landing in the corner of Bartholomew Close. ...caused extensive damage to Butchers' Hall, blowing out all the stained-glass windows in the Banqueting Hall. Fortunately, most of the ...rniture and all the pictures were in store as the Hall was being remodelled after the purchase of 89 Bartholomew Close. The windows ...ere all replaced through donations from the Livery.

10a. The Banqueting Room, 1927, restored to its former glory. The portrait of William Collins hangs centre top of the far wall. It turned up for sale in a New York gallery.

10b. The remains of Butchers' Hall after a V-I bomb landed in the courtyard, July 1944. The bomb also destroyed an eiderdown factory in Little Britain, filling the air with light feathers so it looked as if it was snowing in July.

11b. The Master Jos Swain, with the Beadle, William Long, visiting Smithfield Market during his tour of Great Britain promoting the Company after World War II and raising funds to rebuild Butchers' Hall.

11a. The proposed 'Argentine Tower' (1946) by Howard Kelly, the company's architect, who designed the sixth Hall.

c. During his progress through South America Jos Swain entertained the President of the Republic of Argentina, General Perón and Señora Perón at a dinner at the Plaza Hotel, Buenos Aires, 1946.

12. The Beadle, Ernest Dewey, precedes the Master, James Blofeld, Deputy Master Fred Bonser, and the Clerk, Lancelot Hall, back t
Butchers' Hall after the service at St Bartholomew-the-Great, 1929

Up to the second half of the nineteenth century vast herds of cattle and flocks of sheep were built up in Australia, New Zealand and the Argentine. When supplies greatly exceeded local demand the only parts of the beasts that were exported were the hides, skins, wool and tallow, the meat often being abandoned when the local market became saturated. However, the ever-increasing demand for meat in Britain created a ready and lucrative market for anyone who could transport it halfway around the world. Clearly, some way had to be found to utilise this cheap source of meat. Due to the great distances involved live transport was not an option. In 1863 a prize of £70 and a medal was offered by The Society of Arts to anyone who could effectively find a way of transporting fresh meat from Australia and New Zealand, which prompted a rash of inventions to do with mechanical refrigeration.

One alternative to transporting carcases was to turn beef into a concentrated meat extract which was then easily transported. Baron Justus von Liebig set up a meat extract plant in Uruguay, as did Robert Tooth in Australia. Another alternative was canning, and a large plant had been set up in New South Wales by the Dangar brothers in 1847. Three years later, the gold rush hit Australia. The demand for beef soared and with it the price of cattle, which put the cannery out of business. The market soon recovered, however, and exports resumed from Australia to join those from both South and North America, where Chicago had become the centre of the United States canning industry. However good the canning industry was, clearly the way forward was to be through refrigeration.

It was on Queen Victoria's birthday, 24 May 1882, when the *Dunedin*, an iron sailing ship of 1,320 tons, was secured in St Katherine's Dock, London, having completed the 12,000-mile voyage from New Zealand in just under a hundred days. She had been fitted out in Glasgow with a Bell-Coleman refrigeration plant, the very best on the market, and was carrying a full cargo of the finest frozen mutton and lamb, along with some pork. It was the first shipment to arrive from the Colony, but the voyage had started badly when the steam engine powering the plant broke down in Port Chalmers, her home port, and the cargo was unloaded and sold locally, so the first frozen New Zealand lamb was actually consumed by the New Zealanders themselves. Once the engine was repaired, another batch of top-quality sheep and lambs was chosen, slaughtered and then frozen on board. The meat arrived in perfect condition with only one carcase out of 5,000 being condemned. It was well received at Smithfield where it averaged 6d a pound, the mutton being slightly dearer than the lamb. The whole consignment was sold in just under two weeks. One of the first lamb carcases was taken to Buckingham Palace, where it was butchered in front of Queen Victoria, and New Zealand lamb chops were on the menu that night. The consignment caused a great stir. A sheep farmer in New Zealand had sent two sheep and three lambs to his son, an undergraduate at Jesus

College, Cambridge. The lamb was roasted on a spit in the College kitchens, then served cold the next day to his college rowing eight. Despite the heavy lunch of lamb, or possibly because of it, the Jesus boat was Head of the River, having bumped all rivals.

In a leading article, *The Times* described the shipment as 'a triumph over physical difficulties as it would have been incredible, and unimaginable a very few years ago. It is impossible to say how this will end and how it will affect the destinies of this country'.[8] Landowners were worried at the effect of flooding the country with cheap meat – the Duke of St Albans 'demanded fair play for the English farmer'. Questions were asked in the House of Lords, while the New Zealand Agent-General assured the public that the supply would be constant, and better coming from a Colonial source rather than a 'Foreign' one. But the trade was a hazardous one. The *Dunedin* made a further sixteen voyages between New Zealand and England, but in 1890 she disappeared without trace with her cargo of frozen meat and wool, probably in a storm as she rounded Cape Horn or when she struck an iceberg.

But the importing of frozen meat was here to stay.

It is not surprising that efforts to produce an efficient freezing unit that could be installed in a ship should have initially born fruit in Australia, for clearly at the end of the century it was the only way possible to export their meat (other than canning) which, after wool, was still the mainstay of their economy. Chilling and freezing meat had long been an option. Ice houses had been a prerequisite in all country houses in the seventeenth and eighteenth centuries, although that was mostly for chilling drinks rather than preserving food. The *Experienced Butcher,* written in 1816, tells of 'the freezing temperature, . . . namely 32 degrees on the scale of Fahrenheit's thermometer, [for] complete preservation of putrefaction, . . .Hence the common practice of keeping meat in snow in the frozen climates of the North; and of packing fish in ice, and sending them in that state from Scotland to the London Market'. At about the same time, Sir Humphry Davy, President of the Royal Society, was writing of the 'antiputrescent quality of cold climates' that was 'fully illustrated in the instances of the rhinoceros and mammoth lately found, in Siberia, entire beneath the frozen soil, in which they must probably have existed from the time of the deluge'.[9] In St Petersburg, there was even an annual fair known as the Winter or Frozen Market, 'for the sale of frozen provisions'.[10] With the advent of the railways, however, carcases could be kept fresh, like the fish, packed in ice. There were even shipments from North America with meat surrounded by large quantities of ice, but it was soon found to be impractical as it needed the same amount of ice as meat to preserve it on the transatlantic crossing. In the beginning scientists worked on developing an ice-making machine, there being an unprecedented demand for it – natural ice was even shipped to England from North America for such appliances as butchers' cold stores. The early patents were either English or French, but by

1855 James Harrison, an Australian engineer, was the first to make a machine to produce ice commercially – up to then ice was even exported from the United States to Australia. Using Harrison's method of compressed ammonia, Eugene Nicolle, a brilliant French engineer who had emigrated to Australia, later patented a machine for freezing meat, and with his patron, Thomas Mort, opened the first meat freezing plant in Darling Harbour in Sydney. This plant was adapted for installation in a ship, and after some initial difficulties was eventually made to work successfully. The first shipment of frozen Australian carcasses to Britain was brought aboard the *Strathleven*, a 2,436-ton sailing ship with an auxiliary engine chartered from the Burrell shipping line and, like the *Dunedin*, fitted with a Bell-Coleman refrigeration unit. Her cargo of forty tons was landed in London in February 1880 when the meat was found to be in excellent condition. The *Daily Telegraph* reported that it had been 'tested by ordinary methods of cooking and found to be in such good condition that neither by its appearance in the butchers' shops, nor by any peculiarity of flavour when cooked for the table could it be distinguished from fresh-killed meat'.[11]

Although the Company had the Foreign and Colonial Meat Bill thrown out, Parliament still found it necessary for butchers to differentiate between home-produced and foreign meat and to sell them separately. Again, the Committee of the London Central Meat and Poultry Markets Association put together a petition against the proposal, but this time they put it in their own name. Although the Company of Butchers gave their advice, the Association went ahead on their own, fighting hard all the way through the Committee stages of the Bill, and in the House of Lords, but the Agricultural Produce (Marks) Act was passed in January 1897.

The Private Slaughterhouse Bill introduced into Parliament at the close of the nineteenth century was another instance of the Company protecting the trade. The Bill proposed that all private slaughterhouses in London should 'cease to exist'[12] and that they be replaced by public ones, erected by the London County Council. In their 'humble petition' the Company acknowledged that the private slaughterhouses admirably filled the needs of the London butcher, and, as no complaint from any of their neighbours had been received as to their suitability, that they should be allowed to continue under the scrutiny of properly-qualified inspectors. They further maintained that the meat from a private slaughterhouse was infinitely superior to anything coming out of a public one, and that, 'notwithstanding the vast supplies of dead meat which pours into English markets from abroad, there is still a demand for home killed meat'. They cited all the well-known criteria of good meat, such as that it should rest after slaughter, something not possible in a public slaughterhouse, and doubted whether there would be proper lairage before slaughter. Transport would also pose a problem, and offal sales were 'not practical'. At that time, there were 450 private slaughterhouses in London, and it was proposed that they should be replaced by just six public ones. Thus, each one should do the job of seventy to eighty private slaughterhouses, regardless of the expense and space needed to set them up. Finally, it would be inconvenient for the slaughterman/butcher to have to travel to the public slaughterhouse, leaving his shop unattended. The Company was indeed fortunate in their Clerk, Harry Philpot, a solicitor, who drafted the petition, ending prosaically with: 'Pray take no steps to establish public slaughterhouses or to suppress private slaughterhouses and your Petitioners will ever pray, Etc. Etc.'[13] The petition was successful at that time, and earned the thanks of the London Butchers' Trade Association for the 'very valuable assistance'.

It was indeed appropriate that the Company of Butchers should continue in their support of the Smithfield Club. A grant of 50 guineas was voted by the Court towards the expenses of the Club each year. By the end of the nineteenth century the Club nominated a butcher, usually from the Company, to be one of the two judges for the carcase section of the Smithfield Show, the other being a farmer-grazier. At that time the carcase competition used 'the block test' which relied on the judge's visual assessment of just what sort of carcase the live animal would produce. But this led to fierce arguments, as the two judges were continually at odds as to what 'sort of meat best met the needs of the public, the butchers' customers'. In each of the four classes an umpire who was both a breeder and a London meat trader invariably 'had to be called in [when] in every case the umpire sided with the butcher judge'.[14] The difficulty arose because there was no slaughterhouse at the Agricultural Hall, and the butchers who purchased the winning beasts invariably failed to send in the returns as to how they killed out. The problem was solved when a slaughterhouse was added to the Agricultural Hall, so that the carcases themselves could be judged during the Show. This put paid to the grossly over-finished beasts winning the live-dead classes as they had in the past.

At the turn of the century the Master, John Bridgewater, proposed that the Company of Butchers should donate 50 guineas prize money annually and present three cups for the best beef, sheep and pig carcases, then still known as 'the Block Test'. The Smithfield Club were rather embarrassed, as up until that time, 1904, they had stuck to the rule that only Royal Patrons could give cups. Queen Victoria had donated the cup for the best-beast-in-show, the supreme sheep cup had come from the Prince of Wales, while his son, the Duke of York and future George V, presented the pig champion cup. The Butchers' offer was therefore politely declined by the Committee of the Smithfield Club, explaining that no exception could be made to their rules, whereupon the Butchers withdrew their offer. When the President of the Club, Prince Christian of Schleswig-Holstein (who was married to Princess Helena, Queen Victoria's third and favourite daughter) heard that the offer had been turned down, he immediately reversed the decision. The Company then set up a committee to choose the design, and three sterling silver cups were ready for presentation in December 1904. All three cups have been competed for each year, except during the War years and the foot and mouth epidemics. At the time of writing, the Best Carcase of Beef is on its tenth Challenge Cup, Champion Lamb Carcase is on its sixth Challenge Cup, while the Challenge Cup for the Champion Pork Carcase is on its eighth incarnation. The first Pork Cup was won two years in a row by the Duchess of Devonshire (1904 and 1905) for her Berkshire boars, and it 'became Her Grace's absolute property'.[15] In 1995 the cup was lent by the then Duchess as 'an item of special interest at the celebration of 100 years of the carcase competition'.[16]

Since its very foundation, first as a Guild then a Company, the Butchers have always engendered great loyalty amongst its members. Frequently this loyalty extended to generosity, either to the Company itself or to the Poor Fund for relief of others. Towards the end of the nineteenth century, the way was led by William J. Bonser who marked his year as Master (1887) by investing £500 in India 3% stock to provide a pension of £15 per annum. This was to be given to 'a decayed liveryman'[17] or the unmarried daughter or widow of a Liveryman of the Company. There was another gift of £500, invested in 1890 in the same India stock, donated by Emily and Ann Game, in memory of their father Charles Game, Master in 1864. This Fund paid out £15 a year to 'a Freeman of the Company in distressed circumstance', or the daughter or widow of a Liveryman. Soon after, in 1896, Benjamin Bloomfield Baker (twice Master, in 1869 and 1870) followed suit with his Baker Pension, a similar legacy for the same. One of the greatest benefactors of this time, however, was another Master, Alfred Lyon, an active Liveryman for forty years and a successful salesman at the Central Meat Market. At a Court meeting in 1892 he announced that he was 'prepared to hand over to the Court of the Company by deed of gift' a freehold house and shop, number 381 High Cross, Tottenham, together with a circular piece of land known as Clyde Circus. Part of the annual income from the property, not less than £26 but no more than £30, was to be used to help 'a widow or daughter in necessitous circumstances of a freeman of this Company who shall have carried on the trade of a Butcher, or failing such a widow or daughter of a master butcher not of the Company who had carried on business for at least fifteen years within fifteen miles of the General Post Office'.[18] The Company were also to pay 10 guineas a year to the Churchwardens of Adwick-on-the-Green, Doncaster, while £21 went annually to the Butchers Charitable Institution. When the lease eventually fell in the property was sold, the house and shop to the Metropolitan Electric Tramway Company for £1,650, with the proceeds being invested in India 3% stock, while Clyde Circus went for £740 to a builder to be developed.

Not all the bequests were for charity; in 1910, the Company of Butchers received a legacy through the will of Peter Meech for their benefit. Meech, a passionate Liveryman and active on the Court, gave his address as 101 D Avenue, Central Meat Market, although his home was in Romford in Essex. The Company received a 'farmhouse and farm with several parcels of land and buildings belonging thereto known as Higher Meerhay Farm situate in the Parish of Beaminster [Dorset] and two cottages and an orchard called Swaffield and limekiln upon trust for and to be held by the Masters, Wardens and Commonality of the Worshipful Company of the Art or Mystery of Butchers'.[19] Higher Meerhay Farm, that included Kitwhistle Farm, was a stock and dairy unit of around 255 acres. The land was very hilly, although much of it had been lyncheted, or terraced, originally to grow cereals, while the house was a typical Dorset longhouse built around a cobbled courtyard. Harry Philpot, as one of his last acts in over thirty years as Clerk and solicitor, applied to hold the property in mortmain, which was granted in May 1910. Peter Meech was generous in death as in life; after providing for his widow he left other farms that were sold to pay for the demolition of two houses and the erection of the Peter Meech Homes of '6 houses, five to be rented to the poor of Poorstock'.[20] He also gave legacies to his employees of Frederick Fletcher All and Peter Meech & Co, along with £500 to the Butchers' Charitable Institution for the relief 'of decayed or distressed Master Butchers (pork or cattle), meat commission salesmen, hide or skin salesmen, their widows or orphans'.[21] There was just one condition, which was a 'tablet fully setting forth the same being immediately erected and maintained in perpetuity in the Butchers' Hall'.[22]

The Company, however, struggled with its inheritance. Although they had a land agent to manage the property it was in poor condition and much money had to be spent on repairs. It was decided that they should sell Higher Meerhay Farm, and in May 1919 it realised £3,950 at auction in the White Hart Hotel in Beaminster. After various bank loans in connection with the farm were paid off, £2,000 was invested in Railway Stocks.

A further loan was needed in 1913 to pay for improvements to Butchers' Hall. The Company had tried to purchase 86 Bartholomew Close in 1883, when they had offered the parish of St Bartholomew-the-Great £1,000 for the freehold. Unfortunately, it was subject to 'Bryce's City of London Parochial Charities Bill . . . and the Vestry did not consider themselves free to deal with the offer'.[23] Later the Company was able to acquire 89 Bartholomew Close – which adjoined their existing premises – for £3,500 from a Mrs Sarah Salaman. With this new building in their possession, the company engaged the architect George Vickery, from the firm of T.S.Vickery, to draw up plans for the improvements to the Hall incorporating their new purchase. Shortly before the Great War was declared everything was removed from the hall, and work began. By September 1915 they were well under way when on the night of the 8th September, as *The Times* reported, 'German airships were over the Eastern Counties and London, and [although] our airplanes went up, they failed to find them'.[24] One Zeppelin slipped through on that moonless night and indiscriminately dropped its bombs over London. One landed on the corner of Bartholomew Close, diagonally across the street from the Butchers' Hall. Judging from the photograph of the crater and of the damage done to the houses opposite it must have been a massive bomb. These houses, including two which had at one time been occupied by two famous Americans, Benjamin Franklin, during his stay in London as a printer in 1725 and the novelist Washington Irving, were severely weakened and had to be pulled down.

The Clerk, Arthur Pearce, author of the second history of the Company, immediately called an emergency meeting of the Court at the Guildhall. There he reported on the considerable damage done to the Hall and the surrounding buildings by the Zeppelin's bomb, including: 'the destruction of the stained glass windows in the Hall and on the stairway landing to the hall . . . The pictures had fortunately been removed from the Hall owing to the alterations which were in progress at the time of the raid'.[25]

Having inspected the damage the morning after the raid Pearce immediately called in the Company architect, George Vickery, and surveyor, J.W. Roper, to assess the damage 'for the purpose of claiming under the Policy of Insurance which had been taken out for the purpose of providing against loss by damage from Aircraft'. At the outset of the War, there had been considerable debate as to whether such insurance cover was necessary, but the proposal in favour of it was eventually carried by a single vote. Roper and Vickery both confirmed that after their 'exhaustive examination of the building, . . . the result was that they were of the opinion that structurally the building was in sound condition and that the damage was confined to the Fabric and the contents and the destruction of the windows',[26] virtually the same words used after the fire that destroyed the Hall in Pudding Lane. Pearce reported that he had already prepared a claim for the damage, and the Court approved the figure of £4,267, with another £100 for fixtures and fittings, not including the stained glass windows. In the end, Lloyds settled the claim for £3,562. Despite the threat of further air raids the Company repaired the damage with the insurance moneys and completed the improvements, moving back into the Hall a year later in May 1916.

When the Armistice was signed, like the rest of the Country the Butchers were counting their dead, and one of their earliest resolutions was to commission a Roll of Honour 'to contain those Liverymen, sons, daughters and grandchildren killed in the War'[27] to hang on the staircase – so long as 'the cost did not exceed £50'. The Armistice was also marked by a new stained glass window called PEACE, to replace the one showing the Arms of the Company. It was funded by all twelve of the new Liverymen, the first to be admitted after the Great War. There was now an extra window in the enlarged Banqueting Hall, and for this the Master responsible for the improvements, John Gow, presented a stained glass portrait of George V. The other windows were also replaced with the same subjects (although not always the same images) by consortiums of Masters, Masters elect and Liverymen in the case of the Daniel Defoe and Queen Victoria windows, while the windows depicting the three 'Charter Kings', James I, Charles I and George II came from J.G. Jenkins, W.F. Archer and G.W. Potts respectively. Finally, two comparatively recent Liverymen, Sir William Vestey and Sir Edmund Hoyle Vestey, donated £750 each to replace the Shakespeare and Cardinal Wolsey windows. Dudley Forsyth, the leading artist in stained glass of the day, was chosen, drawings were made and the final design was approved. The cost of both these windows was £1,350. The pair of fine watercolour cartoons showing Shakespeare and Wolsey, along with that of Charles I, hang on the landing outside the general office in Butchers' Hall. In the same Court Minutes as this entry, oenophiles will be distressed to read that '6 dozen bottles of Warre's [18]89 Port [were] disposed of at 42/- a dozen'.

At a special Court meeting held in March 1914, Sir William Vestey, who would be raised to the peerage in 1922, had been 'admitted to the Freedom and Livery by redemption and made and subscribed the Declaration in the terms of the Ancient oath and was admitted and clothed and entered accordingly'. The fine at that time was £54 17 6d. His brother, Edmund Hoyle Vestey (who was to receive his baronetcy in 1921) had been admitted in the same year. The two brothers, Managing Director and Chairman respectively of the Union Cold Storage Company, were typical of the new breed of butcher, steering the considerable change in the meat industry, and, like their rivals the Borthwicks, were to become great benefactors of the Company of Butchers.

Before the Great War, millions of industrial workers desired meat rather than bread and potatoes, but it was not readily available and beyond the means of most of them. Beef was a luxury, mutton expensive and poultry scarce largely due to seasonal production, poor distribution and, before cold storage, spoilage. This was to change towards the end of the nineteenth century, in part due to the foresight and entrepreneurial skills of the two Vestey brothers, William and Edmund. At the age of seventeen, William Vestey was sent to Chicago by his father, Samuel, a provisions broker from Liverpool. In the abattoirs William saw the dreadful waste of trimmings and cheaper cuts. These he bought and sent to England as canned, corned beef. From America he and his brother moved on to Argentina, where the hide of an animal was almost of more value than the meat. They began by sending home a shipment of chilled partridges, unwanted in the Argentine, but highly prized, particularly out of season, in England. The trial worked so well that the brothers built their own cold store in Liverpool, and with it came the founding of their Union Cold Store empire. This led to a second, larger cold store in Liverpool and another in the Argentine by when they had moved on from partridge to beef. With cold stores at both ends to control both supply and distribution, they could now assure year-round supply to overcome the seasonal fluctuations in price. The Vestey brothers' maxim for success was never to let others do what they could do themselves, and this led, among many other ventures, to their founding the Blue Star shipping line to transport their own produce around the world.

Other family companies, like Thomas Borthwick & Co, were also early to take advantage of 'the opportunities offered by the frozen and chilled meat trade, not only as importers, wholesalers and distributors but also by becoming very much involved in the New Zealand, Australian and Argentine ends of the trade', being the official selling agents of the New Zealand Loan and Mercantile Company. Over the years the Butchers have benefited greatly from the generosity of the owners of these family conglomerates, not only in monetary terms, but through their support of the Company. They, along with their numerous staff, have added knowledge of another side of the meat industry to share with their fellow members. Traditionally, the role of the Butchers was not only to keep a watching brief on the meat trade, but, through their fellowship, to pool knowledge for the benefit of all. At the end of the Great War another dimension was added to this fellowship.

As in many other Livery Companies there was a move to establish a Masonic Lodge within the Butchers, there being 'a great surge of Masonic activity in the five years after the War when 700 English Lodges were founded'.[28] To this end, W Frederick Bonser, Master in 1922, applied to the Court 'for permission to found a Masonic Lodge in connection with the Company'. Bonser also applied to use the Company's Arms and motto for the Lodge. The motions were carried unanimously, and under the sponsorship of the United Smithfield Lodge the Taurus Lodge No 3981 was consecrated at Butchers' Hall on 1 December 1919. The Lodge had also adopted the Company's motto, but changed the *boves* to Taurus, hence its nomenclature. The Butchers were the fourth City Livery Company to have a Lodge, but the first to use their own Hall for Lodge meetings. Bonser then asked for the use of the Hall for Lodge dinners in February, April, September and December, which was again granted on the nod, although this was later amended to the fourth Tuesday in September, November, January, and March. The Lodge flourished from the outset, and is stronger today than ever before, with a record membership. Taurus milestones were always marked in style – even their Silver Jubilee in December 1944 was celebrated with a fine dinner, notwithstanding war-time restrictions. The menu was exotic and filled with long-forgotten delights, but a note attached to the card read 'any relation between the menu and the food actually provided is purely coincidental'.[29]

Another thriving society within the Butchers' Company was the Golfing Society, founded in 1927. It started with a small group of Liverymen who formed themselves into a team to take part in the first 'Prince Arthur Cup'. This was a competition open to all Livery Companies and organised by the Worshipful Company of Coachmakers and Coach Harness Makers in honour of Prince Arthur of Connaught, third and favourite son of Queen Victoria, who was made an Honorary Freeman. The first competition was held at Walton Heath in Berkshire. The winners were Lt Col Walter Scott-Miller, Master in 1925, and William J Parsons, Master in 1929. Not only did the Butchers team win the inaugural match, they also won the Cup two years later. The third Butchers' plaque to be added to the base of the cup was in 2004, won by John Harwood (Captain), William Lickorish, Michael George and Dennis Phillips.

But this close bond of fellowship within the Company was not entirely secular. During celebrations of the eight hundredth anniversary of the founding of the Priory Church of St Bartholomew-the-Great in 1923, Bernard Parsons, the then Master, proposed that it became the Butchers' church. It had had a rich and varied history, being the oldest place of worship in the City after the chapel in the Tower of London. It was founded by Rahere, courtier to Henry I, as an Augustinian Priory in 1123, along with the Hospital. After the Reformation the Priory became a parish church, but it was thought to be too large and the nave (the site of the present garden and graveyard behind the original west door) was allowed to fall in. The Lady Chapel was secularised and was used variously as the printing works (where Benjamin Franklin was employed in the early eighteenth century) ending up as a lace and fringe factory. When the church was restored at the end of the nineteenth century a blacksmith's forge was removed from the north transept. Unlike the Company's halls, St Bartholomew's survived the Great Fire, also the Zeppelin raids in the Great War.

The church itself, not the incumbent, was affiliated to the Butchers' Company. At W. Frederick Bonser's suggestion the Master once again appointed his own personal chaplain to take the service in St Bartholomew-the-Great after Common Hall. The first year (1925) the Master's Chaplain was the Bishop of London, the Right Reverend Arthur Winnington-Ingram, and the year after it was the Reverend W. Besley, Rector of St Lawrence Jewry and 'Honorary Priest to His Majesty the King'. It would appear that the post of Honorary Chaplain was a haphazard one as the names change at random. At the outbreak of the Second World War, the Reverend Canon Savage, the Rector of St Bartholomew-the-Great, took over as Chaplain to the Master. He was succeeded in 1944 by his curate, the Reverend Dr Newell Wallbank, MA, Mus.D, Ph.D who remained as Rector and Chaplain to the Master until his retirement in 1979. Wallbank was much loved, and in his turn had a deep affection for the Company. After thirty years as Chaplain he was made an Honorary Freeman of the Company, and when he retired he was given a lunch in his honour where his guests included the Archbishop of Canterbury, the Reverend

Dr Coggan (the son of a butcher and Honorary Freeman of the Company), and the Bishop of London, the Right Reverend Gerald Ellison.

And so the business of the Company was carried out between the Wars very much as before, as indeed it would be in the future. The Minutes and agenda books are full of the Company's varied business, their triumphs and failures, important decisions and mere detail. The receipt of a replica Company Mace from James Blofeld was 'acknowledged with thanks'[30] – his portrait, painted for his hundredth birthday, cigarette in hand, hangs above the stairs outside the Court Room. Lengthy discussions took place about whether to change the blue ribbon of the badges of office to the livery colours of blue and white: plain blue held. At an emergency meeting, it was decided that sixty special constables from the Stock Exchange Division could be billeted in the Hall for the duration of the General Strike, and that the livery dinner be moved to the Poulters' Hall. Two mahogany chairs were stolen – 'carvers bearing the Company Arms was reported missing by the House committee'.[31] They were never found. Shy of publicity, the Court turned down out of hand a request from the *Daily Telegraph* for an article on the Company, but the Clerk was happy to report at a lengthy meeting in the Hall that the 'Meat Pitchers Strike had been brought to a termination'. The Clerk told, too, of the blue plaque to be erected by the London County Council on 'the Post Office building on the West side of Roman Bath Street to commemorate the site of Butchers' Hall burned in 1666'.

Various gifts to the Company were faithfully recorded at Court Meetings, such as Howard Bonser's bookcase, along with a silver gong and hammer. Another interesting item came from the Honourable Samuel (later 2nd Baron) Vestey, with the gift of a 'Chinese [Export porcelain] bowl with the arms of the Company and the name Edward Fisher, a freeman of the Company in 1775 thereon'. These pieces of Chinese Export porcelain bearing the Arms of the Butchers are extremely rare, with only five recorded services, three from the Qianlong period of around 1775 (as with those bearing the names William and Susan Robinson), and two others of the Ch'ien Lung of about the same date, inscribed with the name of Edward Fisher or the initials G.M.F.C. A small teapot and three tea bowls of this Fisher service are displayed in the cabinet in the present Hall.

After the invasion of Poland on 1 September 1939, war was declared on Germany. The Master of the Company of Butchers, Fred Burton, proposed that 'in view of the National Emergency . . . and in consultation with the Clerk, the Common Hall called for Monday September 4 1939 be adjourned to October 5 1939 and the meeting of the Court be cancelled. The outbreak of war to be regarded as cancelling'.[32] This somewhat bald statement was very necessary, for having lost their charter in 1743 (see page 96) for their failure to hold Common Hall, the Master did not want a repeat, even for such a dire reason. The same day an offer was received from Lloyd Bank to store the Company's Charters in the vaults of a provincial branch, which was politely declined. Mindful of the damage caused by the bomb dropped by the Zeppelin, the Butchers' first action was to order the stained glass windows to be boarded up, each with a ¼-inch steel plate. They were further protected by cellophane. The basement of the Butchers' building in Little Britain was requisitioned as an air raid shelter under the Defence Regulations.

On the night of the 11th and 12th May 1941 there was a full moon. Wave after wave of German bombers crossed the Channel and an 'intense and indiscriminate attack was made on London with high explosives and incendiary bombs'.[33] But 'thirty-three night raiders, the largest number since the War began, were shot down on Saturday night and Sunday morning'.[34] Casualties were high. Much damage, too, was done by the bombs, particularly those that fell on Westminster Abbey, the British Museum and the Houses of Parliament – and Butchers' Hall.

Three days later the Court was summoned by the Master, Herbert Jackman. It was he who read the report of the damage that night. He began by saying that the Beadle, Mr Long, and his wife were asleep at the time of the air raid and had 'escaped injury'. But the Hall 'had suffered severe damage by enemy action, a High Explosive Bomb of heavy calibre having fallen into Bartholomew Close, and though the structure seemed to have stood up well, the windows and doors throughout the building had been blown out, and damage done to the pictures, furniture and stained glass windows'.[35]

The Master continued, telling the Court that the Company Surveyor, the architect Mr Vickery, had made an inspection of the building, and as far as he could see there was no serious damage to the structure, just to the roof 'which would be necessary to strip and new roof timbers would have to be supplied'. The cost of the essential repairs was impossible to assess at that time, as no contractor would give an estimate. As the Deputy Master, W Fred Bonser, later pointed out, temporary repairs were made to the roof 'at a cost of £1,700'.

It is surprising that more damage was not done to the building, considering that it received a direct hit from 'a High Explosive Bomb of heavy calibre', thought to be of 500 lbs. For the second time in less than thirty years all the stained glass windows were blown out, but this time the separate 'little pieces were collected up, carefully labelled and stored'[36] against the day that they could be reinstated. The better pictures had been removed from the walls and stored in the crypt of St Bartholomew-the-Great and survived intact, along with some pieces of furniture. By comparing the inventories of 1926 and 1947, it would appear that virtually all the Company's effects came through the War unscathed.

Four months before the blast in Bartholomew Close the City Livery Club had been bombed out of their premises in Old Broad Street. They were, however, fortunate that Fred Bonser, then Deputy Master of the Company, was also on the Club's committee. He arranged that they should take over Butchers' Hall, 'excluding the Committee Room, one office room and the Beadle's quarters, for the period of the War and twelve months thereafter'.[37] Part of the agreement was that they should pay half of the cost of installing a lift.

It can be said that the Company of Butchers have been extremely unlucky to have lost five out of their seven halls (including the Saxon Hall) to fire. The Tudor Hall so nearly escaped the Great Fire of London, being only a few hundred yards from where it finally burned itself out. Likewise, when the German V-1 struck the Butchers' Hall just before midnight of 31 July 1944, the end of the Second World War was in sight. That 'doodlebug', one of 'a small number of bombs [that] were sent over'[38] the Home Counties and London, scored a direct hit on the Hall. The Beadle William Long, a Fire Warden, was away at the time with his son, but his wife, daughters and son-in-law were in the building. They heard the V-1 and 'realised that it was very close. When it cut out' they 'counted 22 seconds and there was the most almighty explosion when all the windows were blown out'.[39] The bomb also destroyed an eiderdown factory in Little Britain, so when the Fire Brigade arrived the whole area looked as if it had been snowing.

Yet again another Master, this time Michel Oppenheimer, followed in a long line of his predecessors as he gave the Court his report on the damage to their Hall in the offices of Josiah B. Swain, St John Street, by the Angel. Exactly like the previous report on the damage to the Hall, he began by saying how pleased he was that 'Mrs Long and her daughter who were sleeping in the Beadle's quarters on the top floor, though suffering from shock and cuts from broken glass, had miraculously escaped from more serious injury'. The Hall, he said, had 'received a direct hit on the roof . . . which had caused very severe damage . . . [and that it] will require very extensive repairs, at any rate partial rebuilding before it will be available for further use'. The Company's Architect, the same George Vickery who had carried out the improvements to the Hall, was also there to report on the condition of the building. He began by saying that he had been all over the ruined Hall and had made a thorough inspection. It appeared that the roof and the top two floors had been blown apart, and that the fabric of the building, especially the upper part, was badly damaged. According to Vickery it was the fireproof floors that he had put into the 89 Bartholomew Close end of the building, during the 1913 improvements, that had protected that part of the building and 'probably saved the lives of Mrs Long and her daughter'. Although there was an enormous amount of debris on the top two floors, he felt, as far as he could see, that the lower walls appeared to be sound, but he suspected that, behind further mounds of debris, the panelling and joinery would prove to be badly damaged. Vickery recommended that the upper walls be pulled down immediately and the debris cleared, and then a further assessment of the damage made, as 'until that was done, there could be no estimate of cost of the repair'. As it turned out, 'no general movement of the part below the [second] floor of the Hall could be detected', which meant that the two floors and the basement were serviceable when cleared of debris. After a long discussion it was moved that Mr Vickery be instructed to arrange with a firm of contractors for the removal of the debris, and for an asphalt roof to be constructed over the floor. A committee consisting of the Master, the Deputy Master, Montague Abrahams (Master in 1942) and Josiah B. Swain (Master in 1946 and 1947) was set up to monitor progress, and to pursue the 'claim under Part II of the War Damage Act with respect to the loss and damage to furniture and chattels as to removal and storage of the part that could be salvaged'. Finally it was resolved that Mrs Long should be given a two-week holiday with her family 'forthwith to enable her to recover from the severe shock she sustained and that the sum of £31 10 shillings be paid to her for this purpose'. With the Hall in ruins and the Beadle's apartment destroyed there was nowhere for them to go *but* on holiday. Fortunately, the Longs owned a house on the Isle of Sheppey.

With the War over, and VE and VJ Days celebrated, the reconstruction of the country began. The Company of Butchers were fortunate in the energies and dedication of their new Master, Josiah B. Swain. His first act after being sworn in was to swear a pledge to:

> use my best endeavours to further the cause among the members of the Meat and Allied Trades of the social, economic and cultural life of the industry. I pledge myself to visit all the centres of our widespread Industry at home and overseas to carry a message of goodwill to all who cross my path.
>
> I fully believe that the erection of a new Butchers' Hall at Smithfield, London will raise our industry to a new high level and in years to come, will be looked upon as one of the crowning events of our trade.[40]

Josiah Swain, always known as Jos, became the prime mover in replacing the Butchers' Hall. Soon after it was damaged he reported to the Court, drawing attention to 'how best the Company could exert its influence in the benefit and advancement of the trade'.[41] Swain was proposing, as 'a memorial of the War that was now happily drawing to a close', a joint scheme with the London County Council for 'the provision of a new hall for the Company and the building of a technical institute . . . [that would serve] as a meeting place, adequate in size and consistent with the dignity of the Company which would afford a meeting place for all the organisations in connection with the trade'.[42] He produced an artist's impression of what the building might look like, and suggested that the meat industry should not only contribute towards it, but manage the institute as well. In the end nothing came of this far-sighted and grandiose scheme, but not for want of trying on Swain's behalf.

On New Year's Day 1946 Josiah Swain, accompanied by his wife and by the Beadle, William Long, with the Company's mace and banner, set off for Plymouth, where they were entertained the next day by the Lord Mayor. He thought it a fitting place to start his pilgrimage, as it was from there that Sir Francis Drake had set off on his 'voyages of discovery and riches'.[43] The Master's progress took him around the country, criss-crossing from the Fleshers of Glasgow to the Butchers of York. He visited places such as Portsmouth and Bristol, Norwich and Stoke-on-Trent, Liverpool and Hull, and all the important cities and towns, the likes of Birmingham and Manchester, in his quest to raise awareness of the Company and to solicit contributions for the rebuilding of the Hall. The meat institutions, such as the Smithfield Market Traders' Association, also entertained them, all signing his book of goodwill. But that was just the beginning. On 2 July 1946, the Master and Mrs Swain, accompanied by the Beadle, left England aboard the *Highland Monarch* for Rio de Janeiro, taking with them a new, leather-bound book of goodwill. Again, he had written his pledge on the title page:

As Master I am taking this book with me on my pilgrimage overseas to the meat producing countries of the world.

In every country I expect to meet Presidents, Minister of State, members of Church and Civic authorities, farmers, members of the Meat Industry, Port Authorities and Hospitals from whom I will ask for a message of goodwill to be recorded herein.[44]

This South American progress began well with an audience with General Enrico Gaspar Dutra, the recently-elected President of Brazil, who, along with a host of other dignitaries from the State and Church, signed the book. Swain reported back to the Court that 'he had everywhere received a warm and enthusiastic welcome, and felt that his presence in South America had not only furthered the main object of conveying goodwill from Great Britain and the Meat Industry, but had done much for the improvement if International relationships'.[45]

Three weeks later on 12 August 1945, the Swains were in Uruguay at an audience with President de Amézaga, followed by another round of receptions and audiences. The trip was going extremely well, Swain being treated more like a Government Minister than the Master of a City of London Livery Company. Although the book was filling up with important names, including those leading figures in the meat industry, there was still no money in his 'begging bowl'. But matters were to change during the following week when he arrived in Buenos Aires, the capital of the Argentine Republic.

In early October, the Butchers held their Court Meeting in the Cutlers' Hall in Warwick Lane. Amongst the usual business, Dr Lancelot Hall, the Clerk, read out a letter he had received from the Master. The beginning was an account of how well the trip was going, but then came the bombshell when Swain informed the Court that he had 'arrived in Buenos Aires and was desirous that the Court should pass a resolution to confer the Honorary Freedom on the President of the Republic of Argentina, General Perón'.[46] The Court was stunned. Hall, a solicitor, reassured them that all, in fact, was well. He continued:

> the City Chamberlain had very kindly explained the procedure and that there was no objection to the passing of a resolution, but it would not be possible actually to admit him [Perón] as the taking of the Freedom involved a declaration of loyalty to the British Crown, a copy of such resolution could be handed to General Peron if he visited London, but it was contrary to the custom of the City of London to present any document at all outside the City of London.[47]

Hall informed the Court that he had sent a copy of the City Chamberlain's letter to the Master, and, after a long discussion they decided that 'with regret' they were 'unable to concur with the Master's suggestion'. The Court did decide to form a small committee to look into the possibility of conferring the Honorary Freedom on the President, and that a 'resolution be passed to confer the Honorary Freedom upon General Perón and that when General Perón is able to visit the City, a special meeting of the Court and Livery is held and a copy of the resolution duly engrossed be presented to him'. It was an admirable compromise.

Meanwhile, the Master was busy in Buenos Aires. On 9 October, Swain hosted a dinner for the President and Señora Perón at the Plaza Hotel. It was a lavish affair, funded by the Company, but what it did achieve was exactly the right kind of publicity. Photographs of the Master with the Peróns under the Butchers' Company banner, flanked by the Beadle Mr Long with the Mace, appeared in the press in the Argentine and at home. However, far from home and no doubt flushed with the success of the evening, the Master entered into another agreement with the Argentine Government, this time 'for a gift of £100,000 for rebuilding [the Hall] on condition that a portion be known as Argentine Tower'.[48] The Clerk reported the Master's negotiations to the next Court meeting, adding that Swain had further agreed that part of the completed Hall should be 'leased to the Argentine for 99 years at a peppercorn rent'. When the proposal was read out by the Clerk the Court were appalled. This was clearly totally unacceptable on every score. The Clerk, an eminent lawyer, with the backing of the Court, wrote to Swain in the strongest terms:

Dear Jos,

Your letter with the suggested arrangements with the Argentine has come to hand and was most carefully considered . . . I made it quite clear to you long since, and it was also made quite clear by members of the Reconstruction Committee that under no circumstances would it be possible to offer free accommodation for anyone as it is impossible to know exactly what our capital commitments or income commitments will be when the hall is erected in due course. In the first place, we have not acquired the site and have no idea of the cost to obtain the necessary land to put up the building. Judging by the price such sites are fetching in London today it might cost several hundred thousand pounds to acquire the land alone.

Secondly we have not got the slightest idea of the cost of erection . . .

Thirdly we have not got the slightest idea what the outgoings will be . . .

Fourthly . . . the idea of selling a future building for a premium payable now without any idea of our cost commitment is an impossible arrangement financially . . . [and] any such arrangements made now without adequate advice from experts in building and finance would land the Company into a position of bankruptcy. Any idea of such commercial arrangements was never for a moment considered by the Court or by me. It was anticipated that you might be able to persuade the Latin American countries and others to make substantial gifts for the erection of a suitable building, and some arrangement might be made on a proper and financial basis to give them the opportunity of using the Hall, but certainly not on the lines which you indicate in your letter. The Court were quite emphatic . . . that under no circumstances can you make any offer to person or persons in respect of the matter unless such an offer has previously been approved by the Court.

I am sorry to have to put the matter so very bluntly but I can personally see disaster ahead for any such arrangements as those you indicate,

Signed,

Lancelot Hall.

The letter was waiting for Swain at the Plaza Hotel on his return from a tour of Chile, where he had an audience with the Vice President, Juan Antonio Iribarren. Swain was furious and immediately sent a long cable back to Lancelot Hall, which he read out at the next meeting. The Master wrote that 'unless he could be given a free hand in the matter' he proposed to return home (by that time the Swain party had in fact already sailed on the *Gaelic Star* of the Blue Star Line which arrived in England on 18 January).

Understandably the Court 'learned with much concern the abrupt return of the Master and the cancelling of his visit overseas'. To justify their actions over this sorry affair, in which Swain was conferring the privileges of the livery and allocating parts of the proposed hall without their consent, they were at pains to record their position clearly. 'It is therefore necessary', the Clerk wrote,

> to record in view of the Master's likely presence at the next Court Meeting, the sentiments of the members of the Court that all self sacrificing efforts of the Master put forward, the arduous experiences he has undergone and the courage and tenacity with which he has faced up to the endless difficulties he encountered. The Court however deeply mindful of its rights and responsibilities to preserve and maintain the dignity of the traditional status of the Company was bound firmly to prove its assertive views to make them abundantly clear to the Master. It must be remembered that the Court gave its unanimous approval and co-operation and support to the Master from the first date in which the rebuilding scheme was conceived on so ambitious a plan. They agreed to the many functions that were held, the provincial tour by the Master to the civic centres and finally to the enterprise overseas upon which the Master embarked with heartiest good wishes from the Court. That the Master's journey should have ended in so unsatisfactory a manner has caused the Court the deepest feelings of misgivings and regret and this should be emphasised to the Master in the fullest measure.

The Master was indeed present at the next meeting in February 1947. The Court gave him a vote of thanks for all he had done on the Company's behalf over the last year, seven and a half months of it spent out of the Country. In his absence he had been elected Master for the second year in succession. The balance of Swain's expenses was repaid, and with that the matter of the Argentine débâcle was at an end, as was the 'suggested trip to the Dominions'. Jos Swain had intended to go on to New Zealand, New South Wales, Queensland and Victoria, where the 'Pilgrimages and Greetings Books', beautifully bound in tooled leather with the date (1946) and the country and states, had already been prepared. When Señora Perón was due to visit London in 1948 there was a suggestion that 'she be entertained', but this was 'left on the table'.

But Jos Swain's peregrinations were not quite over, for the next year, 1948, he visited the United States. This trip was a great success. As before, he aimed high and met the President, Harry S. Truman, and Thomas Dewey, Governor of the State of New York, both of whom signed his book of goodwill, as did the Mayor of New York, William O'Dwyer. The Swains went on to Chicago, the home of the meat packing industry, where the Company's banner had been seen in the past at various exchange visits and exhibitions. There, not only did the Mayor of Chicago, James Kennedy, receive him but also the heads of all the major meat firms

– John Holmes from Swift, Thomas Wilson of Wilson and Co., and G. Eastwood from Armour and Co.

It can only have been deeply frustrating for the Court, and indeed the rest of the Livery, that the plans to replace their bombed-out hall were proceeding so slowly, since it appeared that every Government body was conspiring against them. The basic problem was that St Bartholomew's Hospital wanted to modernise and rebuild, but their plans included the site of Butchers' Hall. Although the War Damage Claim had long been agreed at £56,935 with fees of £4,413, the Ministry of Works would not grant the Company a licence to rebuild. Then the planning department of the London County Council would not entertain any application for the new hall until St Bartholomew's Hospital had made up their minds. To avoid the stalemate the Company offered to transfer the site of the Hall and their properties in Little Britain to the Hospital, in return for a similar site where a building of the same size as the present Hall could be erected, along with a payment of nearly £70,000. Still the Hospital prevaricated, and as the impasse dragged on the Hall became tatty and run down. But the Company could not refurbish it with the threat of a compulsory purchase hanging over them. Playing for time, the Hospital agreed that they would part-fund the renovation, with a straight gift of £5,000 and a further amount based on a sliding scale up to £10,000, which was eventually accepted. But the Company was losing patience with the Hospital, who refused to meet their deadlines. Instead they kept renewing their plans, one of which even included the new Butchers' Hall 'set on an island in the middle of the new Hospital complex'. This was clearly unacceptable. The Butchers, however, were basically quite amenable, pointing out that all they wanted was a new hall, and that if they could not rebuild on their present site then the Governors should provide them with an alternative, comparable site. Another year passed as the Hospital and the London County Council demurred. The Corporation came up with a site in Cloth Fair, which the Butchers seriously considered, but turned down on the grounds that reinstatement would cost £155,000. Eventually the Butchers lost patience with the Hospital Governors. When it was pointed out that the War Damage Claim could not be transferred if Butchers' Hall was built on another site, and that the amount of the award (some £61,000 in all) would therefore have to be added to the purchase price, the Hospital Governors were stirred into action. They were finally persuaded to rethink their plans, and after yet another short delay the Butchers were free to rebuild their Hall (and develop 42 – 44 Little Britain) on the original sites.

The Company had long since commissioned Howard Kelly to come up with plans for a suitable Butchers' Hall. The first plans were presented to the Reconstruction Committee in 1950, the artist's impression of the building being framed and now hanging in the general office. There was another design in 1956 on which planning permission was finally granted in November, with a final version, the one that was built, being delivered in 1957. These plans were a complete breakthrough in design. It was one of the first modern City Livery Halls to be built in London, far removed from the utilitarianism of post-war Britain – rationing, after all, had only ended three years before. Kelly had also incorporated radical features, such as dressing the building with reconstituted stone, and in place of the stained glass windows of old he used small panes of hand-made glass, translucent from the inside but opaque when seen from outside. It was decided then that the stained glass windows should not upset this unique design feature.

To divorce the rebuilding costs from the routine affairs of the Company, the site of 87, 88 and 89 Bartholomew Close was leased to 'The Butchers' Company Estates Limited', a limited liability company, for eighty years. The job was put out to tender, and a year later it was decided that Messrs Griggs and Sons, the lowest of five tenderers, would rebuild the Hall at a cost of £89,629. They estimated that it would take forty-nine weeks to complete the task, and the Clerk made arrangements that the Company would have the use of the Cutlers' Hall in the meantime. But it was all very well having the site, the plans, the planning permission, and the War Damage Claim – the balance of the necessary funds was still needed to be raised.

When planning for the new hall began an extra two guineas per annum were added to the quarterage of the Livery. The Master approached Ronald Vestey, Chairman of Union International, who advised him that in order to raise the money 'personal representation be made to all the leading importing companies, so long as it was on a sound commercial basis'. The plan paid off, for soon after the 'profound gratitude of the Court' was given to Mr Chisholm on behalf of the New Zealand Meat Producers for their 'generous, heart-warming contribution' of £10,000. Other interest-free loans followed from the likes of the London Retail Meat Traders Association, the Smithfield Market Traders Association, importing and fatstock marketing companies as well as many banks. By the end of the year, the Company had the additional money needed to start the rebuilding – £30,000.

2 April 1959 was 'a capital spring day',[49] when the Court, a few Liverymen and friends gathered in Bartholomew Close. There was a definite air of excitement amongst the small group that had assembled to witness the Master, George Montague MC, lay the foundation stone for the new hall. There was also a crowning sense of achievement, for they had overcome almost insuperable odds, and triumphed over ten years of disappointment. As the foundation stone, suitably inscribed with the names of the Master, architect, builder and the date, was eased into place on the right-hand side of the front door, it marked the dawn of another important era in the history of the Worshipful Company of Butchers.

7 The Sixth Hall

1957–

'Will the Court please stand to receive the Master.' The Beadle, Charles Woods, wearing the robe of his office almost for the first time, marched into the Great Hall ahead of Samuel Fletcher. As the Court and Livery rose as one for the 1961 Common Hall, they reflected with justifiable pride on their surroundings, since they were back once again in their new Butchers' Hall. Although the backdrop was relatively new, the form of Common Hall was well-known to all but the fourteen new Liverymen that year. As ordained in the 1749 Charter, they had been summoned 'to appear on Monday 4th Day of September 1961 at 11 o'clock in the forenoon at the *PRIORY CHURCH OF ST BARTHOLOMEW-THE-GREAT SMITHFIELD* to attend Divine Service at which a sermon suitable to the occasion will be preached by the *REV^d Dr. N. E. WALLBANK, M.A., MUS.D., PhD*, and afterwards personally to be and appear at Common Hall . . . to give Voice, Vote and Lot, who shall be MASTER, WARDENS AND ASSISTANTS of the said Company for the year ensuing'.[1] The notice had been signed by Norman L. Hall, the 'worthy and learned' Clerk, so described as he, like his father and immediate predecessors, was a practising lawyer and partner in the distinguished firm of solicitors, Halls of Cloth Fair. The notice was accompanied by a list of nominations, under Bye Law 2 of the recently-reworked Ordinances. The list was headed by the single nomination James Arnold Brewster for Master along with five names for Warden. Among the fifteen names nominated to serve on the Court as Assistant was that of Herbert J. Jackman.

The proceedings continued in exactly the same manner as they had for centuries. The Master called upon the Clerk to read the Notice convening Common Hall, and the Minutes of the previous year, which, when passed, were duly signed. The Clerk was then called upon to 'read the names the Liverymen put in nomination for Master'. James Arnold Brewster, being the only nominee, stood and was duly elected 'Master for the ensuing year'. The Clerk read the declaration:

Now that you are elected and chosen to be Master of the Art of Mystery of Butchers of The City of London, you swear that you shall and will so long as you continue Master, endeavour yourself so near as you can well, truly, faithfully, honestly and diligently to execute the said Office and that with indifferency with every respect. And also to the utmost of your power you shall and will endeavour to put in due execution all the good and lawful ordinances made or to be made touching the same Mystery sparing no person for favour or affection nor punishing any person for hatred or Malice. And that every such Goods, Plate, Jewels, Money and other things which by reason of your said Office shall come into your hands possession or Custody you shall make a good true plain and perfect account of them to such person and persons and in such manner and at such times as by the Rules Orders and Ordinances of the said Company or Art of Mystery aforesaid is or shall be directed or appointed – So help you God.[2]

Brewster assented to the declaration, and the Clerk proceeded with the election of the five Wardens who, unusually at that time, included only one Past Master. After they too had made their declarations, the 'worthy and learned' Clerk then read out the names of the fifteen Assistants, adding that 'Past Master Jackman being absent from Common Hall his name was withdrawn from the nominees'. His place as Assistant was taken by the Reserve candidate, John Silver, who subsequently went through the Court to become Master in 1971. Technically, Jackman was also liable to a fine of 'thirteen shillings and four pence to the said Master Wardens and Commonalty' for his absence, although this was not legally enforceable. Under the terms of the Company's original Ordinance of 1607, anyone who was not physically present at Common Hall could not be elected on to the Court. Jackman was, in fact, terminally ill in hospital, and died soon after. He had served the Company loyally through the Court, rising to Master in 1940. After his year of office he remained, as was the custom, on the Court for the next twenty-one years, serving (as a Past Master) both as Warden and Assistant. At his valedictory nomination, he was eighty-two years old. Another member of the Court who was present at that 1961 Common Hall was the Reverend Thomas Parker, a great theologian, who had become a Freeman of the Company through patrimony, his father Thomas John Parker having been a butcher and Master in 1885. Parker himself never became a Liveryman, but under the 1637 Charter, the Court can be drawn from Freemen and Liverymen alike. He went on to become Master himself in 1962.

'Reserve elections' were rare. Some, like Ernest Gunner, who became Master in 1967, were elected on to the Court mid-term when a member of the Court died. Dispensation could be given through 'just cause', such as illness, at the discretion of the Master. When Robert Cornell was nominated as Assistant, but could not attend Common Hall, he was 'excused by the Master' and took his oath at the next Court

Meeting. At the same Common Hall, Edwin John Noël Canvin 'was not present and had not asked to be excused' and so had his name withdrawn. Canvin, a keen sailor, was caught in a storm and could not make it back for Common Hall, or even contact the Master. So 'In accordance with the Byelaws, John Kenneth Curran was proposed by the Master, seconded by the Deputy Master as an Assistant' and Canvin was off the Court.

Although there was nothing in the Ordinances to prohibit members of the Court nominating each other *ad infinitum*, to the younger members of the Livery it seemed most unjust: W. Fred Bonser, who served as Deputy Master for thirty years, retiring a little over two years before his death in 1957 aged eighty-five, and Sydney Blofeld, Master in 1941, who as an Assistant received the congratulations of the Court on his ninetieth birthday, are typical cases in point. The Clerk, Norman Hall, who had succeeded his father Lancelot in 1948, was deeply committed to the Butchers and mindful of their future. He could well foresee that the current system of election by the 'Kingmakers' *on* the Court *to* the Court would eventually rebound on the Company. In theory, Liverymen were elected on to the Court in strict seniority, 'Buggins' turn' (where appointments are made by rotation rather than merit), although, for a nominal fine, a nomination could be refused. As there were no admissions to the Livery during the Great War, there was a four-year gap in seniority by the time Liverymen came up for nomination in the 1950s. Progress to the Court was extremely slow, which meant that the nominees were all of a certain age by the time they were eligible for election. With the consequent predominance of septuagenarians, and not infrequently octogenarians, the average age of the Court was considerable. As early as 1953 Hall drafted a proposal for William Goldstein, Master in 1938, to be considered by his fellow members of the Court:

At the Court of this Worshipful Company having considered the composition of the Court and the tenure of office of its members, the manner of their appointment or election, it is of the opinion that in the best interest of the Company and to ensure the goodwill, understanding and cooperation of the Liverymen, the existing method of appointment and election be abolished and the practice of filling vacancies by rotation from the livery list be replaced by the regular retirement of a specified number of the senior members of the Court at specified periods as may be finally decided upon. That the liverymen be accorded the privilege of nominating candidates for election to the Court who will present themselves by the liverymen at Common Hall or at a specified date during the year if found preferable. That this resolution should not debar any retiring member of the Court from accepting nomination from such election except that members of the Court should not be granted the right to nominate a retiring member for such re-election and that a sub-committee should be appointed by the Court to consider the foregoing and further to give general consideration to the whole question of nomination of candidates for election to the Court.[3]

The proposal was not well received, though the Court did vote to set up a committee to look into the question. But Hall persevered. He could see the problems of running a Company on an ancient Charter, and went to the City Chamberlain who 'pointed out that it was for the Company to construe its own Charter', and, if difficult to run as such, then 'the spirit of the Charter should be interpreted'.[4] Hall went to the original 1605 Charter and, finding much of it faded and illegible, sent it to Scotland Yard to be photographed with their new 'infa-red process'. The Chief Inspector was rewarded for his services with a lunch. Hall could see that the vital changes he had worked out could in fact be implemented within the framework of the existing Charters and Bye-Laws. But the matter dragged on unresolved as Hall and Goldstein produced more and more draft resolutions. Finally, in 1954, they came up with the one that was acceptable to the Court and which was finally passed:

I   That the nomination of candidates for election as Master, Wardens and Assistants is in the hands of the individual Liverymen.

II That in consequence the Court as a formal body should no longer as part of its business arrange for candidates to be approached to accept nomination or recommend nominations to the Livery.

III That the Master and each Warden and Assistant has individually the right of nomination no less than any other Liveryman.

IV That no Liveryman shall be improperly approached to withdraw his candidature.

V   That the conduct of proceedings at Common Hall if under the control of the Master or Senior Warden in the chair, it is desirable that the opportunity be afforded to the nominator to speak in favour of his candidates so long as exercising his discretion and that the Chairman is consistent between all the Candidates.

VI That a printed copy of the Charter Byelaws be made available to each Liveryman with the summons for Common Hall and that Liverymen be reminded each year of the electoral procedure in a suitably worded covering letter.[5]

Past Master Goldstein further suggested that two or three of the senior members of the Court should not offer themselves for re-election, but clearly this was not to their liking. The Committee pointed out that, as a body, the Court had no right anyway to nominate or recommend candidates, and so this should not apply. Although the resolution was approved, the age of the 'kingmaker' had not yet passed. Nothing changed. But in March 1970, Norman Hall set up a Committee under the Chairmanship of Alfred Anderson, Master in 1968, and made up solely of Past Masters, to resolve once and for all the question of the make-up of the Court and the route to Master. Under the system prevailing at the time those who lived long enough would eventually make it on to the Court by right of seniority, Buggins' turn', but this would take anything between twenty and thirty years, making the candidate at the very least fifty-five years old. Add the very minimum of another ten years to Master, then he would be too old 'for the enjoyment' of the position, and that good men would be lost if they joined the Livery late. With this in mind it was agreed that, in making nominations:

a The Court should ensure the continuity that there should, if possible, always be at least five and preferably eight (but not more) Past Masters on the Court.
b That an Assistant should not be nominated for the Court unless he intended, (other things being equal) and was considered in all ways suitable, to go forward to Master.
c That the nominees of members of the Court should be chosen on the advice of five selected members of the Court in close touch with the trade by seniority in the Livery, but having careful regard to the recommendations of (b) above.

This was accepted in principle by the Court, and the Livery was informed. There were, however, drawbacks to these proposals. With the ever-expanding Livery it was thought inappropriate to commit every member of the Court to remain until he 'had passed through the offices and served the office of Master', along with the limited period as Past Master 'to add experience to the Court's deliberations'.[6] As it stood, this would have committed the nominee to at least fifteen consecutive years of continuous service, which could have been 'inconvenient' to the Liveryman still active in business. Another point was that once on the Court, having made the undertaking to proceed to Master, the Assistant might be too embarrassed to leave should he subsequently change his mind.

It was all very well agreeing such matters in committee, but changing the system would be a great deal more difficult. With change on the cards but not fully implemented, at 'any other business' stage at the Common Hall of 1976 Douglas Noakes, then a Liveryman, raised the question,

of nominations to membership of the Court and quoted . . . [from] a letter on the subject in 1970 [see above]. He said obviously only a small proportion of members could become Master and suggested that the list of nominations each year should be circulated to Liverymen with the first notification of Common Hall meeting.[7]

Norman Hall, the Master and former Clerk, confirmed that the matter was very much in his mind, and that a committee to study the procedure would be appointed and a report made. While it was realised that the proposed new system would naturally have some transitional problems, as all those who were then on the Court had theoretically agreed to progress right through the system to Master and beyond, there were those (and one in particular) within the system who had no intention of going forward to Master. By not becoming Master and subsequently a Past Master, such individuals would therefore not be obliged to leave the Court when their turn came, which naturally upset the system.

At the Committee meeting held on 16 February 1977, Ronald Lickorish, then an Assistant but Master in 1982, proposed that the undertaking to go through to Master should be abolished. Further, it was suggested that 'newly elected Assistants should not be expected to be re-nominated for more than 2 or 3 years' unless they wished to go 'forward through the five offices of Warden and Renter Assistant to become Master'. This all seemed eminently sensible, as although there would be no accelera-tion to the office of Master, more Liverymen could in future serve on the Court as Assistants, and those who could not serve for fifteen consecutive years for business reasons could return 'to become Master at a later date' (this provision was later abolished). Thus by divorcing 'the initial election as Assistant. . .[from] the sub-sequent election to the senior offices' it became possible to 'bring to the Master's Chair a senior Liveryman who for good reason was unable to remain on the Court for the fifteen years or more'. For this to work, at least one Past Master had to 'decline his nomination', but to soften the blow it was proposed that Past Masters could attend the Court and speak, but would not be entitled to vote.

The system was further refined when it became mandatory to create two new positions on the Court annually – one from a Past Master (originally they stayed for five years, now reduced to four) and the other an Assistant who came off after two years. At a stroke the average age of the Court was almost halved, much to the envy of the other Livery Companies as the Butchers were the first to adopt such a system. The system was improved even further when it was decided that Past Masters might stay on the Court for a maximum of four, but usually three, years even if they served as Deputy Master. That way, at least one, on occasion more, Past Masters came off every year. Under the Charter, there have to be fifteen Assistants. With the new system, three (or in exceptional circumstances, four) Assistants are elected on to the Court from the Livery every year, but however many vacancies there are, only one of them goes the whole way through the system to Master.

Thus, with one of the largest Liveries in the City, at least three vacancies to the Court are created each year. Within this new system, every year there is one unfortunate Liveryman – the reserve. Once nominated, he or she is not eligible to go on to the Court afterwards, unless a vacancy is created during that year.

As a consequence of the first clause of the 1953 proposal (see page 153) 'that the nomination of candidates for election as Master, Wardens and Assistants is in the hands of the individual Liverymen', nominations for the Court, and even that of

Master, have, on occasion, come from 'the floor' – the Livery. At the end of the 1990s there were two such challenges, one for a position on the Court and the other for Master. In the end both nominations were defeated in the ballots among the Liverymen 'in accordance with The Charter and Bye Laws 2', and in both cases the Master's nominations carried the day.

The new Butchers' Hall, where those ground-breaking meetings on the Constitution took place, was completed in 1960. There was in the end not enough money to construct the fourth floor to accommodate the Beadle, so the original plans were amended to provide for three floors, a ground floor and basement. At last the Hall was ready for opening, although it would have been opened sooner but for the stone for the staircase in the hall being held up by a strike at the Portland Stone quarry. The Master was disappointed that the Duke of Edinburgh was not free to perform the ceremony as he was out of the country at the time. But the Duke did promise to 'visit in the autumn' – in fact he came to dinner in December that year. Instead, the honour went to the Right Honourable the Right Reverend Henry Montgomery Campbell, Bishop of London, who performed the ceremony on 4 May 1960 after a service at St Bartholomew-the-Great. The Butchers were delighted with their new Hall, and the Clerk wrote to the contractors, Griggs and Sons, 'informing them of the pleasure it had given members of the Court to see the work of rebuilding their Hall carried out with such care and high standard of workmanship'.[8]

Such a major undertaking was naturally a great drain on the company's finances, particularly as the balance of the building costs (those above the War Damage Claim) were interest-free credits and not straight gifts. It was decided that these would be paid off as and when finances allowed. The promissory notes (mostly for around £1,000) were placed in the deeply carved *Waka-huia*, literally translating as 'feather canoe' but actually a treasure box to hold the feathers of the *huia* bird and other items of great value. It was a gift from Sir Thomas Macdonald on his departure as High Commissioner for New Zealand in 1968. Just one 'treasure' or promissory note was drawn out each year, until they were all paid off. Often the longer the payment was left, the more difficult it was to trace the benefactor, that company having been taken over or amalgamated in the meantime. Besides the straight donations of cash, there were other gifts in kind, such as the Black Bean (*Castanospermum australe*) panelling in the Court Suite, a gift from the Government of Australia, while the New Zealand Government donated the panelling of Southland Beech (*Nothofagus menziesii*) in the Great Hall. The floor, presently acoustically covered up with a carpet, is of Canadian Maple (*Acer rubrum*). It has long been a tradition that the High Commissioners of Australia and New Zealand have been made Honorary Freemen of the Company on arrival at the Court of St James, in recognition of their country's trading links with the meat industry.

One of the prime movers in tidying up the loose ends of the building works and the refurnishing of the Hall was Jos Swain. Although a butcher by trade he had a great interest in, and knowledge of, antiques. He began by visiting the Whitefriars Glassworks, off Fleet Street, where the shards of the stained glass windows had been stored. They advised him that as they had 'no commercial value' they would dispose of them for him free, and not charge for their storage since 1940. Swain also found pieces of furniture, glass and ceramics, and suggested that they be donated by a company or individual to the Butchers' Hall. Messrs Armour & Co., Swift & Co and Herbert Woodley paid for the chandeliers. The Livery clubbed together to provide 115 dining chairs, each upholstered in 'butcher's blue' leather with the Company crest on the back. The fine white marble chimney-piece in the Court Suite was a gift of Howard Potts, and came from Henham Hall, the seat of the Earl of Stradbroke, when it was demolished in the early 1950s. The Earl wrote to the Master:

> it affords me much pleasure to know that the fireplace and chimney-piece out of the drawing room of my old house is in the [Butchers'] Hall . . . It was supplied by Messrs Benin Fils, 96 Rue Blanche, Paris and is shown in the firms accounts as Salon: *une cheminée en marbe blanc* £2,500 (*sic*).[9]

In fact Stradbroke translated the entry '2,500 *livres*' as pounds sterling, whereas at that time, 1794, there were 12 *livres* to the pound, so the chimney-piece originally cost £200. Even so this was a staggering sum, as the whole house, designed by James Wyatt, cost only £20,000 (estimate £12,000).

In the initial plans of the Hall, Howard Kelly the architect had allowed for a tapestry to fit into a plaster surround at the end of the Great Hall. Various suggestions were put forward for the design, and a tentative estimate of £1,700 was received from the Royal School of Needlework. When Liveryman Ronald Vestey heard of the plan he immediately agreed to present the Company with a tapestry in memory of his father, Sir Edmund Vestey, and uncle, Lord (William) Vestey (see Plate 5a). He commissioned Lucien Fleury, a French artist in his mid-thirties of the *Salon de la Jeune Peinture* school in Paris. His work has been described as 'figurative, but reveals a highly stylized approach to nature'.[10] Fleury was an ideal choice, having painted several very large murals and made a number of tapestry cartoons for both the Gobelin and Aubusson factories. The initial cartoon 'of the proposed layout which is to include St Paul's Cathedral, the Meat Market and the church of St Bartholomew-the-Great' was shown to the Court. It 'was also to have the Arms of Lord Vestey [left] and Sir Edmund Vestey [right] . . . inserted in the top corners with a suitable inscription at the bottom in memory of Lord Vestey and Sir Edmund'. In fact beside the penned stock in the foreground there are other Vestey landmarks, such as the tower of Liverpool Cathedral, 331 feet high, designed by Sir Giles

Gilbert Scott and paid for by them. The whole was surmounted by a butcher's blue border, inset with representations of the tools of the butcher's trade. Vestey commissioned the Aubusson factory to weave the tapestry, and once work had started various members of the Court made frequent excuses to go to Paris to report on its progress. After two years it was ready to be shipped to Butchers' Hall, but was delayed by a railway strike. At last it arrived in October 1964, and was hung in the appointed space by the local builder with large nails. James Brewster, chairman of the Fine Arts Committee, was horrified to see it sagging so badly and immediately called in an expert from the Victoria and Albert Museum, who was even more horrified. He arranged for the tapestry to be taken down, the large nail holes repaired, and re-hung properly on a batten. The next problem was that it hung nine inches short of the bottom. The factory was consulted, but they assured Brewster that it would stretch into place in two to three year's time. They were right, and it now fits perfectly in the space.

The Vestey tapestry is the largest in the City. In the days of heavy smokers it soon became yellowed, and various estimates were sought to have it cleaned. When all these proved prohibitively expensive, Aubusson were again consulted for advice. Their answer was simple and inexpensive – to take it off the wall, lay it on the floor, and clean it with an ordinary vacuum cleaner.

Just as the windows of the Great Hall were designed not to have stained glass panels, so it was originally intended that there should be no pictures on the walls either. Before the first bomb fell on the former Hall, there were sixteen portraits of former Masters hanging in the Banqueting Hall and half a dozen in the Court Room, with two more on the stairs. All these were first taken down and stored in the basement, then some were taken to the Crypt of St Bartholomew-the-Great for safe keeping with the remainder going to Herbert Jackman's farm at Chertsey in Surrey. After the War, Jackman mentioned that he wanted rid of the pictures. Some were hung, with the remainder stored in the basement of the Hall. With the new Hall and the no-pictures policy in the Great Hall, it was decided in 1965 'that Mr Swain be given the authority to contact any family who might be interested in having any of the old pictures in the basement otherwise to dispose of them',[11] after they were appraised by the Director of the City Corporation Art Gallery. It was not long before portraits reappeared between the fluted Corinthian columns.

One addition to the Great Hall that was very much in keeping with the overall decorative scheme was the wall plaque of the Company's Arms donated by John Brewster to commemorate his year as Master in 1983. It was created by Simon Timmins, then a student at the City and Guilds of London Art School, who was recommended by Sir Roger de Grey, then President of the Royal Academy. It was carved out of a single block of lime wood that had come from Germany and took four men to lift, but when Timmins had finished carving two years later he could lift the wedge-shaped plaque by himself. For many years a photograph of the massive plaque, painted and gilded, was used for the menu covers.

Another major piece of artwork came to the Company in 1975. It was an engraved glass screen, with two doors, and was donated by Thomas Borthwick & Co. as a memorial to members of the family in the meat trade who were Liverymen of the Butchers' Company. The screen was dedicated in particular to Algernon Borthwick, tragically killed while driving to Scotland with his wife when a lorry blew over on top of the car. At the time, Borthwick was Renter Assistant and so due to become Master the following year.

Sir John Borthwick, Chairman of Thomas Borthwick & Co., met the artist John Hutton at an exhibition at New Zealand House and admired his work that included a series of glass panels in Coventry Cathedral depicting Angels and Saints. After taking him to Butchers' Hall, Sir John commissioned Hutton to design and engrave a suitable glass screen to go across the reception hall. Hutton returned to New Zealand and started work. Unfortunately he died before completing the panels but his son, Warwick, who was also an artist and competent glass engraver well versed in his father's pioneering technique, took over with Sir John's encouragement, and completed the screen.

The two large glass panels of the screen depict the Four Seasons (see Plate 5a). The panel on the left shows a figurative Spring gazing expectantly past a flight of swallows to Summer, basking in the sun depicted with a stylised corona. Below, a few sheep are standing beside a host of trees, flowers and other vegetation. On the right hand side is Autumn, clasping the newly-harvested fruit, beside the figure of Winter, arms crossed and shivering against the cold. Above is a flight of departing swallows. Beside Autumn is a waning sickle moon, again surrounded by more New Zealand flora and a standing bull. The two small panels in the centre are in fact sliding doors. Here are etched the Arms of the Butchers' Company beside those of the Borthwick family, one large and two smaller cinquefoils (a heraldic design with five lobes in a circle, like a rose with five petals) below their crest, the *couped* head of a Moor on a helm. Below the Butchers' Arms is a New Zealand Tree fern, kowhai (*Sophora microphylla*), flax and clematis, while plants from Australia, the Australian wattle, bottlebrush, waratah (*Telopea speciosissima*), the floral emblem of New South Wales, and an orchid are below the Borthwick Arms. This rich mixture of plants represent the two countries where the Borthwicks had been trading in meat for well over a century. When the doors slide back the two sets of Arms fit exactly in the sun and the moon. During the renovations in 1996, it was decided to remove the screen to its present position in the reception hall, to create a passage behind and where it is seen to better advantage. The wall behind was plastered and polished, leaving a mottled sky-blue decorative effect as a suitable foil to the delicate engraving.

The Company of Butchers have shown themselves to be thoroughly progressive, not only with their building and decoration, but also in their practices. Although the Clerk, Norman Hall, had on the advice of the City Chamberlain been advised to interpret the 1749 Charter as the Company thought fit, there were certain aspects of it that made it unworkable. A number of amendments were mooted in 1951 and these were finally ratified in the 'Supplemental Charter of 23rd November 1968',[12] better known as the Queen Elizabeth II Supplementary Charter. It was basically the same as the 1749 Charter, but with just a few alterations to fit into the modern world. Where the original confined the Company's jurisdiction to the City of London and a two-mile radius, the 1968 supplement widened the scope to 'all other persons using or exercising the said Art or Mystery or who shall of their own pleasure' submit to the authority of 'the Master, Wardens and Commonalty of the Art or Mystery of Butchers of the City of London'. The date of Common Hall, the first Monday in September, was relaxed to any day (except Saturday or Sunday) from July to October so long as no more than fourteen months elapse between meetings. Further, it was no longer necessary for members of the Court to reside within the City of London and the two mile curtilage in order to be nominated for Master, Warden or Assistant. It also became allowable to be absent at Common Hall, with due reason, but the Oath of Declaration had to be made within two months of election. Finally, the 1749 Charter and the Supplement

> shall be in all things valid and effectual in law according to the true intent and meaning thereof and shall be taken, construed and adjudged in the most favourable and beneficial sense for the best advantage of the Company . . .[13]

And so the Queen Elizabeth II Charter brought the Company right up to date.

The Crown and the City of London have existed side by side for centuries, generally, but not always, in perfect harmony. The Butchers' Guild (and later Company) was often at variance with both, but in the main they have been true and loyal subjects of the Monarch. The Company's close association with the Royal Family was strengthened by the first visit of Queen Elizabeth The Queen Mother after her visit to Smithfield in 1968, during the Market's centenary year. The visit included not only a walk through the Market but a service in St Bartholomew-the-Great as well. As there was nowhere suitable in the Market for the Queen Mother to 'freshen up', Douglas Noakes, the Superintendent, suggested that she repair to Butchers' Hall. When she arrived at the Hall hot foot from the Market, she was clearly moved, for there she had been serenaded in the Grand Avenue under the clock by the whole staff of the market who, accompanied by a concertina, gave an entirely impromptu rendition of *If you were the only Girl in the World*. Some time after, on 24 March 1976, Queen Elizabeth was made an Honorary Freeman (No. 4839) of the Butchers' Company, staying to lunch. She was presented with an illuminated scroll of her

Freedom by the Master, Austin Kingwell, and she signed the original Golden Book. It was said that Queen Elizabeth had a great fondness for the Company and always referred to them as 'my butchers', and boasted that she was 'the only butcher in the Royal Family'.[14] She was also the only one within the Royal Family to be proud to be a Trades Union member, albeit an honorary one.

During the 1986 visit to Smithfield Market Queen Elizabeth had been made a *bumaree*. At Billingsgate a *bumaree* is a fishmonger who buys only part of a box of fish, but at Smithfield he is a self-employed porter, licensed by the Market. In her new role the Queen Mother was made to take the oath to abide by the rules that included promising not to use bad language and to notify any change of address within seven days. She was presented with an enamelled *bumaree* badge with her porter number 86, to coincide with her age. The shop steward was upset about the fact that, as the Market was then a closed shop, all *bumarees* had to be members of the Transport and General Workers Union. The solution was simple, and Queen Elizabeth was promptly given honorary union status. Afterwards she lunched at Butchers' Hall as guest of the Master, William Woolhouse. She was to return to Butchers' Hall three years later, this time bearing a silver and enamel *bumaree* badge from her Market visit, which became a prized possession. Queen Elizabeth can only have been delighted to see 'her Butchers' represented in a carriage drawn by two bay horses at her ninetieth-birthday celebrations on Horse Guards Parade and again at her hundredth birthday parade.

On her election as an Honorary Freeman, Queen Elizabeth was presented with 'a golden [and enamelled] brooch, set with diamonds, portraying the Arms of the Company',[15] a gift from the Master, Austin Kingwell. In fact it was one of two brooches made by Tessier, the other Kingwell gave to his wife, Jean, who later donated it to the Company for the wife of every subsequent Master to wear. When The Princess Royal was made an Honorary Freeman of the Worshipful Company of Butchers on 18 February 2003 she too was given a brooch. After the ceremony the Princess lunched at the Hall as guest of the Master, Michael Richardson. She was also a guest of honour at the dinner at the Mansion House in February 2005 to mark the 400th anniversary of the granting of the Royal Charter. This brooch appears in the two portraits of the two Royal Liverymen, Queen Elizabeth painted by Howard Morgan and donated by Henry Tattersall, Master in 1994, and the Princess Royal painted by Michael Noakes in 2005 and given to the Company by Michael Katz 'in memory of his wife, Mrs Ilse Katz, a Liveryman of this Company'.

There was a time when rivalry between the Livery Companies was marked with bloodshed and broken bones, but latterly it has been more good-natured. In November 1982 the Queen Mother was dining as a guest of the Worshipful Company of Fishmongers. Unfortunately she swallowed a fishbone (as she did again in

1993), and was admitted overnight to King Edward VII Hospital to have it removed from her throat. When she had fully recovered, the Clerk of the Butchers' Company, Commander Peter Brook-Cowan, wrote to his opposite number at the Fishmongers, E. S. Earl, with little regard for metre or scansion:

> The Company of Butchers
> Have heard, with disenchantment
> The fishy tale of object lodged in Throat
> Of their Honorary Freeman
> Queen Elizabeth the Queen Mum
> So we really thought we ought to pen this note
>
> To enquire if those purveyors
> Of that icthyoid pseudo protein
> –The Fishmongers is what we mean to say –
> Can show cause or let hindrance
> Why we should not warn the Queen Mum
> To stick to meat for protein, come what may.

The Fishmongers replied, with better rhyme, but equally bad metre:

> Oh! Purveyors of zoonic salmonosis,
> Cysticerus bovis and trichinosis,
> Actinobacillosis and cirrhosis,
> Caused by hepatic fascioliasis.
>
> Oh! vendors of a product cholerical,
> High in fat polyunsaturatedly
> Maximised by methods hormonical,
> That threaten to caponise belatedly.
>
> Remove the beam, wretched fleshmonger
> Before ere you slander the one pure
> Unadulterated food that longer
> May Her Gracious Majesty endure.
>
> Why! Fed on a diet entirely ichthyological
> Which nature provides in variety prodigal
> Your well beloved free lady oughta
> Survive to receive a telegram from her daughter.

Besides the Livery connection there is a very strong service link with the Royal Family. Queen Elizabeth was Honorary Air Commodore of 2600 Squadron, the Royal Auxiliary Air Force Regiment, when the Master, Frederick Jenkins, was asked if the Butchers would agree to adopt the unit. The matter was put to the next Court meeting, and on 2 June 1955 they were formerly affiliated. Soon after, Queen Elizabeth wrote to say how delighted she was with the arrangement. All began well. The Master and members of the Court dined in the Squadron Mess; the Officer Commanding and some of the officers dined in Hall. There was a drinks party for the other ranks. But no sooner had the reciprocal hospitality been completed than the Squadron was disbanded, and their trophies sent to the Hall to be stored, later to be lost in the burglary. That was the last anything was heard of the Squadron until it was reformed in 1959 as No. 1 Maritime Headquarters Unit, Royal Auxiliary Air Force, based at Northolt. As their involvement was purely social the Butchers agreed for the new Squadron to be affiliated, and invited the Officer Commanding, the Adjutant, and two other ranks to lunch. In early 1999, Air Chief Marshal Sir Michael Graydon, Chief of the Air Staff, presided at a No. 1 Maritime Headquarters Unit dinner at Butchers' Hall, with several other senior Air Marshals and Sir Adrian Swire, who had succeeded the Queen Mother as Honorary Air Commodore of the Squadron, among other guests. Being the only Royal Auxiliary Air Force Squadron in the London area, the idea was floated (and adopted in October 1999) that they should 'change designation and inherit the title of 600 (City of London) Squadron, Royal Auxiliary Air Force'.[16] The original 600 Squadron was formed in October 1925 and disbanded in 1957, and their colours laid up in the corner of the Lady Chapel of the Priory Church of St Bartholomew-the-Great. The veterans' Association still uses the church.

Amongst many other regiments and corps, The Princess Royal is Colonel-in-Chief of the Royal Logistic Corps, with whom the Butchers' Company also have a close link. The link is largely social, but they have provided their Corps of Drums to lead the Boar's Head ceremony (see page xii) and the other ranks to carry the facsimile head. In 2005, as a result of negotiations by the Clerk, Commodore Anthony Morrow, formerly Commodore Royal Yachts and Captain of HM Yacht *Britannia*, the Royal Navy is now also affiliated through HMS *Tyne*, a River Class offshore patrol vessel. The Company also has an affiliation with the Incorporation of Fleshers of Glasgow and are honorary members of the Company of Butchers of the City of York. Since the 1950s, the Company has been linked with the *Zunft zum Widder*, the Butchers of Zürich, Switzerland with whom they exchange periodic visits. In 2004, the Company presented the Butchers of Zurich with a cleaver, similar to the one used to summon the Court and Livery to any function. The tradition of 'ringing in' has been inherited from Smithfield Market where traditionally anyone who is late for work, or has a birthday, runs to their stall to the sound of the cleavers being struck, where 'it sounded like a peal of church bells'.[17]

As early as January 1958 it was recorded in the Minutes that 'Mr [G.J.] Dunsmore [Master in 1956] wanted an independent committee to look into the Company's affairs'. The motion was put to the Court but was defeated by fifteen to one, the Company being quite content with the way things were going. It was, however, to take another twenty years before their plight was recognised and the Court acted to put the Company back on a sound financial footing. By the early 1980s the Company was haemorrhaging money – there was an annual expenditure of '£50,000 just to run the hall, that is £200 a working day' before any improvements or repairs, sinking fund or indeed anything else. There was a move to sell the Hall and join up with the Farmers' Company who were casting about for a new hall. Negotiations dragged on for two years, but nothing came of it. Not for the first time the Company were dipping into capital to cover routine expenditure. Then in February 1983 the Minutes recorded:

> Past Master Terence Bonser said that he was extremely concerned about the financial position; things had changed radically and it was a worrying time; should not a high-powered specialist be invited to find out where the Company was going and where it should go; could not certain Liverymen give a hand? The Master said he paid every possible tribute to the House Committee who had been deeply concerned about the financial position; there were signs of stability but it might take another six months for results to show. P/M T.W.Bonser said that everybody on this Court had corporate responsibility and the success of the Hall depended on running a successful catering business; unless the catering business was profitable, the Company could not run this Hall.

Prophetic words. For years the catering had all been in-house, primarily for the benefit of the Company plus a very few outside engagements. Often the food was of questionable quality – at some dinners 'you could only tell if it was pork or beef if there was apple sauce or English mustard on the table'.[18] By the end of the 1970s, the Company had changed its policy and taken on an outside catering company, Thwaites and Mathews. When their catering manager was caught pilfering wine (two clocks had also disappeared while he was at the Hall), he was dismissed, and in April 1980 replaced by their employee Charles Boyd to head-out the small staff of a chef, wine steward and waitress – Helen York 'who had been there forever, followed by her daughter [Gladys Hillier] and granddaughter [Jane Chasney]'.[19] The Company liked Boyd, whom they considered had 'proved to be very competent'. When Thwaites and Mathews sold out to an American firm, two of their number set up on their own under the wing of Thomas Borthwick. The firm, Petergurr, after Peter Gurr one of the partners, was contracted by the Company to run all the catering within the Hall. All went well, initially, with the Butchers taking just 20 percent of the profits in exchange for providing the base for the catering company, the kitchens and dining room. The Court was delighted, and recorded in the Minutes the 'marvellous support of Mr Boyd'. Then came the bombshell – in January 1983 Petergurr went into voluntary liquidation. Fortunately Charles Boyd stayed on to work with Letherby and Christopher, another City catering firm who had stepped in to fill the void. But they were just a stop-gap solution to tide the Company over until something more permanent could be worked out. Mindful of Bonser's directive, some members of the Court clearly thought that something more radical was required to turn the Company's fortunes.

After much 'corridor discussion', three of the younger members of the Court led by Peter Moore approached Charles Boyd and the triumvirate suggested that he and his then wife Liz, an accountant, should form a catering company with the Butchers, not only to service the needs of the Livery, but also to promote their Hall for outside events. Boyd and his wife leapt at the proposal. He raised £10,000 capital from his father and sold his beloved TR6 sports car. The Butchers provided an office (the site of the present bin area), the fully-equipped kitchen, and the light equipment. They agreed in principle that Charles Boyd should have 40 percent of the new company, his wife Liz 20 percent and the Butchers' Company the remaining forty. The older members of the Court could not countenance the minority shareholding, but eventually the split was agreed. One hundred £1 shares were issued. As with the unpaid fine of one mark for practising as an adulterine guild (see page 6) in 1180, the Butchers' Company £40 share capital has also remained unpaid. The company was called Chester Boyd, Cheshire being the home of the Boyds, and two members of the Court are appointed each year to the Board.

Chester Boyd was launched at Common Hall 1983 when John Brewster was installed as Master and, as a joke, turkey was served at that first lunch. The arrangement with Chester Boyd worked well from the very beginning. The Butchers' Company provided a springboard for the joint company to expand, not only by using the Hall for their own and outside events, but for Chester Boyd to operate elsewhere in the City. Besides many of the other City Company functions, at the time of writing they provide the catering service at the Mansion House. Although the Company benefits financially from the arrangement through potential dividends and an annual licence fee, Boyd admits that he also profited, not least in drawing on the wealth of expertise within the Company in the preparation of meat, 'particularly their strong areas of salt beef, steak and kidney pudding and roast beef'.[20] Such was their success that after three years it was decided that the kitchens needed updating. By great good fortune, the time coincided with the abolition of the Greater London Council and the demise of County Hall. One kitchen there had never even been used, and Boyd was able to buy two vast cupboard ovens with hanging rails, large enough to cook a baron of beef, for £50 each, and a range for £200. By 2005, Chester Boyd was employing 120 full-time staff and had a turnover in excess of £10 million. It would be going too far to suggest that the arrangement was the turning point of the fortunes of the Butchers, but with a competent caterer, Butchers' Hall became one of the preferred places in the City to entertain.

While the Company was wrestling with financial and catering problems, they received another devastating blow. Over the 1981 Easter Bank Holiday, thieves broke in to Butchers' Hall through the kitchens. They first went to the wine cellar in the basement, kicking in the lower door panel but without taking anything. They then went on to the strong room at the end of the passage, forced their way in, and blew the door off the safe. It was a very professional raid, possibly conducted to order, as they knew exactly, to the troy ounce and date, what they would find, for the complete schedule of silver is detailed in Philip E. Jones' *The Butchers of London*.[21] What the thieves did not know was that the Master, David Cornell, was moving house that very weekend and had lodged his own silver in the Company vault. It was a devastating loss. The Court regalia, the Master's badge and chain, the Deputy Master's and the Renter Assistant's badges were all stolen, along with the Clerk's badge. The Master's badge was comparatively new, having been replaced during the Mastership of Jack Clarfelt in 1978. Much of the silver was Victorian and elaborate and of great sentimental value, having been donated by various Liverymen in recognition and appreciation of the Company. The earliest piece of plate owned by the Company at that time was a beaker engraved with the Butchers' Arms and foliage dated 1669, all the earlier silver having been sold in 1640 to fund Charles I's fight against Parliament (see page 65). Also taken was the replica beaker presented to the Company by Terence Bonser. Another notable piece was the cup presented by Nathanial Edwards in lieu of the fine for not serving as Master in 1724 (see page 95). One of the largest pieces to be lost was a fine early-nineteenth-century silver gilt cup and cover, with snake handles and a shell finial, that had been found and presented by Jos Swain. Another great loss was the 'Pitts Plate', a collection of Victorian silver gilt service from a Glasgow silversmith made in 1879–80, a gift from the widow of Horace Pitt, Master in 1905. There were flagons, plates, tazzas, candelabra, candlesticks, sugar sifters and the like that were 'truly wonderful. The service was used in the small Court Dining Room, and looked marvellous when lit by candlelight'.[22]

Amongst this sorry catalogue of stolen silver, there was just one particularly valuable piece which did survive: the original mace or Beadle's staff, presented to the Company by Jasper Stocker when Master in 1718. The replica, provided by James Blofeld, Master in 1928, was lost in the robbery. The whole matter was very suspicious. The Beadle's staff should obviously have been *in* the safe, particularly over a Bank Holiday weekend when the Beadle and his wife were away for the weekend. Yet it was found after the robbery outside the safe behind the open strong room door. However, the mace was the one piece of plate that was readily identifiable – it had been exhibited at the Festival of Britain in 1951, along with the Charles II beaker and the Nathanial Edwards cup – and could not possibly have been sold without being recognised for what it was. Also to survive the robbery was a silver cigarette box that was out of the Hall being repaired, and the sails and pieces of rigging that fell off the model of the *Flying Dutchman* as the thieves thrust it into a sack. These were mounted on a block of wood, a testament to the Butchers' loss. The thieves also left five Sheffield plate candlesticks behind; these were of lesser value, giving credence to the belief that they knew exactly what they were taking.

The silver was never recovered. Fortunately, it had been appraised by Tessier just two years before, so there was an accurate description and valuation. The reward of £5,000 offered for information leading to its recovery was increased by a further £2,000 from the loss adjusters. The burglary appeared on the BBC programme *Police Five*, but there was absolutely no response. Some thought that the haul went straight to the United States, others would have it that it went to the Soviet Union.

Also stolen from the safe was one of the Company's greatest treasures – the original Golden Book of the Worshipful Company of Butchers. The idea for a Golden Book was born of the Victory Banquet given by the Butchers at Guildhall in 1946. It was a great meeting of all the most senior representatives of the meat trade from both home and abroad. The moving force to create a Golden Book was Richard Christmas Hammett, Master in 1949, who over the next seven years was in constant discussion with the Royal College of Arms. The book was finally ready in 1953, in time for the Coronation. Within the pages were:

> the Company's Arms, the Royal Arms, the Arms of the City of London, with a preface for signature by the Lord Mayor . . . the donor's Arms . . . the Arms of all the Meat Producing Countries of the World and finally, a series of open pages for signature from time to time as suitable subjects suggested themselves.[23]

Hammett died before the project was finished, and it was taken over by Jos Swain. When it was at last finished, it was declared a triumph. The front and back were covered in red silk-velvet. The silk came from the same silk-farm in Lullingstone in Kent as did the silk for the heavily-embroidered Purple Robe of Estate worn by the Queen at her Coronation. The corners, spine and edge embellishments were in heavy silver gilt which, like the Company's Arms in gold and enamel that adorned the front, were made by Garrard & Co, the Royal jewellers. When it was placed in the cabinet in the Hall the book rested on a golden damask cushion, covered by an embroidered purple velvet cloth. The first signatures in the book were those of the new Queen, followed by the Duke of Edinburgh. The Duke of Norfolk, in his capacity as President of the Smithfield Club, Richmond Herald, the High Commissioners of Australia and New Zealand, the Ambassadors of Uruguay and the Argentine Republic, and Major Lloyd George, Minister of Food in charge of 'Derationing' all signed the book. There were also sections 'to record the names of Masters and Deputy Masters of the Company, Clerks to the Company, Honorary Freemen and distinguished visitors'.

The insurance claim for the robbery was finally settled at £107,000, which was immediately ring-fenced and invested pending new purchases. One of the first projects was to reinstate the Golden Book, which was eventually achieved with a donation from Liveryman Frank Burton. Like the original, the replacement was 'copied from the Bath Book commissioned by George III listing members of the Order of the Bath and their coats of Arms'. After the pages devoted to the development of the Company's Coats of Arms, the Masters, Deputy Masters, Clerks, distinguished guests, Honorary Freemen and the like are faithfully recorded in its five hundred and seventy-one pages. The first signature, with her Royal Arms, is that of Queen Elizabeth The Queen Mother when she visited the Hall in 1986.

A Silver Committee was set up under David Cornell to decide how the money should be spent. There was, however, a faction within the Court who thought that the insurance money should be diverted to other areas within the Company. But the Committee stood firm. They began by replacing the badges of office; Tessier, who had the experience and submitted the best quotation, were given the order. Then, after the safe had been repaired, the Livery was asked if they had any silver that they would care to donate. Some pieces came from outside the Company, like the 'Gadsden rose bowl', given by Lady Gadsden 'to commemorate her husband's year [1979] as Lord Mayor'.[24] But the real objective of the Silver Committee was to replace the lost plate. They began by discussing whether to replace the Company's silver with what they had had in the past, mostly Victorian pieces, or to go for something contemporary. It was decided that it would be unsatisfactory to mix the two, and that it would be better to 'go for modern on the basis that it reflected the thinking of the Court to be in the Twentieth Century'.[25] The Committee began by commissioning four loving cups from Grant Macdonald, a London silversmith specialising in City Livery Company commissions and whose work David Cornell had admired. Macdonald, who trained at the Central School of Art and the Sir John Cass College, had set up his workshop in Bear Street, Southwark (see page 51). He was steeped in the traditions of the City through the Barbers, his family's Company where he too was Master (in 2002), and also the Goldsmiths' Company (where he was a Warden in 2005). This background meant that he fully understood the practicalities of Company plate, in particular the loving cup. He came up with a number of drawings for the Committee's approval, even making a model of the preferred version. The design was radical with three handles placed below the bowl, which meant that the cup was well-balanced and made it much easier to pass from one to another. Two of the lids have the Company's Arms set within a finial, a bull and a sheep are on the other two. The Butchers' Arms are on two of the bowls, with scenes of Smithfield Market set in a silver gilt frieze on the other two. The price was £6,500 for the four cups. The final touch was a deep, curved bezel so that the lid is easily replaced as it is passed on. These were infinitely better than the Royal Wedding Commemorative Cup that 'was used for the first time at the Ladies Dinner [and] was [found] difficult to drink from . . . it was thought that it should go on permanent view in the Hall somewhere'.[26] A pair of important loving cups were presented to the Company by William Woolhouse, Master in 1984, to commemorate Queen Elizabeth The Queen Mother's ninetieth birthday. They are very fine and are decorated to reflect Queen Elizabeth's interests, with bulls' head castellated finials and a moulded frieze showing galloping horses, with her Arms and a representation of Glamis Castle engraved on one cup, the Company's Arms and Smithfield Market on the other.

After the badges, the Master's chain and these loving cups were purchased, the Committee decided to slow down on new commissions. Grant Macdonald has since made many other pieces for the Company, including a set of four candelabra, two of them being donated by Michael Katz, and an ornate pepper and salt grinders that features the winged bull of St Mark. Another particularly fine pair of candelabra were presented by Lord Vestey. Other pieces have been donated over the years. When the Queen Mother visited the Hall in 1997 Michael Katz, the Master, presented her with a silver port decanter which he had commissioned from Grant Macdonald to mark the occasion, whereupon 'Her Majesty graciously requested that it remained with the Company, albeit, perhaps, a trifle reluctantly'.[27] Another special feature of that visit was the 1900 Madeira, the year of Queen Elizabeth's birth, drunk in her honour. In the same vein as the Company holding onto its presents, the pen-holder presented to her by David Franks, Master during her visit in 1986, was taken back and held in the Hall 'for safe keeping', just like the silver gavel presented by Graham Sharp when he was Master in 1989 (uniquely, Sharp went on to become Clerk between 1997 and 2003). With the high interest rates on offer at that time, the Silver Committee was able to spend the interest and maintain the capital at £110,000. The sum was later taken over into the general funds, monies being made available to the Fine Arts Committee to purchase relevant pieces as and when they come up for sale, as agreed by the Court.

To do something once is an occasion, to do it twice it becomes a tradition. Starting with the Boar's Head Ceremony (see page xii), the Butchers' Company have, over the years, built up their particular traditions within the City of London. When one of their own is Lord Mayor, as with Roger Cork in 1996, or even

Thomas Challis in 1852, then their role in City affairs becomes even more special, such as entering a Butchers' float for the Lord Mayor's Show. Even before the Lord Mayor elect is sworn in, he breakfasts with the Butchers' Company after the rehearsal for the Lord Mayor's Show. Another breakfast is customary after his visit to Smithfield Market sometime in the summer. The Company's major social event of the year is the Ladies Banquet in the Hall, also attended by the Lord Mayor. The Lady Mayoress returns to the Hall with a lunch in her honour hosted by the Company.

When the Beadle, Charles Woods, arrived at Butchers' Hall, he moved into a prefabricated building on the roof with his wife and family. It was not ideal, but it did at least provide accommodation so that the Beadle could live, if not *in* the Hall, at least *on* the Hall, and Mrs Woods could create a roof garden. The Company valued Woods' services highly. After an interim Beadle, he was replaced by John Clarke and, when he retired, the prefabricated building was used for storage until well past its useful life. Clearly by 1995 the whole structure of the Hall needed to be rethought. The original concept of the Hall was to replace its predecessor, very much as a gentleman's London club, but over its first twenty years the new Hall had become a highly successful venue for commercial functions. But nothing is forever, and it was realised that, where they had once led the field as a desirable venue they were now lagging behind other Companies offering a similar service. The kitchens needed updating, there was no air-conditioning, and the noise from the traffic could be clearly heard in all the rooms for hire. Even more important was the lack of proper offices for the staff.

The original office was on the ground floor, the site of the present Gunner Mallion library. It is a small room, yet it housed four and on occasion five members of staff. One particular feature of the Butchers' Company is that they engender great loyalty, and with it longevity of service. One Assistant Clerk, Frank Veal, died in harness aged 85, another, Bob Barron, hoped to beat his record, but died aged 83. Mrs Hilda Gregory began as a secretary and in her twenty-year service became Assistant Clerk. She trained up Lindsey Jones so well that it was a 'seamless movement' when Mrs Jones took over from her. In 1997, Lindsey Jones was promoted to Assistant Clerk 'a distinction well deserved recognising her knowledge, competence and popularity within the Livery'.[28] She retired in 2005 after twenty year's service. In a similar manner Commodore Anthony Morrow was eased into his position as Clerk in 2003.

The House Committee had been discussing the various improvements to the Hall for years, but nothing had been done as it was not known if the foundations would take an extra floor. When Master (in 1992), Fred Mallion commissioned a survey of the whole building, and it was found that it could indeed support a roof extension. By 1995, the problem was properly addressed, and a separate Committee under Douglas Noakes, Master in 2001, was formed to see the project through to completion. Plans were drawn up to make a 'comprehensive and brand new self-contained catering area at 3rd floor level',[29] and for a whole new fourth floor for offices under a mansard roof. There was also a suggestion that the Master should have a flat on the top floor to replace the pokey room he occupied behind the kitchens. Apart from the space needed for this, however, having the building occupied would also have caused a greater problem with the fire regulations. In the end, a small flat was bought for the Master's use in Spencer Heights, a modern block in Bartholomew Close. Then there were other smaller projects, like swapping over the strong room and the wine cellar.

The whole job, including new air-conditioning and secondary glazing, was put out to tender. Finally, the estimate of £1,018,444 (plus fees) was accepted from the building firm of Overbury. There was much opposition to the scheme from within the Court. It was the time of the BSE crisis and a jittery economy. But in the end the Committee prevailed. Funding, always a byword where the Butchers' building plans were concerned, posed the next problem. An appeal was launched by John Jackman, Master in 2002, as Chairman of the Management and Finance Committee, to raise £1.5 million for the improvements. The money was raised 'in two or three months'.[30] Later, the Committee set about building up the liquid reserves of the Company, and almost reached their target of £1 million by the Millennium. Every donor's name was entered in the Golden Book (three anonymously, 'one so that his wife did not know'[31]). Those who gave 'a substantial sum' had a room named after them, thus the Committee Room on the top floor was named after David Walker, while the General Office became known as the 'Michael and Ilse Katz Suite'. Other donors included Bernard Matthews and George Adams (Master in 1997) who had the Reception hall and the old Master's office respectively named after them. The Library was called the Gunner Mallion Library, Mrs Ernest Gunner providing much of the money in memory of her husband, Master in 1967. The funding for the restoration of the Great Hall came from Lord Vestey and his cousin, Edmund Vestey, and is marked by a discreet plaque. They also paid to have the Vestey tapestry properly illuminated.

It was essential that the works be carried out as quickly as possible. The Hall was cleared, the contents stored, and work began on 31 May 1996. The work completed, Alderman Roger Cork formally re-opened Butchers' Hall on 5 October 1996, a mere eighteen weeks later, when he also unveiled a stained glass window of his Arms to celebrate his election as Lord Mayor. The structure and fittings were seen as a success and the space provided by the new top floor deemed a godsend. But that was only phase one, as it was left as little more than in builder's finish. For the redecoration of the Hall another four-man Committee was appointed, under a

'Chairman with proper vision in only one eye and two of the Committee colour-blind'.[32] Notwithstanding these optical handicaps, the Committee set to and appointed the Kingston Design Group to come up with a radical decorative scheme. There was much 'anxiety expressed in the early stages about the change of style envisaged, but in the end it was accepted as bold, imaginative, forward-looking and definitely different without losing the reference to the past'.[33] It appears that the greatest discussion of all raged around which way up the arms should go on the new, blue carpet in the reception hall. The Company had been presented in the past with two large carved and gilded wall mirrors, but it was decided that they did not fit into the new décor and they were sold at Sotheby's. The money was used to buy an impressive pearlware jug with the polychrome Arms of the Company and the legend 'William Pain of Child Ockford' (today's Childe Okeford) Dorset and dated 1787, along with a fine painting of cattle by Thomas Sydney Cooper, a mid-Victorian artist. The companion picture of a group of Herdwick sheep was presented to the Company by Robin Pooley, Master in 1987, in memory of his father W. Melville Pooley.

Part and parcel of the physical expansion of Butchers' Hall was the increased responsibilities of the Company, as they were soon to take over the administration of other related charities, most notably the Butchers and Drovers Charitable Institution, and the administration and membership of the Worshipful Company of Butchers' Guild, the voice of the industry principally charged with the responsibility for education.

The whole *raison d'être* of first the Guild, then the Company, of Butchers was to preserve standards in their trade. To this end, they began with the rigorous training of the apprentice butcher. But clearly, with the changing practices of the trade in the twentieth and twenty-first centuries, a more scientific approach was needed. The technical education for the meat industry began with the meeting of a practical meat trader, the farsighted Richard Christmas Hammett, Master in 1948 and 1949, and the educationalist W. H. Nevill, principal of a technical college in Battersea, South London. Nevill inaugurated the first Meat Trades Classes in 1923, and became the first principal of the Smithfield Meat Trades Institute, then housed in Saffron Hill. In 1948 it became The Smithfield College of Food Technology (within the National College of Food Technology) under Dr Mountfield. As one of his first acts as principal, Mountfield attended a Court Meeting, 'looking for ten scholarships of £60 per annum for three years' and to fund the examinations with an annual contribution of £140 towards their cost. He also hoped that 'the Company would take a leading part in the National College'.[34] The matter was discussed at length and it was Jos Swain who proposed that a single scholarship be funded by the members of the Court contributing 2 guineas each for seven years, the shortfall to be made up from the Livery, although they did keep a watching brief on the

Smithfield College, awarding the prizes of silver and silver gilt medals to the successful students and later holding the prize-giving in the Hall. In June 1948, an Education
Committee was established within the Butchers' Company.

By 1946, there were various bodies representing the meat industry, but it was in
part due to the influence of the Butchers' Company that the Institute of Meat was
founded to manage the practical and theoretical training in those immediate post-war
years, and to speak for the industry. The Institute of Meat also set the standards, as well
as conducting the examinations and awarding the coveted Certificates of Merit at
various grades. The emphasis was on technology, hygiene and skills in meat cutting
and the preparation of meat products. By the end of the 1980s, however, the Institute
was becoming outdated. Furthermore, the food retail industry was changing very
fast, with the supermarket taking over as the major driving force. Many functions
of the butcher, along with most sausage and pie production, were being transferred
away from the point of retail sale back to the specialist cutting plants that could
cope with mass production, weighing and price-labelling of meat. The smaller
abattoirs were giving way to huge modern plants which could cope with the
volume demanded by the supermarkets, and could afford to comply with ever more
demanding European Union regulations. This was a fast-changing industry.

There was clearly an urgent need for modernisation to meet the industry's require-
ments. The cudgels were taken up by some of the Council Members of the Institute,
the likes of Philip Proven, Colin Cullimore and Douglas Brydges, all Liverymen,
but it was Fred Mallion, a former pupil, lecturer and finally Principal of the Smithfield Institute who was the prime mover in the educational field within the Company. Largely through his energies the Meat Training Council was established in
1991, and it became the entirely new and independent organisation that set new
standards 'and spread the skills base across the whole industry, from the farm gate
to the retail shelf'.[35] In addition, the awards were reformed to fit in with the
Government's new National Vocational Qualifications (NVQs), and further education went on to degree level. Lord Vestey was appointed chairman of the MTC,
with the council members coming from the Butchers' Company. It was funded
partially by them and partially by the Meat and Livestock Commission. It was
considered a great success, and it went on to become the model for the whole food
industry.

What was left of the Institute of Meat continued as a professional body working
in tandem with the Meat Training Council and the Butchers' Company. But its
main purpose had been hived off, so when the Company took over its membership
activities in 2000, largely through the direction of a team led by John Edkins, Renter
Assistant in 2005, the ailing Institute of Meat was re-launched as the Worshipful
Company of Butchers' Guild, with the remit to 'regenerate the activity of the
Institute and to raise its profile significantly within the industry'.[36] Then in May

2004 there was an even more significant breakthrough when the functions of the Education Committee of the Butchers' Company were merged with those of the Guild. It was a splendid marriage. Butchers' Hall was obviously 'the place for the housing and provision of one professional and educational body for the entire industry'.[37] The two bodies complemented each other perfectly. While the Education Committee was a reactive body, responding with funds generated by the Educational Charity Investments as and when the need arose, the Guild was a membership body whose aim was to be more pro-active' and to 'create projects with professional industry interest'.[38] Thus the pooling of the resources and experience meant that 'these two bodies would be able to respond to the need for effective delivery of programmes of great interest to members, whilst providing a watchful eye on the future of the Meat Training Council and other educational opportunities'.[39] When John Edkins stepped down as Chairman, he was succeeded by Douglas Brydges, who by then was also President of the Meat Training Council.

While the Worshipful Company of Butchers' Guild had little or no funds to spare, the old Education Committee had built up a useful portfolio. Up to the late 1950s there was no specific education fund. When the well-liked liveryman George Lonsdale died in his early fifties, an appeal was launched in his name, and a little over £7,000 was raised to start the educational fund. Ernest Gunner left £10,000 to the Company's Education fund, with the same amount to the Institute of Meat Education Foundation. But as the Institute was scaling down its activities these funds, amounting to some £67,000, were amalgamated with the Lonsdale Memorial Fund, as the Company's own education fund was then called. Another very considerable contribution was the Ilse and Michael Katz Trust of £100,000. In 1998 this combined fund was renamed The Worshipful Company of Butchers Education Charity. Each year it supports a wide range of projects, as well as funding research. It sponsors youth competitions, both national and international, and holds seminars, as well as funding visits at home and abroad. It also supports existing schemes, such as those offered by other charities like the Prince's Trust. The Charity also funds various six month secondments to such places as Canada, a scheme initially set up by Ernest Gunner (Master in 1967) who had considerable pork trading interests there. Other students might go to an abattoir in Scotland for three months, and for a time there were scholarships for students to spend three to six months with a German butcher to gain valuable Continental experience.

Outside the Court Room is a print of a typical butcher's shop of the early nineteenth century. As a print it is not especially remarkable, but the subject is interesting as the shop is in New Bond Street (on the site of Asprey, the London jewellers), and it was owned by William Giblett, a notable figure who was three times judge and a steward of the Smithfield Club. His lasting legacy, however, was that he founded the Butchers' Charitable Institute in 1829. By the turn of the century the charity had grown in stature and funds and when the charity set up to help drovers became obsolete (after the final two they were supporting died at the turn of the nineteenth century) the Drovers' Charity amalgamated with the Butchers' Charitable Institution. This combined charity owned a row of almshouses in Walham Green, now a salubrious part of Fulham but formerly a run-down part of South West London, called 'Smoothfield'. They were intended for retired butchers and their dependants, but by 1921 the almshouses had been sold and the residents moved out to Hounslow. For many years the charity had been administered by a committee and a secretary, but when he retired in 1997 Douglas Noakes, who became the President of the BDCI in 2003, suggested that the Butchers' Company should take over the management for a fee. It was an inspired move. Noakes was also President of the Fishmongers and Poulters Institution, formed in 1835 to 'look after needy colleagues in their trade', and he brought them into the same scheme. Naturally, there is much cross-pollination between the Company and these Charities, and the Livery is conspicuous in its support for their functions.

The Company engaged a full-time administrator, first Martyn Craddock then Roy Sully, to look after all aspects of these charities. The brief was also to manage the Butchers' Company General Charities, formed in 1969 out of all the separate trusts, to which had been added various appeals over the years. When the Butchers' charities were first founded, grants tended to go to individuals in need who were directly connected with the trade, but the policy later changed to giving lump sums of money to other charities, generally those connected with the City and the surrounding boroughs. This support is wide and varied, and ranges from a number of children's charities to the Guildhall School of Music.

The Butchers continue in their support of the Smithfield Club (since 1960 the Royal Smithfield Club) as ever they have in the past. The cross-pollination has been strengthened by members of the Court of the Butchers' Company also serving on the Council of the Club – a prime example being Terence Bonser, Master in 1973, serving variously in every office in the Club including President in 1979. But his contribution to the Club, as indeed to the Butchers' Company, went far further than a mere titular head. Along with Ernest Gunner, Master in 1976 and President of the Club in 1981, they 'steered the carcase competitions on a course that set standards which became the model for organisations throughout the industry, with regard the judging process and attractive presentation'[40]. Another Master of the Butcher's Company (in 1963), farmer and Vice President of the Club was A. W. (Bill) Hedges. Apart from his contribution to the Council over forty-eight years, it was as an exhibitor that he is also remembered, winning the Pig Supreme Champion with a pair of Welsh in 1976. His daughter, Patricia Dart, one of the few women on the Council, serves as a carcase steward. Roger Moore, Master in 1998, is another active member of the Royal Smithfield Club, as is Lord Vestey, President in 1986 and 87, whose company, Dewhurst, often bought the Supreme Champion of the Show. Many of the meetings of the Club are held at Butchers's Hall, where the three Kings' Cups won outright by J. J. Cridlan are on display, a permanent reminder of the special relationship between Club and Company.

The 400th anniversary of the granting of the first Royal Charter to the Company of Butchers was celebrated throughout 2005. At the '400th Charter Banquet' at the Mansion House on 17 February, an appeal to raise £400,000 to boost the Company's General Charity, while also benefiting two specific charities (the Treloar Trust, for the treatment and training for 'the little crippled children of London', and St Bart's and London Childrens' Trust) was launched by the Master, Colin Cullimore. A new stained glass window was commissioned from the artist Mel Howse, a Freeman of the Worshipful Company of Painter-Stainers, for the reception hall. In keeping with the Butchers' modern outlook, the design was contemporary (see Plate 7). According to the artist, it 'conveys the meeting of minds with a common goal, a forum for the exchanging of experiences especially whilst entertaining. The shaking of hands repeated across the table conveys the continuous process of development within the industry'. On a more traditional theme, Patrick Hawes was commissioned to compose a new anthem to the words of *Psalm* 8, adapted by the Master.

In the thousand or more years between the feasts held in the first Butchers' Hall in Farringdon and that great Butchers' dinner, the butcher's trade has changed out of all recognition, the transformation escalating through the last one hundred years and accelerating even faster in the last twenty years. Though obviously the same animals, modern livestock bear little resemblance to the scrawny beasts slaughtered in the streets of medieval London. The first and (so far) last Butchers' Halls share only the name – one a draughty wooden building, the other a five story modern building of concrete, steel and glass, which is both the administrative hub of the Company's hugely expanded activities and interests and the setting that keeps the Company alive. While the members of that original Butchers' Guild were drawn solely from within the City of London, the present members of the Company of Butchers are drawn from all over the United Kingdom, even from Europe. But notwithstanding these natural differences between the original Guild of Butchers and the present Worshipful Company of Butchers, over a thousand years apart, they have the same, fundamental, rationale – to honour their Guild, to protect and guard the high standards of their ancient trade, and to promote fellowship within their organisations.

The role of the Worshipful Company of Butchers is every bit as important today as ever it was in the past, but unlike the Worshipful Company of Fishmongers, who still appoint and pay for inspectors in Billingsgate Market, the Butchers have long been released from such workaday duties in the meat markets. Nor do they have a direct role within their trade, like the Goldsmiths who still hallmark items made from precious metals, or the Gunmakers who test and mark small arms gun barrels. Although the Worshipful Company of Butchers no longer has any direct control over their trade, being apolitical, they are from time to time requested to 'warn, influence and advise' on matters within the meat industry. With the wealth of experience and knowledge they have to draw on, from all aspects of the trade, it is sage advice. As with the Mystery Guild of Butchers, the Company is equally dedicated to preserving the standards of their trade, not least by investing in education, the successor to the rigorous apprenticeships of the past.

It is not just the rare roast beef at the Court and Livery luncheons that makes them invariably oversubscribed, but the opportunity that such gatherings afford for members and their guests to meet on common, neutral, ground to foment friendships and exchange ideas. The Company is made up of many different factions of the trade – retailers, wholesalers, importers, slaughterers and the like – often factions at complete variance one with another, yet within the Company they are as one. The fellowship of the Butchers' Company is as strong as ever it was when those first few butchers gathered together to form the Guild and to feast in honour of St Luke, their Patron Saint. The Butchers still have that strong sense of giving, and care for their own and the less fortunate. The bonds of good fellowship extend to the golf links, the shooting field, the sailing waters, the green turf of Sandown Racecourse and the green baize of the bridge table.

There can be few trades that have changed so much over the centuries as that of the butcher. No sooner was one practice established, or a taste accepted, than it was replaced by the next development in their business. The drover disappeared when livestock was transported by ship and rail, then imported livestock was replaced by refrigerated carcases. Then came the rise of the carcase butcher in the nineteenth century, followed by the chains of butcher's shops in the twentieth, until they too, along with many an independent retailer, were superseded by the supermarket. Yet by the very nature of their trade, butchers are practical people and the Butchers' Company is, as it always has been, proud that over 95 percent of its members are still connected with the trade. By the nature of their trade too, there is little room for sentimentality, and so they move easily with the times and survive. Although the Worshipful Company of Butchers naturally values its traditions, this pragmatic trait makes for a thoroughly modern company, yet *plus ça change, plus c'est la même chose* – the more it changes, the more it stays the same.

3a. HM Queen Elizabeth The Queen Mother with the Master, Alfred Anderson, and Mrs Anderson, during her first visit to utchers' Hall. The Hall provided a useful respite between a tour of Smithfield and the service at St Bartholomew-the-Great, 1968.

3b. HM Queen Elizabeth The Queen Mother after she was made an Honorary Freeman of the Company in 1976, largely at the nstigation of the Master, Austin Kingwell. He is flanked by the Beadle, Charles Woods, and the Clerk, William Collins.

14a. Students in a cutting and boning class at the Smithfield Institute, 1929. The Company has always supported training programmes to ensure excellence within their trade since the very first apprenticeships in the 13th century.

14b. The decorated Boar's Head, 1968, that was actually carried through the streets of the City before the practice was banned for health and safety reasons.

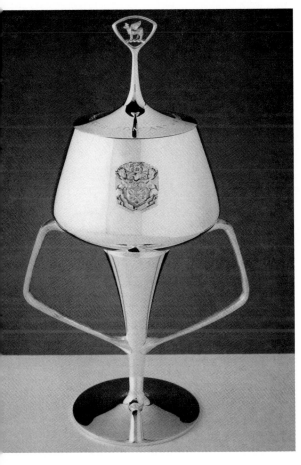

15a. One of four Loving Cups designed and made by Grant MacDonald after the Company's silver was stolen in 1981. It was decided to commission contemporary pieces rather than to recreate the stolen plate.

15b. One of a pair of The Queen Mother Loving Cups presented by the Master, William Woolhouse, to commemorate her 90th birthday.

15c. HRH The Princess Royal signing the Golden Book after her election as an Honorary Freeman, 2003, with the Master, Michael Richardson.

16. Butchers' Hall, 2005. The Butchers' Company has always been innovative and forward-thinking as seen by Howard Kelly's radical design of 1957. The planned top storey was finally added in 1996.

Appendix I

Masters of the Worshipful Company of Butchers
1605 – 2004

The year denotes the date of election at Common Hall.

1605 Francis Greene (16 September–18 October)
1605 Henry Bowers
1606 Robert Warde
1607 Francis Green
1608 William Pawle
1609 Henry Bowers
1610 Robert Warde
1611 William Cleaver
1612 Thomas Mouse
1613 William Pawle
1614 Robert Greenly
1615 Robert Brookbanke
1616 William Cleaver
1617 William Pawle
1618 Philip Greenly
1619 Robert Clements
1620 William Pawle
1621 Philip Greenly
1622 William Parker
1623 Robert Clements
1624 Robert Brookbanke
1625 William Parker
1626 John Oswyn
1627 Robert Clements
1628 Samuel Stone
1629 Benjamin Blackboragh
1630 Edwyn Fisher
1631 Robert Clements

1632 George Stretton
1633 William Woodfield
1634 Thomas Wight
1635 William Scrugges
1636 William Stretton
1637 George Stretton
1638 Thomas Wight
1639 William Scrugges
1640 John Levett
1641 William Ardington
1642 Michael Phillips
1643 John Levett
1644 William Forniss
1645 Michael Phillips
1646 – 1670 records missing
   although the following
   were all Past Masters:
   William Nevill
   Thomas Thompson
   Richard Packe
   Mr Pert
   Richard Hodgekins
   Edward Aylett
   John Virtue
1671 John Kirbey
1672 Edward Aylett
1673 Richard Hodgekins
1674 Edward Aylett

1675 Thomas Tympson
1676 William Payne
1677 Alexander James
1678 William Holmes
1679 Edward Pick
1680 Theodore Nicholls
1681 Francis Follansby
1682 Thomas Judd
1683 Roger Harris
1684 Edward Newins
1685 Edward Newins
1686 Roger Dixey
1687 John Jewkes (to February 1688)
1688 John Sergeant (March to October)
1688 Samuel Wakelin
1689 Samuel Trowell
1690 George Crowder
1691 John Campion
1692 John Jeffries
1693 James Benn
1694 Henry Wrigley
1695 James Hubbard
1696 George Clipson
1697 Thomas Roberts (October–November)
1697 William Quilter
1698 John Chilham
1699 Thomas Jenkins
1700 William Fryer
1701 John Browne
1702 Richard Smythe
1703 Samuel Pigeon
1704 Isaac Holford
1705 Thomas Warner
1706 Thomas Hemley
1707 Lawrence Martin
1708 Robert Roger
1709 Samuel Tomlinson
1710 Joseph Mallard
1711 John Paine
1712 Edward Winston

1713 William Fuller
1714 William Ileford
1715 Geoerge Crowder
1716 Read Vanner
1717 William Kemmis
1718 Jasper Stocker
1719 Thomas Lee
1720 Richard Crockett
1721 Joseph Mallard
1722 Lawrence Tinley
1723 William Ileford
1724 William Elliott
1725 Ingles Prescott
1726 Edward Markham
1727 John Thorpe
1728 Thomas Bourne
1729 Thomas Bourne
1730 Josais Oately
1731 Benjamin Fielder
1732 William Barnett
1733 Francis Phillpott
1734 Samuel Cobley
1735 Marmaduke Hornby
1736 Richard Goater
1737 Edward Rogers
1738 George Lewin
1739 William Tompkinson
1730 Charles Dolley
1741 Geroge Carter
1742 –
1743 Thomas Shadd
1744 William Rolfe
1745 William Rolfe
1746 William Rolfe
1747 William Rolfe
1748 Thomas Shadd
1749 Thomas Shadd
1750 –
1751 –
1752 John Olney

1753 Samuel Saunder
1754 Edward Kibble
1755 James Holland
1756 William Pearson
1757 Joseph Gamble
1758 John Furniss
1759 William Furley
1760 William Gifford
1761 Thomas Orton
1762 John Pantree
1763 Christopher Maynard
1764 John Collier
1765 Benjamin Bentley
1766 John Stogdale
1767 Edward Worth
1768 William Hickling
1769 John Avery
1770 Robert Arrowsmith
1771 John Pocklington
1772 William Worth
1773 John Cheese
1774 Thomas Dalby
1775 James Halliday
1776 Thomas Pocklington (died)
1777 William Looseley (March–September)
1777 James Druce
1778 Thomas Cox
1779 William Lindus
1780 Thomas Love
1781 George Scrivener
1782 John Lunn
1783 Devereux Wall
1784 Thomas Seear
1785 William Tyler
1786 John Ackland
1787 Thomas Haynes (died)
1787 Richard Wace
1788 James Cook
1789 Aaron Bateman
1790 Thomas Watts

1791 Richard Markham
1792 William Francis
1793 James Horwood
1794 John Fisher
1795 Thomas Dalby junior
1796 William Parnell
1797 Charles Fisher
1798 James Boote
1799 Jeramiah Radborn Hewer
1800 Peter Mellish
1801 John Dryland
1802 William Mellish
1803 Henry Fountain
1804 John Stepto
1805 Thomas Slaughter
1806 Henry King
1807 Robert Hulme
1808 Thomas Wace senior
1809 William Lambert
1810 John Needham
1811 Thomas Boys
1812 George Cross
1813 Thomas Ackland
1814 Joseph Fisher
1815 John Warmington
1816 William Macey
1817 George Bishop
1818 William Lindus
1819 Thomas Challis
1820 Solomon Bennet
1821 William Comfort
1822 William Field
1823 Robert Hulme
1824 Stephen Neate
1825 Valentine Rutter
1826 John Over
1827 Benjamin Stubbing
1828 William Collins
1829 Giles Silverside
1830 Joseph Pocklington

1831 John Briggs
1832 Richard Hicks
1833 William Collingwood
1834 William Bayley
1835 Robert Pocklington
1836 John Emblin
1837 William King
1838 Edmund Collingwood
1839 Thomas Challis
1840 William Giblett
1841 Samuel Hawkins Jutsum
1842 Charles Simpson
1843 Daniel Cork
1844 John Sharp
1845 John Wilson
1846 John Sharp
1847 Richard Hicks
1848 John Henry Lucy
1849 Richard Cooper
1850 John Banister
1851 Joseph Warmington
1852 William Henry Vicars
1853 William Collins
1854 William Collins
1855 Claus Hinken
1856 George Hill
1857 John Collins
1858 Francis Healey
1859 Thomas Hatton
1860 Charles Comfort
1861 William Cox
1862 William Cox MP
1863 William Collingwood
1864 Charles Valentine Game
1865 Edward Hill
1866 Henry Thomas Woods
1867 Charles Hewer
1868 Charles Thomas Jenkinson
1869 Benjamin Bloomfield Baker
1870 Benjamin Bloomfield Baker

1871 James Halliday Whitchurch
1872 Samuel Dance Morey
1873 Benjamin Venables
1874 William Henshaw Comfort
1875 William Weedon
1876 Wilfred Lyon
1877 James Horwood
1878 James Matthews
1879 Rowland Faulkner Potter
1880 James Killby
1881 Albert Bannister
1882 James Killby
1882 John Arthur Garton
1883 Thomas Killby
1884 Alderman Edward Hart
1885 Thomas John Parker
1886 George Bullas
1887 William James Bonser
1888 Charles Game
1889 Peter Meech
1890 Robert Prowd Lambert
1891 John Ashbridge
1892 George Herbert
1893 Alfred Lyon
1894 William Wilberforce Jenkins
1895 William Edward Stoner
1896 Francis Whitfield Wragg
1897 Thomas Gurney Randall
1898 Frank Clayton
1899 William Haydon LCC
1900 John Hill
1901 Thomas Hankins (died)
1902 John Hill
1902 Edmund Dean
1903 Edward Garnet Man JP
1904 John James Bridgewater
1905 Horace Thomas Pitt
1906 Joseph Gurney Randall
1907 Frederick Seymour Banks
1908 Charles Game CC

1909 Sir William Purdie Treloar B^t
1910 Herbert Hill
1911 Henry Shiply Fitter
1912 James Blofeld
1913 John Thomas Gow
1914 John Ashridge
1915 William Wilberforce Jenkinson
1916 John Thomas Hart, CC
1917 John Toulson Gardner
1918 Frank Clayton
1919 Charles Alfred Allin
1920 William West
1921 Philip John Rutland JP
1922 William Frederick Bonser, OBE
1923 Bernard William Parsons, JP
1924 Howard John Bonser
1925 Col Walter Scott Miller, DL
1926 Charles Randall Olliff
1927 Percy Winterbon Killby
1928 James Blofeld
1929 William James Parsons
1930 Benjamin Killby
1931 Norman Gow
1932 Leopold van Zwanenberg
1933 John P Ashbridge
1934 William Ried, junior
1935 James Blofeld
1936 Ernest C. W. Oldham
1937 Herbert Valentine Game
1938 William Goldstein
1939 Fred G. Burton
1940 Herbert J. Jackman
1941 Sydney Blofeld
1942 Montague G. Abrahams
1943 Thomas Throup
1944 Michel Openheimer
1945 Josiah B. Swain
1946 Josiah B. Swain
1947 Thomas C. Price
1948 Sheriff Richard C. Hammett, CC

1949 Richard C. Hammett, CC
1950 George W. Wheeler
1951 Hugh Wright, MBE
1952 Edward J. Baldwin
1953 I. Arthur Franks
1954 William Lee, JP
1955 Frederick G. Jenkins, FCA
1956 G. J. Dunsmore
1957 Frederick E. Martin
1958 G. R. Montague MC
1959 Robert Garnham
1960 Samuel H. Fletcher
1961 James A. Brewer
1962 The Rev. Thomas M. Parker, DD, MA
1963 Andrew William Hedges
1964 Arnold A. van Zwanenberg
1965 Samuel H. E. Franks
1966 Charles J. F. Greenham
1967 Ernest R. Gunner
1968 Alfred M. Anderson, MA
1969 Harold F. Minter, OBE
1970 Harold B. Swain
1971 Thomas A. V. Lawrence
1972 John Silver
1973 Terence W. Bonser, MBE
1974 Frederick F. Barrett
1975 H. Austin Kingwell
1976 Norman L. Hall, CBE, CC
1977 Frederick W. Brewster
1978 Jack G. Clarfelt
1979 Robert C. Cornell
1980 David F. Cornell
1981 Robert H. A. Connell
1982 Ronald J. Lickorish
1983 John W. Brewster, OBE, CC
1984 William A. Woolhouse
1985 David l. Franks
1986 Norman C. Poultney
1987 Robin Pooley

1988 Richard W. Baker
1989 Graham J. Sharp
1990 Ronald W. H. Covell, OBE, JP
1991 Ronald E. Stedman
1992 Frederick J. Mallion, MBE
1993 Hyman Arnold, FCA
1994 Henry T. Tattersall
1995 Roy E. Seeman
1996 Michael R. Katz

1997 George C. Adams, OBE
1998 Roger Moore
1999 Graham A. Jackman
2000 John F. Jackman
2001 Douglas J. Noakes, MBE
2002 Michael J. Richardson, MBE
2003 William J. Parker
2004 Colin S. Cullimore, CBE, DL

Appendix II

Clerks of the Worshipful Company of Butchers
1605 – 2005

Harrey Woodlond	1544 – 1552
John Pynchyn –	
Nicholas Pawlyn	1560 – 1576
– Dixon	? – 1617
Henry Awdley	? – 1624
Thomas Thorneton	1624 –?
John Philpott	? – 1680
Thomas Stamp	1680 – 1700
John Stamp	1700 – 1701
Robert White	1701 – 1703
Samuel Trowell junior	1703 – 1729
John Leadbater	1729 – 1743
James Head	1743 – 1746
John Lucy	1746 – 1750
John Miles	1750 – 1753
Thomas Benn	1754 – 1769
Thomas Benn junior	1769 – 1784
Thomas Gale	1784 – 1792
Thomas Street	1792 – 1839
Thomas W. Gilbert	1839 – 1847
Joseph Daw	1847 – 1880
Harry J. V. Philpott	1880 – 1910
Arthur Pearce	1910 – 1927
Lancelot E. Hall, LL.B	1927 – 1948
Norman L. Hall, MBE, LL.B	1948 – 1961
Henry T. Kennedy	1961 – 1964
A. Peter Coleman	1964 – 1969
William M. Collins	1969 – 1979

Peter Brook-Cowan	1979 – 1985
Alan H. Emus	1985 – 1996
J. C. Martin Chapman	1996 – 1997
Graham J. Sharp	1997 – 2003
Anthony J. C. Morrow, CVO	2003 –

Appendix III

Equivalent Contemporary Values of the Pound

(as of February 2005)

£1 in 1270	£530. 20	£1 in 1888	£59.42
£1 in 1300	£515. 10	£1 in 1900	£56.79
£1 in 1350	£426.62	£1 in 1913	£55.29
£1 in 1400	£445.17	£1 in 1916	£36.21
£1 in 1450	£498.22	£1 in 1920	£21.11
£1 in 1500	£483.80	£1 in 1930	£33.27
£1 in 1550	£199.56	£1 in 1940	£28.59
£1 in 1600	£100.16	£1 in 1945	£25.83
£1 in 1660	£75.21	£1 in 1950	£22.67
£1 in 1700	£77.72	£1 in 1957	£15.93
£1 in 1750	£84.76	£1 in 1965	£12.80
£1 in 1800	£32.02	£1 in 1970	£10.23
£1 in 1830	£49.26	£1 in 1975	£5.55
£1 in 1840	£43.89	£1 in 1980	£2.84
£1 in 1850	£58.25	£1 in 1985	£2.00
£1 in 1860	£42.96	£1 in 1990	£1.50
£1 in 1870	£45.49	£1 in 1995	£1.27
£1 in 1880	£48.08	£1 in 2000	£1.11

Selected Bibliography

ACKROYD, Peter, *London, the Biography*, London, 2000

ALAN, Thomas, *History and Antiquities of London*, London, 1828

ALFORD, B. W. E. and BARKER, T. C., *A History of the Carpenters Company*, 1968, London, p. 243

BEDE, The Venerable, (Ed. Giles), *Ecclesiastical History of England*, London, 1884

BESANT, Sir Walter, *Mediæval London*, London, 1906

—— *London in the time of the Tudors*, London, 1904

—— *London in the Time of the Stuarts*, London, 1903

—— *London in the Nineteenth Century*, London, 1909

BLACKHAM, Robert J., *The Soul of the City London's Livery Companies*, London, 1931

BOYLAN Henry (ed.), *A Dictionary of Irish Biography*, Dublin, 1998

BROMLEY, John, *The Armorial Bearings of the Guilds of London*, London, 1960

CHARTRES, John, *Agricultural Markets and Trade, 1500 – 1750*, Cambridge, 1990

CHEW, Helen & KELLAWAY, William, *London Assize of Nuisance 13021 – 1431*, London, 1973

COLLEGE OF ARMS, Vincent Collection, *Two Ears of Wheat*, folio K, circa 1530

CUNNINGHAM, Peter, *Hand-book of London*, London, 1850

CUNNINGTON, Phillis, and LUCAS, Catherine, Occupational Costume in England, London, 1967

CURL, James Stevens, *The Londonderry plantation, 1609–1914: the history, architecture and planning of the estates of the City of London and its Livery Companies in Ulster*, Chichester 1986

DAVENANT, Charles, *Discourses on the Publick Revenues, and on the Trade of England, by the author of Ways and Means*, London, 1698

DITCHFIELD, P.H., *The City Companies of London and their Good Works*, London, 1902

DRUMMOND Sir J. C. & WILBRAHAM, Anne, *The Englishman's Food*, London, 1939

EKWALL, Eilert, *Street Names of the City of London*, Oxford, 1954

EXPERIENCED BUTCHER THE, London, 1816

FABYAN, R., *The New Chronicle of England, London*, 1811

FORSHAW, Alec, *Smithfield Past and Present*, London, 1980

HALDANE, A. R. B., *The Drove Roads of Scotland*, Edinburgh, 1952

HERBERT, William, *Livery Companies*, Vol. II, London, 1834

HORNE, Thomas, *Treatise on Live Stock*, London, 1810

JENKINSON, H., *Exchequer Tallies*, Archælogia, lxii, part ii

JONES, Philip E., *The Butchers of London*, London, 1976

LATHAM, Robert, and Matthews, William, editors,

—— *The Diary of Samuel Pepys*, Vol. V London, 1962

—— *The Diary of Samuel Pepys*, Vol. VII London, 1972,

LIPSON, E., *Economic History of England*, Vol. I, London, 1956

—— *Economic History of England*, Vol. II, London, 1959

MEDVE, Victor Cornelius & THORNTON, John L, Ed. *The Royal Hospital of St Bartholomew, 1123–1973*, London 1974

MITCHELL, R.J., & LEYS, M.D.R., *A History of London Life*, London, 1958

MUFFETT, Thomas, (Corrected and Enlarged by Bennet, Christopher), *Health Improvement: to Rules Comprising and Discovering the Nature, Method, and Manners of Preparing all Sorts of Food used in this Nation*, London, 1655 THORNTON, John L

NACENTA, Raymond: *School of Paris – The Painters and the Artistic Climate of Paris Since 1910*, London, 1960

NICHOLS, E. G. (ed.) *The Diary of Henry Machyn*, London, 1848

NICHOLS, J. G., Ed. *Camden Society*, London, 1848

OWEN, W., *A New and Complete Dictionary of Arts and Sciences Comprehending all the Branches of Knowledge . . . by a Society of Gentlemen*, London, 1754

PASTON-WILLIAMS, Sara, *The Art of Dining, a history of cooking and eating*, London, 2001

PEARCE, Arthur, *The History of the Butchers Company*, London, 1929

PERREN, Richard, *The Meat Trade in Britain 1840–1914*, London, 1978

PORTER, Roy, *London, A Social History*, London, 1994

REED, Charles, *An Historical Narrative of the Origin and Construction of the Honourable the Irish Society*, London, 1865 RYE, W. B., *England as seen by Foreigners in the Days of Elizabeth and James I*, New York, 1885

RICHARDSON, John, *The Annals of London*, London, 2000

RILEY, H. T., *Liber Albus, The White Book of the City*, London, 1861

—— *Liber Custumarum*, London 1873

RIXON, Derrick, *The History of Meat Trading*, Nottingham, 2000

SCHLESINGER, Max, *Saunterings in and about London*, London, 1853

SHARPE, Reginald, *London and the Kingdom*, Vol. II, London, 1894

SMOLLETT, Tobias, *The Expedition of Henry Clinker*, London, 1771

STOW, John, *A Survey of London*, London, 1598

—— *Annales, or Generall chronicle of England*, London, 1615

STRYPE's edition of Stow, London, 1720

STRONG, Sir Roy, *The Story of Britain, London,* 1996

—— *The Corporation of London, Origin Constitution Powers and Duties*, London, 1950

TOULMIN SMITH, Lucy, *English Gilds*, London, 1923

TROW-SMITH, R, *A History of Livestock Husbandry*, London, 1957

—— *History of the Royal Smithfield Club*, Bath, 1980

WALLER, Maureen, *1700 Scenes from London Life*, New York, 2000

WALTHAM, Richard, *History of the Royal Smithfield Club*, Bath, 1998

WEBB, Edward Alfred, *The Priory Church of St Bartholomew-the-Great*, London, 1921

WHITELOCK, D., *English Historical Documents*, Vol. 1, 500 – 1042, London 1979

WYNTER, Dr Andrew, *The London Commissariat*, Quarterly Review, 1854

YOUATT, William, *A Treatment on the Breeds, Management, and Medical Treatment of Swine*, London, 1847

YOUNG, T. Dunlop, *The Retail Meat Trade*, London, 1929

Source Notes

GL – Guildhall Library

CHAPTER I

1 Quoted in Pearce, p. 3
2 Owen, W., *A New and Complete Dictionary of Arts and Sciences Comprehending all the Branches of Knowledge . . . by a Society of Gentlemen*, London, 1754, p 248
3 Toulmin Smith, Lucy, *English Gilds*, London, 1923, p. 62
4 Ibid, p. 74
5 ibid., p. 82
6 Bede, The Venerable (ed. Giles, S.), *Ecclesiastical History of the English Nation*, London, 1884, p. 54
7 *The Corporation of London, Origin Constitution Powers and Duties*, London, 1950, p. 4
8 Trow-Smith, R, *A History of British Livestock Husbandry*, London, 1957, p. 69
9 Whitelock, D., *English Historical Documents*, Vol. 1, 500 – 1042, London, 1979, p. 7
10 Ackroyd, Peter, *London, the Biography*, London, 2000, p. 36
11 ibid., *Anglo-Saxon Chronicles*
12 Stubbs, *Select Charters*, p. 97
13 Ackroyd, p. 56
14 Riley, H. T., *Liber Albus, The White Book of the City*, London, 1861, p. 219
15 Birch, H. *Introduction to Historical Charters*, London, 1957, p. 41
16 Besant, Sir Walter, *Mediæval London*, London, 1906, p. 34
17 Ekwall, Eilert, *Street Names of the City of London*, London, 1954, p. 1
18 Quoted in Ackroyd, p. 329
19 Letter Book E, p. 20
20 Riley, H. T., *Liber Custumarum*, London 1874, p. 5
21 Letter Book C, pp. 54, 55
22 Stow, John, *A Survey of London*, London, 1598, p. 87
23 Quoted in Rixon, p. 111
24 Riley, (*Liber Custumarum*), p. 53
25 Ibid., p. 57
26 Riley, H. T., *Liber Albus*, London, 1861, p. 230
27 Letter Book E, p. 110
28 Stow, John, *Annals of England*, London, 1912, p. 75
29 Letter Book C, p. 173
30 Letter Book A, p. 217
31 Chamber's *Book of Days*, 17th January
32 Stow, pp. 69, 70
33 Ibid.
34 Letter Book C, p. 239
35 Ibid.
36 Letter Book E, p. 137
37 Letter Book C, p. 239
38 Ibid.

39 Letter Book A, p. 217
40 Letter Book E, p. 137
41 Riley, (*Liber Custumarum*), p. 602
42 Letter Book E, p. 231
43 Riley, *Memorials*, p. 194
44 Letter Book G, p. 174
45 Riley, (*Memorials*), p. 356

CHAPTER 2

1 Chew, Helen & Kellaway, William, *London Assize of Nuisance 13021 – 1431*, London, 1973, Order Number 569, p. 142
2 Fuller, Thomas ed., *The Worthies of England*, London, 1952 p. 200
3 Letter Book F, p. 84
4 Wardens' Accounts, 1545–46
5 Letter Book G, p.31
6 Letter Book G, p. 43
7 Ibid., p. 31
8 Stow, I, p. 211
9 Letter Book H, Folio 337
10 Ordinance 1402–3 Henry IV, Book H, folio 337 Guildhall Chamber
11 Riley, pp. 339–340
12 Letter Book G, p. 249
13 Letter Book H, p. 392
14 Rep.2, of.20
15 *Plea and Memoranda Rolls*, Vol. 1, pp. 288, 289
16 Besant, Sir Walter, *Mediæval London, Vol. I Historical and Social*, London, 1906, p. 71
17 Letter Book H, p. 299
18 Riley, (*Memorials*), p. 540
19 Alford, B. W. E. and Barker, T. C., *A history of the Carpenters Company*, 1968, London, p. 243
20 Harleian MS. 279
21 Chaucer, Geoffrey, *Canterbury Tales*, London, Prologue, line 365
22 Stow, p. 197
23 St Thomas, A. H. & Thornley, I. D., *The Great Chronicles of London*, Gloucester, 1983, p. 115
24 Besant, p. 108
25 Letter Book K, pp. 2, 3
26 Ibid.
27 St Thomas, p. 115
28 Herbert, G., *Livery Companies*, Vol. II, London, 1902, p. 218
29 Nichols, E. G. (ed.) *The Diary of Henry Machyn*, London, 1848, p. 294
30 Fabyan, R., *The New Chronicle of England, London*, 1811, p. 38
31 Muffett, Thomas, (Corrected and Enlarged by Bennet, Christopher), *Health Improvement: to Rules Comprising and Discovering the Nature, Method, and Manners of Preparing all Sorts of Food used in this Nation*, London 1655
32 Ibid.
33 Letter Book K, p. 10
34 Letter Book L, p. 67
36 Journal VIII, f. 82
37 Ibid., f 9d

38 Jor. 8, fos. 88v,90,97
39 C.R.L.O., Book of Fines, of. 2
40 Rep. 10, fos. 10v,17v
41 Rixon, p. 142
42 Jor. 9, fo. 60
43 Strype's Stow, p. vol 2, pp. 344, 345
44 Young, T. Dunlop, The Retail Meat Trade, London, 1929, p. 145
45 Rep. 3, fo. 129v
46 Stow, p. 234
47 Ibid., p. 239
48 Letter Book Q. of.45v
49 Letter Book X, of. 219v
50 Jones, p. 108
51 Lipson, p. 112
52 Jones, p. 109
53 24 Henry VIII, c.3
54 Letter Book P, of. 18v
55 See Jones, pp. 110, 111 for list of names
56 Letter Book P, of. 31
57 Rep. 9 fo. 56
58 Rep. 10 fos. 159v, 173v
59 Ibid.
60 Rep. 11fo. 60v
61 Mitchell, R.J., & Leys, M.D.R., A History of London Life, London, 1958, p. 48
62 Letter Book L, p. 163–4
63 Wardens' Accounts 1577–78
64 Riley, (Memorials), p. 669
65 Mitchell, p. 50
66 Harleian MMS 541
67 Stow, p. 112
68 GL MS 6464 (10)
69 Coll. Arms. Grants 90, p. 19
70 Bromley, John, The Armorial Bearings of the Guilds of London, London, 1960, p. 34
71 Revelations, chapter iv, verse 7
72 Ezekiel, chapter 1, verse 10
73 Bromley, p. 34
74 College of Arms, Vincent Collection, Two Ears of Wheat, folio K, circa 1530
75 Bromley, p.36

CHAPTER 3

1 GL 6440 p. 87
2 Rep. 12 (2), fos. 490, 491
3 Quoted in Pearce, p. 53
4 Quoted in Ditchfield, P.H., The City Companies of London and their Good Works, London, 1902, p. 212
5 Quoted in Strong, Sir Roy, The Story of Britain, London, 1996, p. 183
6 Quoted in Paston-Williams, Sara, The Art of Dining, a history of cooking and eating, London, 2001, p. 18

7 Quoted in Medvei, Victor Cornelius & Thornton, John L, Ed. *The Royal Hospital of St Bartholomew, 1123–1973*, London, 1974, p. 23

8 Rep.11, fo. 373v

9 Letter Book Q, fo. 229v

10 GL 6440 p. 93

11 Ibid., p. 97

12 Rye, W. B., *England as seen by Foreigners in the Days of Elizabeth and James I*, New York, 1885, p. 245

13 Bestant, Sir Walter, *London in the time of the Tudors*, London, 1904, p. 152

14 Shakespeare, *Henry IV* Part II, Act 2, s. iv

15 Quoted in Ackroyd, p. 106

16 Ackroyd, p. 105

17 Ibid.

18 Lipson, E., *Economic History of England*, Vol. 1, London, 1959, p. 232

19 Quoted in Ackroyd, p.106

20 Ibid.

21 Letter Book G, p. 310

22 Chaucer, Geoffrey, *The Canterbury Tales*, (The Miller), line 550

23 Ibid., (The Tale of Sir Thopas) line 51

24 Letter Book O, fo. 270

25 Quoted in Ackroyd, p. 107

26 Shakespeare, (*The Winter's Tale*), Act IV, scene III

27 Rep.27, fo.63

28 Nichols, J. G., Ed. *Camden Society*, entry for 28 October 1561,London, 1848, p. 270

29 Rye, p. 118

30 Quoted in Silven Crossroads.com. Laneham, Robert, 1575

31 Mitchell, R. J., & Leys, p. 117

32 Rep.70, fo. 126v

33 Journal 22, f.24

34 GL 660/1 Vol 1, p.352

35 Ibid., Vol 2, p. 2

36 Ibid., 1597–98

37 Boylan. Henry (ed.), *A Dictionary of Irish Biography*, Dublin, 1998, p. 156

38 Ibid., p. 158

39 GL 6440/1, Vol. 1, p. 531

40 Ibid., p. 549

41 The Charter can be viewed at the Guildhall Library reference number GL MS 9804

42 GL 6440/1, Vol. 1, p. 531

43 Ordynances for the Butchers, Item 4

44 Ibid., Item 5

45 Ibid., Item 5

46 Ibid., Item 7

47 Ibid., Item 10

48 Ibid., Item 11

49 Ibid., Item 18

50 Ibid., Item 33

51 Ordinance: 49 Item 19 August 1607

52 Ibid., Item 52

53 Cunnington, Phillis, and Lucas, Catherine, *Occupational Costume in England*, London, 1967, p. 115

54 Shakespeare, Henry VI, Part II, Act IV. Scene VII

55 Blackham, Robert J., *The Soul of the City London's Livery Companies*, London, 1931, p.53

56 Curl, James Stevens, *The Londonderry plantation, 1609–1914: the history, architecture and planning of the estates of the City of London and its Livery Companies in Ulster*, Chichester 1986, p. 30

57 The Honourable the Irish Society official handbook, London 2002, p. 2

58 Ibid., p.3

59 Ibid., p. 5

60 The Great Twelve are, in numerical order, the Mercers, Grocers, Drapers, Fishmongers, Goldsmiths, Skinners, Merchant Tailors, Haberdashers, Salters, Ironmongers, Vintners and Clothworkers

61 Curl, p. 89

62 BBC *War and Conflict* transcription, *The Ulster Plantations*

63 GL MS. 10 563A

64 Reed, Charles, *An Historical Narrative of the Origin and Construction of the Honourable the Irish Society*, London, 1865, p. 86

65 Pearce, p. 92

66 Letter Book M, fo. 147v

67 Ibid.

68 GL. MS 6464, Deed No. 10

69 GL. MSS 6467, no. 15

70 Ibid., 6464

71 Jones, p. 210

72 Ibid., p. 35

73 Wardens' Accounts, 1634–35

74 Ibid., 1635–36

75 Wardens' Accounts 1639–40

76 Quoted in Richardson, John, *The Annals of London*, London, 2000, p. 131

77 Ibid., 1641–42

78 Rep.42, fo. 142v

79 Rep.67, fos. 272

80 Besant, Sir Walter, *London in the Time of the Stuarts*, London, 1903, p. 75

81 Evelyn, John, (ed. de la Be'doye're Guy), *The Diary of John Evelyn*, p. 412

82 Besant (Tudor), p. 70

83 Latham, Robert, and Matthews, William, editors, *The Diary of Samuel Pepys*, Vol. V, London, 1972, pp. 199, 200

84 Quoted in Potter, p. 80

85 GL MS. 64431/1, fo. 26v

86 Latham, Vol VII, p. 183

87 Quoted in Richardson, p. 142

88 Ibid., p. 268

89 Quoted in Porter, p. 85

90 Ibid.

CHAPTER 4

1 Latham, Robert and Matthews, William, (editors) *The Diary of Samuel Pepys*, London, 1962, Vol. VII, p.267

2 Porter, Roy, *London, A Social History*, London, 1994, p. 89

3 St Bartholomew's Hospital Journal, Vol 4., fo. 171

4 Rep. 74, fo.19

5 *Strype's edition of Stow*, London, 1720, p. 90
6 Alan, Thomas, *History and Antiquities of London*, London, 1828, p. 73
7 GL 6443/4, February 1735
8 Allan, Vol. III, p. 129
9 GL 6443/1, 13 January 1687
10 Ibid., 12 January 1688
11 Davenant, Charles, *Discourses on the Publick Revenues, and on the Trade of England, by the author of Ways and Means*, London, 1698
12 Trow-Smith, Robert, *History of the Royal Smithfield Club*, Bath, 1980, p.10
13 Horne, Thomas, *Treatise on Live Stock*, London, 1810, p. 132
14 *Pictorial Half Hours, Shepherds' and Drovers' Dogs Compared*, London, 1851
15 Haldane, A. R. B., *The Drove Roads of Scotland*, Edinburgh, 1952, p. 68
16 Chartres, John, *Agricultural Markets and Trade, 1500 – 1750*, Cambridge, 1990, p. 158
17 Essay on *The Graces and Anxieties of Pig Driving*.
18 Quoted in Waller, Maureen, *1700 Scenes from London Life*, New York, 2000, p.177
19 Rep. 91, fo. 193
20 GL 6443/1 5 March 1688
21 Ibid.
22 Sharpe, Reginald, *London and the Kingdom*, Vol. II, London, 1894, p. 519
23 Waller, p. 176
24 Ibid., p. 178
25 Ibid., p. 180
26 Ibid., p. 181
27 *Calendar of State Papers Domestic*, 7 June 1661
28 Quoted in *The Shorter Oxford Dictionary*, Oxford, 1983, p. 903
29 Besant (*Stuart*), p. 123
30 GL 6443/1, 29 July 1624
31 Quoted in Waller
32 Cunningham, Peter, *Hand-book of London*, London, 1850 p. 104
33 Quoted in Ackroyd, p. 270
34 Ibid., p. 268
35 Ibid.
36 Ibid.
37 Ibid.
38 GL 6443/2, 26 October 1693
39 Ibid., 16 October 1695
40 Ibid., 8 October 1696
41 Court of Aldermen, misc. papers 1709
42 Ibid.
43 GL 6443/2, 4 October 1713
44 Wardens' Accounts, 15 November 1697
45 Journal 52, fo. 142
46 Sharpe, Vol.II, p,605
47 Ibid.
48 Letter Book K, p. 220
49 Rep. 30, fo. 308
50 Quoted in Pearce, p. 160
51 Ibid., 161
52 Drummond, Sir J. C. & Wilbraham, Anne, *The Englishman's Food*, London, 1939, p. 205
53 City's Cash 1/1 fo. 13

54 Jones, p. 200
55 Ibid., p.201
56 Quoted in Pearce p. 114
57 Jones, p. 42
58 Pierce, p. 114
59 Ibid., p.115
60 Ibid.
61 Ibid., p.116
62 Smollett, Tobias, *The Expedition of Henry Clinker*, London, 1771, p. 146
63 BBC.co.uk, *Historic Figures, Robert Bakewell*
64 Rixon, p. 217
65 Youatt, William, *A Treatment on the Breeds, Management, and Medical Treatment of Swine*, London, 1847, p. 203
66 Ibid., p. 207
67 Rixon, p. 223
68 Horne, p. 78
69 Trow-Smith, Robert, *History of the Royal Smithfield Club*, Bath, 1980, p. 95
70 *The Experienced Butcher*, London 1816, p. 98
71 Quoted in Jones, p. 103
72 *The Experienced Butcher*, p. 104
73 Perren, Richard, *The Meat Trade in Britain 1840–1914*, London, 1978, p. 119
74 Dickens, Charles, *Oliver Twist*, London, 1838
75 Pearce, p 136
76 Ibid.
77 Wynter, Dr Andrew, *The London Commissariat*, Quarterly Review, 1854, No. cxc, vol. xcv
78 Quoted in Pearce, p. 167
79 *The Experienced Butcher*, p. 115
80 Ibid., p. 116
81 Quoted in Rixon, p. 232
82 Ibid.
83 Quote in Pearce, p. 183
84 *The Times*

CHAPTER 5

1 GL MS 6443/16
2 *The Times*, 25 April 1829, p. 2, f
3 GL MS 6443/16
4 Ibid.
5 Ibid.
6 Ibid.
7 Ibid, 1 December 1842
8 Ibid.
9 Ibid.
10 Ibid
11 Ibid.
12 Quoted in Forshaw, Alec, *Smithfield Past and Present*, London, 1980, p. 57
13 Cunningham, Peter, *Hand-Book of London*, London, 1850, p. 28
14 GL MS 6443/16, 12 December 1836

15 Ibid.
16 Schlesinger, Max, *Saunterings in and about London*, London, 1853, p. 189
17 BOPCRIS, House of Commons Select Committee on Smithfield Market Removal Bill
18 City Press, quoted in Pearce, p. 172
19 *The Times*, 25 November 1868
20 Ackroyd, p. 331
21 Forshaw, p. 79
22 Strong, p. 420
23 GL. MS 6459, 7 April 1859
24 Ibid.
25 GL MS 6443/16
26 Ibid.
27 Wardens' Accounts, 1595–96
28 GL MS 6465, 10, 581
29 Ibid.
30 Jones, p. 167
31 GL MS 7341
32 Pearce, p. 127
33 GL MS 6443/19
34 Ibid.
35 Ibid.

CHAPTER 6

1 *Billiard News*, Vol. 1, No 6 10 September 1883
2 GL MS 6443/20/150 2 August 1883
3 Ibid.
4 Ibid.
5 Oxford Concise English Dictionary
6 GL MS 6443/20
7 Ibid., 21/248
8 *The Times*, 27 May 1882
9 Quoted in Rixson, p. 268
10 Ibid.
11 *The Daily Telegraph*, 5 February 1880
12 GL MS 6334/22/11 October 1897
13 Ibid.
14 Trow-Smith, Robert, *History of the Royal Smithfield Club*, Bath, 1980, p.55
15 Ibid. p. 150
16 Waltham, Richard, *History of the Royal Smithfield Club*, Bath, 1998, p. 30
17 Pearce p. 264
18 GL MS 6334/196/92
19 GL MS 10 566
20 Ibid.
21 Ibid.
22 Ibid.
23 Webb, Edward Alfred, *The Priory Church of St Bartholomew-the-Great*, London, 1921, vol. ii, p. 21
24 *The Times*, 9 September 1915
25 GL MS 6334/24 15 October 1915

26 Ibid.
27 GL MS 6334/24
28 John Tuckwell to Author
29 Ibid.
30 GL MS 6443/25/226
31 Ibid. 2 September 1929
32 GL MS 6443/26
33 *The Times*, 12 May 1941
34 Ibid.
35 GL MS 6443/26/352 15 May 1941
36 Terence Bonser to Author
37 GL MS 6443/26, 16 January 1941
38 *The Times*, 2 August 1944
39 Miss Rosemary Smith to Author
40 Great Britain Book of Goodwill, p. 3
41 GL MS 6443/26 6 November 1945
42 Ibid., 7 November 1946, p. 15
43 Book of Goodwill, Vol. 1, (UK) 1946, p. 7
44 Book of Goodwill, Vol 11, (South America), 1946, p. 1
45 GL MS 6443/26 3 October 1946
46 Ibid.
47 Ibid.
48 Ibid., /24, 7 November 1946
49 John Jackman to Author

CHAPTER 7

1 Common Hall Minute Book, 1956 – 2004, 1 August 1961
2 Ibid.
3 Court Minute Book 1946, 3 October 1955, p. 375
4 Ibid., September 1950
5 Ibid., p. 373
6 Constitution Committee Report, 16 February 1977
7 Common Hall Minutes 1956–2004, p. 122
8 Court Minute Book 1957, 5 May 1960, p. 143
9 Ibid., 2 June 1960
10 Nacenta, Raymond: *School of Paris – The Painters and the Artistic Climate of Paris Since 1910*, London, 1960, p. 308
11 Minute, 4 November 1965, p. 480
12 *The Royal Charters and the Bye-laws made thereunder of the Worshipful Company of Butchers of the city of London*, London, 1969, p. 19
13 Ibid., p, 21
14 Personal Comment to the Author
15 Court Minute Book 1972, 24 March 1976
16 Colin Cullimore to Author
17 Terence Bonser to the Author.
18 Anon. Personal comment to the Author
19 Terence Bonser to Author
20 Charles Boyd to Author

21 See Jones, Philip E., *The Butchers of London*, London, 1976, pp. 65–70
22 Terence Bonser to Author
23 Supplement to the *Meat Trades Journal*, June 1953, p. 2
24 Court Minute Book, 1972, 8 October 1981, p. 421
25 Graham Sharp to Author
26 Court Minute Book 1972, 4 March 1982, p. 440
27 *Worshipful Company of Butchers Bulletin*, 1997, Autumn edition
28 Court Minute Book, 1996–99, 19 September 1996
29 Paper delivered by Douglas Noakes, Common Hall 1997, p. 2
30 John Jackman to Author
31 Anon. to Author
32 Douglas Noakes to Author
33 Ibid.
34 Ibid.
35 Douglas Brydges to Author
36 John Edkins to Author
37 Minutes of the Educational Committee, 6 May 2004
38 Ibid.
39 Ibid.
40 Waltham, Richard W., *History of the Royal Smithfield Club*, Bath, 1998, p. 32

Picture Credits

The Worshipful Company of Butchers: 2a, 2b, 2c, 4a, 4b (courtesy of the author),7a, 7b, 8c, 9a, 9b, 10a, 10b, 11a, 11c, 12a, 13a, 13b, 14a, 14b, 15a, 15b, 16. Colour: 1, 2a, 2b, 3, 5a, 5b, 6a, 6b, 8
By kind permission of The Guildhall Library, Corporation of London: 5a, 5b, 6b, 6d, 8b, 11b. Colour: 4a
Science Museum/Science and Society Picture Library: 1a; National Railway Museum/Science and Society Picture Library: 7c
National Archives: 1c
By kind permission of the Folger Shakespeare Library, Washington DC: 3a, 3b
Clinton Howell Antiques, NYC: 6a, 6c
London Borough of Lambeth Archives Department: 8a
By kind permission of The Worshipful Company of Drapers: Colour 4a
By Kind permission of Heirloom & Howard: Colour 6c (Overton Collection: *Chinese Armorial Porcelain*, Faber 1974. By courtesy of D. S. Howard)
Mel Howse: Colour 7

Index